MASTERING the ART of
VEGAN COOKING

MASTERING the ART of
VEGAN COOKING

OVER 200 DELICIOUS RECIPES AND TIPS TO
SAVE YOU MONEY AND STOCK YOUR PANTRY

Annie and Dan Shannon

Authors of
BETTY GOES VEGAN

GRAND CENTRAL
Life & Style
NEW YORK · BOSTON

Grand Central Life and Style
Hachette Book Group
1290 Avenue of the Americas
New York, NY 10104

www.GrandCentralLifeandStyle.com

Printed in the United States of America

RRD-C

First Edition: May 2015
10 9 8 7 6 5 4 3 2 1

Grand Central Life and Style is an imprint of Grand Central Publishing.
The Grand Central Life and Style name and logo are trademarks of Hachette Book Group, Inc.

The Hachette Speakers Bureau provides a wide range of authors for speaking events. To find
out more, go to www.HachetteSpeakersBureau.com or call (866) 376-6591.

The publisher is not responsible for websites (or their content) that are not owned
by the publisher.

Library of Congress Cataloging-in-Publication Data has been applied for.

ISBN: 978-1-4555-5753-0

For Sarah Kramer
A vegan amazon who also survived a no good, very bad year
with a smile.
Live Long and Prosper.

CONTENTS

INTRODUCTION 1

CHAPTER 1: Mastering the Practical Pantry 5

CHAPTER 2: Developing A Shopping Strategy 15

CHAPTER 3: Breakfast 25

CHAPTER 4: Lunch 65

CHAPTER 5: Dinner. 115

CHAPTER 6: No More Leftovers! 211

CHAPTER 7: Special Occasions 245

CONCLUSION 313

INDEX 315

INTRODUCTION

This book started out with a working title: *Home Skillet*. It was the book I was writing while we prepared for the arrival of our daughter, Piper, and waited for our first book, *Betty Goes Vegan*, to be released. It was going to be a book about finally "growing up" in your thirties and moving to the suburbs and what it means to us to be "homemakers." It also was a book I was deeply in love with. But on the night of October 26, 2012, we lost our baby.

At the time, I was writing an article for *VegNews* magazine about veganizing difficult egg recipes like deviled eggs and chocolate soufflés. I suddenly found myself in a position where I had a book to rewrite. We had people to call and tell. But there was something more important we needed to do first. See, there's this thing that happens when you find out you're going to be a parent: All your plans for the rest of your life change. Now, we had to figure out how to change them back—and I just wasn't up to it.

The process of starting over can sometimes be liberating and full of promise…except when you really loved the life you already had. Prior to October 2012, we had fallen deeply in love with our lives; now we had to learn to love a whole new life.

The first step was the acceptance that life just wasn't fair. The injustice of the world might seem like the most obvious observation for any adult but until we each of us faces our own personal tragedy, do any of us really ever give up on the idea that we might be the exception?

After weeks of hiding out in our remote Brooklyn apartment, I got up to make my first cup of caffeinated coffee in years and opened my laptop to write out a list of all the things we were going to have to change to get our life back on track. The house we wanted to buy in the suburbs would have to wait so we could stay closer to our doctors in the city. There were expensive fertility treatments and adoption home study dossiers we'd have to pay for now. Suddenly, it became obvious that our new life was going to require us to not only reorganize and reprioritize everything, but to streamline our spending in a major way.

We were hardly alone in this situation. In case you haven't been keeping up with the news, we're experiencing an economic crisis on a global scale. At the time we lost our baby, people all over the world were facing foreclosures, unemployment, or underemployment. That's not fair, either. But that's when it hit me that one of the first suggestions almost any modern economist makes to help save money in your household budget is to cut meat out of your diet—even when not forced to due to lack of supply.

We began by mapping out a four-step strategy for reducing waste, spending less, and getting more from our kitchen in a way that wasn't going to feel limiting:

1. The key to making any lifestyle a success is to make sure it's sustainable. That doesn't just mean making it affordable—you also need to enjoy your life. If you feel like you're sacrificing too much, the temptation to cheat or splurge can thwart your progress.

2. Unfortunately, when most people start cutting back on their groceries, they also start cutting back on the quality of the food they're eating. Ramen noodles (there are a few vegan brands) and other "instant" meals can begin to replace the organic pasta in our cabinets and our vegetable crispers empty out.

3. We were going to have to approach our kitchen differently. No meal is an island—that's a saying, right? Most recipes result in leftover ingredients and servings. Figuring out how to get the most out of what you've already got can be crucial to spending less and reducing the amount of food and money you waste. This became the strategy for how we approached our shopping, cooking, and pretty much everything kitchen related. We focused on getting at least more than one meal out of ingredients that aren't considered "cheap," like mock meat, vegan cheese, fancy flours, and fresh herbs. And we found new ways to fall back in love with inexpensive items we'd started to take for granted like beans, potatoes, rice, and cabbage.

4. Life doesn't consist solely of making dinner and packing lunches. Special occasions fall like confetti on our calendars—so finding affordable ways to celebrate is also necessary. I looked to the war brides of World War II and their ability to create the ultimate DIY weddings while being limited by rationing

protocols. I was inspired by baking tips and recipes that went as far back as the Revolutionary and Civil Wars.

And here's where Betty Crocker, with her perfectly coiffed hair and pleasant smile, entered our lives again. During the Great Depression, Betty Crocker's popularity sky-rocketed. The women who grew up in the 1920s writing to her for tips on how to transition from wood-burning stoves to electric kitchens were now looking for ways to retain some normalcy in their lives during the devastating economic crisis and World War that defined the 1930s and '40s. Hundreds of thousands of listeners tuned into *The Betty Crocker Cooking School of the Air* to learn new and creative ways to make do with less.

To quote Betty during her radio show in 1932: "Thrift has always been the banner of housewifely skill and these days of financial strain, everyone is trying to avoid waste of every kind. Scraps of vegetable and bits of meat, which in a time of plenty might have been discarded, must return to the table again, to go just a little bit further."

The financial cutbacks Dan and I needed to make weren't nearly as severe as the ones many families faced during World War II. But as we began to research the recipes of the time, it became very clear in order to make this next cooking project a success, we were going to need to fall back on another culinary

muse to find a little of that joy required to make this next cooking project a success. This is how Julia Child made her grand entrance back into our lives and kitchen.

I pulled my secondhand copy of *Julia's Kitchen Wisdom* off the shelf and started to flip through the pages I had already dog-eared and bookmarked as future recipes to veganize. Many of them could be simplified while retaining their romantic French flare, and I could see a real plan coming together. We would combine Julia's love of food, the creativity of "Wartime Betty," and a mélange of other (mostly) women who had shared their kitchen and homemaking wisdom for generations into our next big food project: the streamlining of our compassionate kitchen into a well-oiled machine that would reduce waste without sacrificing the quality of our food.

In the end, this book became more than just a collection of recipes and tips that'll save you money. It's also a collection of culinary and budgeting insights we discovered during one of the hardest years of our lives. It celebrates the advice and recipes that have been buried in old women's magazines, cooking shows, and faded recipe cards with a vegan spin, and it follows our latest cooking project closely so you can see what little life hacks we discovered along the way. It's a book about making smart choices rather than hard ones. We also hope it's a book that encourages you to take control of your kitchen and empowers you to find your own tricks for getting the most out of your meals. I guess you could say this book took a different path from our original *Home Skillet* manuscript, but it is just as much about growing up and finding domestic happiness as that book was meant to be.

Life still won't be fair—but three times a day we can make the world a better place by choosing to eat a vegan diet that's better for us, the environment, the animals, and our wallets. We can be what is fair and kind in the world while eating pretty damn well in the process.

CHAPTER 1

MASTERING THE PRACTICAL PANTRY

Whether you're Lewis and Clark heading west or Captain Kirk and the crew of the *Enterprise* voyaging out "where no man has gone before," all great adventures start with the boring task of stocking up for your journey. There's no getting out of it.

If we plan and shop right, we can use the same ingredients in more than one recipe. There won't be any forgotten vegetables in the bottom of our crisper next week, and we'll be able to enjoy fresh vegetables, herbs, and even mock meats without going into debt. We'll be able to revamp that last serving of casserole into a taco filling or a pizza topping, so that leftovers from a dish we made on Sunday night will still be exciting and special come Wednesday.

Let's Begin.

The first step to spending less money on food is to figure out what you've already invested in, and then to find new and more effective ways to use those products and ingredients. This is probably the most labor-intensive part of the whole process.

1. Take an afternoon to go through every cabinet in your kitchen. Use a notepad and pen or a tablet to make a list of every utensil, gadget, pot, pan, jar, box of cereal, etc., you already own. There are a few phone or tablet apps that can help you keep track of your inventory such as Prep & Pantry.

2. Read the labels, see what's gone bad, and throw it out. Starting with a clean slate will make a world of difference.

3. Take notes on what needs to be stored better to ensure it keeps fresh, is

protected from bugs, or doesn't get crushed. We'll talk about that more on page 8.

4. Move to your refrigerator and follow steps 1 through 3 again. Knowing what condiments you already have hanging out on your fridge door can save you a few dollars on your next shopping trip. And don't forget your freezer.

You'll be surprised by how much you already have in your kitchen. The first time I did this, I realized I had several meals' worth of ingredients that were just missing a fresh vegetable or two. But some of you might be starting from scratch, so here are some basic items you'll want to invest in. They're not just in a lot of the recipes in this book, they're in like, every vegan recipe ever.

> Agave nectar
> Applesauce
> Baking powder
> Baking soda
> Beans and lentils (a variety of either dry or canned)
> Black peppercorns
> Brown sugar
> Egg replacer powder
> Flours (all-purpose and whole wheat)
> Garlic

SCORING HARDWARE

If you're taking an interest in your kitchen for the first time, you might not have many pots and pans. This is where secondhand stores can come in handy. You'd be surprised how many people have donated perfectly good cast-iron skillets or large stew pots because they've moved or upgraded with their wedding registry. I bought my favorite cast-iron skillet almost fourteen years ago for $3 at a St. Vincent DePaul's thrift store in Olympia, Washington.

Avoid skillets with nonstick surfaces, especially scratched ones. By now you've probably heard that ingesting coatings that have flaked off your nonstick cookware into your food is suspected of being linked to a few forms of cancer, so why take a chance? We recommend going with cast iron whenever you can. It's inexpensive and can last forever if you take care of it properly.

You can also check with friends. When Dan and I lived in Norfolk, Virginia, we were in walking distance of at least a dozen friends from whom we could borrow cookie sheets and pie plates. Since our kitchen at the time looked like something from inside a submarine, it was nice being able to borrow pots and pans from friends to reduce the number of things we had to buy for ourselves—and also to cut down on clutter.

Investing in a ʃpice Rack

A $40, fully stocked rack of twenty or more spices is an investment any kitchen can benefit from and not just because it'll class up the place. The flavors added by spices and dried herbs will do wonders for your meals without adding sodium or fat. When you buy premade meals in the frozen food or deli sections of a grocery store, it may feel like you're saving money by filling your freezer or cabinet with $3 meals. But this is not as cost effective as it seems—each of those boxes represents only a single meal, and most require you to add vegetables, oil, milk, and often meat that will increase the amount of money you are spending— as well as not being vegan. Some brands are honest enough to list MSG on their label and not hide it in long Latin-y terms—but most aren't. That's why we suggest a different route. We viewed our spice rack as an investment that would pay off in at least thirty meals, or even more if we planned well. We were able to make healthier meals that could be enjoyed again as leftovers—a much better use of our money in the long run.

> Hot sauce
> Maple syrup
> Nutritional yeast
> Olive oil
> Dry pasta
> Quinoa
> Rice (jasmine and brown)
> Salt
> Soy sauce, tamari, or Bragg's Liquid Aminos
> Spice rack basics (dried oregano, ground cumin, red pepper flakes, dried thyme, dried rosemary, dried dill, etc.)
> Sugar
> Tofu

> Vegan milk (soy, almond, and/or coconut)
> Vegetable and/or vegan chicken or beef broth

This might seem like a lot, but you don't need to buy every ingredient at once. You'll be surprised by how many of these things you might already own or by how long they'll last once you stock up.

Buying Condensed Broths

I'm going to state the obvious here: Just adding water saves money.

If you've read our blog or *Betty Goes Vegan*, you know we often recommend a product called Better Than Bouillon when a recipe calls for broth. This product comes in vegetable, vegan chicken, and vegan beef varieties that are flavorful while still low in sodium. You will only use 1 teaspoon of Better Than Bouillon per cup of hot water—and 48 teaspoons come in a $6 jar, making this a terrific investment. You can also prepare your broth in advance and refrigerate it in an airtight container if you want to save time. Just give it a good shake before using it to make sure it gets completely mixed together.

MAXIMIZING THE SHELF LIFE OF STAPLES

Okay, so now you know what you already had in your kitchen, and you've stocked up on the stuff you were missing. Now it's time to figure out how to keep your food fresh.

DRY GOODS

Most dry goods—things like pastas, grains, flours, nutritional yeast, dry beans, cereals, cornmeal—are known as "shelf stable," meaning they don't need to be refrigerated to maintain quality and nutritional value. Make sure they're stored in airtight containers in a dry cabinet away from heat to avoid crushing, mildew, and bugs. A lot of kitchen stores sell plastic containers with sealable lids that work great, but since we've been trying to reduce the amount of plastic in our home, we mostly use glass containers with screw-on lids. A good old-fashioned mason jar is perfect.

IS VITAL WHEAT GLUTEN FLOUR A "DRY GOOD"?

Vital wheat gluten can be a tricky ingredient. On one hand, it's a lot like a flour and just requires an airtight container and cool, dry place to hang out; but I've also had readers tell me stories of their vital wheat gluten going bad in their cupboards. I checked a bag of Bob's Red Mill, and it does say to store in your fridge or freezer. We've been keeping ours in the fridge for the past year, and I haven't noticed a difference, but we also use it frequently—so maybe it never has a chance to go bad in our test kitchen. Either way, vital wheat gluten can be very expensive, so I recommend playing it safe and keeping it next to your ice pops.

FRESH VEGETABLES

There are many different vegetables out there in this great big world, so we've broken most of the vegetables we used in this book into groups by how to best store them. Because honestly, there's nothing more frustrating and discouraging than spending your money on some healthy vegetables just to have to throw them away before you even get to eat them. I've seen such tragedies drive strong vegans into the arms of fast-food restaurants and bags of Doritos.

Most vegetables are best eaten two to four days after you bring them home, so keep that in mind when planning your shopping and meals.

FLOWER BUDS/CRUCIFEROUS VEGETABLES

Broccoli is more delicate than you'd think. Those tiny little flower buds can yellow and wilt in just a day or two if you haven't stored the head correctly. For the longest shelf life, keep your broccoli dry and in a plastic bag with slits cut in it to release any moisture.

Cauliflower is sturdier than its green cousin, broccoli, but also does best in a "breathable" bag to release extra moisture. You'll have to toss your cauliflower once you see it start to rust (get an orange-brown tinge).

There's no denying **artichokes** are my favorite vegetable. I love them in pasta sauce and as a vehicle for "buttery" lemon garlic sauce. I also love that like any good partner, they're not high maintenance. Just store them in a dry place in the fridge—but use them within one to two days.

Asparagus should be stored like any other flower. You've got two options: Put the cut ends in a cup of water, wrap the top with plastic wrap, and store the whole thing upright in the fridge; or wrap a wet paper towel around the cut ends and secure a plastic bag around that with a rubber band. We've tried both techniques with success; the key is treating asparagus the same way you'd treat a bouquet of roses—kept cool and watered.

GREEN LEAFY VEGETABLES

We all agree that eating green leafy vegetables like kale, spinach, lettuce, and cabbage is freaking great for you. But when it comes to the best way to store them, there seem to be as many theories out there as there are antioxidants in kale (i.e., lots). After testing many of these theories, the following method appears to be the most effective: First, go through your greens and remove any spoiled or questionable leaves. When vegetables start to spoil, they release ethylene, which makes the good leaves go bad faster. Then, make sure the "good" greens are as dry as possible. Finally, either place them in a "breathable" bag or poke a few holes in the plastic container they came in to release any extra moisture, and store the greens in the fridge.

ROOTS AND TUBERS

Oh, the reliable **potato**. You are the backbone of so many beloved meals and can be fried, mashed, and baked into numerous delicious dishes. You're also one of the most low-maintenance vegetables ever to swim in a soup or roast on a BBQ spit. Keep potatoes dry and store them in a paper bag in a dark cabinet that stays around 50°F. Seriously. They're that easy. Same goes for **sweet potatoes**.

Beets are more work. You need to store them unscrubbed and unwashed in a plastic bag in the fridge. If your beets came with their leafy green tops still attached, cut those off before storing, then follow the instructions on how to store leafy green vegetables on page 9. You can substitute beet tops for spinach in any recipe.

Radishes and **carrots** are a lot like beets, though they don't usually come with their greens attached. If yours do, cut them off and use them ASAP—I recommend tossing them in a green salad. That's the only way I've come to enjoy radish and carrot greens, but feel free to experiment—you might just discover you love them in a vegan quiche or diced up in a sauce. Put unwashed radishes and carrots in a breathable plastic bag and store in the fridge. They should be good for at least a week.

FRESH FRUIT

Fruit is an essential part of a healthy diet, vegan or not. Ever hear of scurvy? It's a disease pirates would get* when they were out at sea for too long and didn't have enough vitamin C. I've never had it, but it sounds pretty painful and unpleasant. All that could be avoided by adding a grapefruit to your breakfast routine. We've broken up some of the most commonly eaten fruit in the United States into categories that'll best explain how to store them, because we like you and are anti-scurvy.

CITRUS

Citrus is pretty easy. Most citrus fruit—oranges, lemons, limes, grapefruits—will be fine for a few days at room temperature on a countertop or in a bowl. If you need them to last longer than that, store them in the crisper drawer of your fridge.

If you're buying citrus to use for zest, buy organic citrus that will most likely not be coated in that wax film they often put on produce to make it shiny.

STONE FRUIT

We recommend buying stone fruits like **peaches**, **plums**, and **apricots** while still very firm and a little unripe. Ripen the fruit

---

* Okay, other people get it, too, but pirates made it famous.

yourself, either in a paper bag or on a kitchen counter at room temperature, over the next few days. Once your peaches and plums have a light sweet fragrance, they're ready to eat.

Cherries are a completely different story. Keep cherries as cold as possible (but not frozen) in an airtight bag to prolong their delightful little lives.

BERRIES

This category includes blueberries, raspberries, strawberries (okay, technically strawberries aren't berries, but they're cleaned and stored the same way), and the like. Depending on where you live and where you shop, fresh berries can be pricey. That's why I don't feel guilty about looking through an entire display of containers before choosing one. I'll inspect it from all angles looking for even a *hint* of one spoiled berry, like a jeweler appraising a diamond. Don't buy berries if there's even one moldy one in the container. They'll all taste weird. Promise.

Many people tell you to wash berries once you get them home to remove any pesticides or other pollutants, but this can be tricky, too—any dampness on the berries will make them spoil faster. The best trick we've found to both deal with pollutants and add a few days to the berries' shelf life came from both the website *The Kitchn* and *Cook's Illustrated*. They recommend washing berries in a bath

made of 1 cup white vinegar with 3 cups water, then using a salad spinner lined with paper towels to dry them. Make sure they're completely dry, though, or all your hard work will get thrown out with your mildew-y berries. Store washed berries in a breathable container lined with paper towels to absorb and release any moisture.

MELONS

Sorry ACLU—whole melons (honeydew, cantaloupe, watermelon, etc.) should go straight into solitary confinement. Melons release ethylene gas as they ripen, so they make any other fruit around them ripen and spoil faster. You can store an uncut melon in the fridge for about a week; just keep it away from your other fruits and vegetables.

Now, do I really have to tell you that buying precut melon is more expensive, and that you're only paying for the little time you might have saved not having to slice up a whole melon? Those packages of precut melons also don't last very long, so unless you plan on eating those melon pieces right then and there, just walk on by.

SQUASH

I feel honesty is best here. I rarely store whole or raw squash (pumpkins, summer squash, zucchini, butternut squash, etc.). I usually buy it in season, prepare it in whatever way suits me at the time, and freeze it that way. I also hate—just cannot stand—the smell of rotten pumpkins. Yes, the weeks following Halloween have always been quite traumatic for me.

The most important thing about storing whole squash is to keep it extremely dry (so no back porches or basements) and between 50 and 75°F. Besides that, anything goes.

MISCELLANEOUS

Apples are a lot like cherries and benefit from going in the fridge in an airtight bag as soon as possible to retain crispness. But they're also a lot like melons and should be kept away from other fruits and vegetables since they emit large amounts of ethylene gas. That old adage "one rotten apple can spoil the bunch" doesn't just apply to teenagers and political parties. Literally, one rotten apple can emit enough ethylene to spoil all the rest. So be strict, and toss any apples with soft spots and imperfections—or turn them into homemade applesauce.

Pears are usually picked unripe, because they can ripen after being picked and have a longer shelf life in the store. Buy pears when they're still very firm and unripe, then store them in either a paper bag or a bowl on your countertop at room temperature. Once they're tender and you can smell a slight sweet aroma coming from the top, they're ready to eat—and should be eaten pretty much that day.

Bananas are the foundations upon which many a smoothie and vegan baked good are built. Versatile, easy to locate, and usually inexpensive, they're a great fruit to have around. Here are a few tips to prolong the shelf life of your yellow friends.

Never store bananas in a plastic bag, even if they come in one. Those bags seal in moisture and make your bananas spoil faster. Instead, wrap the stems in plastic tape to reduce the amount of ethylene gas they emit and keep them from becoming overripe too quickly. Always store bananas at room temperature, and on a hook if possible. As bananas mature they get what are called resting bruises from sitting in bowls or on countertops, and hooks are an inexpensive way to prevent that. You can install a 99-cent hook under a cabinet and start hanging bananas today.

As a half-Sicilian woman, I am ashamed to admit I didn't know the right way to store **tomatoes** until my thirties. Yes, it's times like this that people often ask, "Where were the parents?" but I can't blame Mom and Dad. For most of my life, I've been hoarding tomatoes in my vegetable crisper, and accepting that once a week I had to make marinara sauce from scratch with any that became borderline water-balloon-ish—just like my mother and her mother before her.

Here's what I've learned: Tomatoes should never go in the fridge. They should be allowed to experience the world on your countertop at room temperature. This will allow them to mature into a fuller flavor, maintain better cell walls, and not get that squishiness we all dread.

There seems to be a small window during which whole **avocados** go from being inedible dinosaur eggs to the perfect, delicious, smooth, good-for-you addition to any meal to disintegrating like that scene in *Raiders of the Lost Ark* when the Nazis melt. Because it can be impossible to tell in the store if your lovely little avocado has already started to spoil, we recommend this trick—pop off the little stem nub. If it's brown underneath, it's too late for that avocado; if it's a light yellow and the avocado is firm, it's safe to buy. We recommend storing avocados in a paper bag at room temperature until they're slightly soft when gently squeezed. That's when you know they're ready to be opened and served.

Anyone who has ever loved avocados and is unlucky enough to not live in Los Angeles, California, where they literally grow in people's front yards (yes, I'm talking about you, P.T. and Lisa) has probably exhausted every old wives' tale out there about how to make avocados last longer. Theories range from storing them in a breathable container in the coolest place in your home to storing them in paper bags mixed with whole onions. Everyone seems to swear his or her method is the holy grail of avocado preservation. My personal experience has taught me that pouring a little lemon juice over a cut avocado, wrapping it in a paper or cloth tea towel,

and storing it in an airtight container will usually keep it fresh for a few extra days. But really, your best bet is to eat any cut avocado as soon as possible. That gross brown slime an exposed avocado gets is really the omega-3 fatty acids oxidizing; since those are the most nutritious parts of our little green friend, you don't want to miss out on that.

Whenever **pomegranate** season comes around, I get way too excited. I have a pomegranate for dessert a few times a week until they slowly disappear from the produce section again. To give your precious pomegranates the longest life possible, store them in a paper bag in the fridge. Pomegranate arils (seeds) can be stored in an airtight container in your fridge for no more than three days.

FRESH HERBS

Now this is going to be one of those moments when you ask yourself, "How can this be a book about saving money in the kitchen and include fresh herbs?" Well, for us, it came down to this: If we used fresh herbs in multiple meals, rather than using an entire package or bunch in just one, our meals were not just healthier—because they were flavored with green leaves full of antioxidants instead of the ol' salt and sugar crutches many "budget" meals rely on—but it also encouraged us to stick to our meal plans since we had already invested in these fresh herbs. Letting them go to waste so we could lazily order some pizza felt like we were betraying the fine-tuned machine that our kitchen routine had become. The key to making this system work, though, was storing our herbs properly so that we could get as many meals as possible out of our $1 bunches.

Most herbs should be treated like bouquets of flowers because, let's be honest, that's kind of what they are: flowers that were picked before they had a chance to form buds and bloom.

Basil, parsley, mint, and **cilantro** do best when you trim their stems at an angle and put them in a glass with a little water. **Basil** and **mint** can be left on a counter at room temperature, but parsley and cilantro need to be refrigerated. **Basil** in particular is very sensitive to heat, and will brown quickly in both cold and hot temperatures, so keep it as far away from anything below 40°F or above 50°F as you can, and add it as the last ingredient to a warm dish to keep that fresh basil flavor.

Chives, green onions, thyme, and **oregano** are sensitive to moisture, so keeping them wrapped in a paper towel and then loosely wrapped plastic wrap will stop them from spoiling too quickly. They also don't need to be kept too cold, so appropriating the little hatch on your fridge door labeled "butter" as an herb compartment will also help them last longer.

[†] Seriously, when I lived in Atlanta, I had a single peppermint plant turn into a small hedge that came up to my waist in a matter of two years.

CHAPTER 2

DEVELOPING A
SHOPPING STRATEGY

A lot of "eating on a budget" plans look at each meal in a vacuum, without regard for space and time. They boil down recipes to their foundations, which have shockingly low and alluring price points. I'm pretty sure this "one-meal wonder" effect comes from a need to compete with fast-food restaurants that claim they can feed a whole family for less than $10.*

But when we step back from the immediate low-price-point gratification, we can see this approach has its flaws. As we said before: *No meal is an island.*

Instead, we decided to strategically use and reuse both the ingredients we already had in our kitchen and the new ingredients we bought fresh every week. So we set the bar at no more than $5 per serving for each recipe. If you look through the recipes, you'll see that most of them come in much cheaper than

that, with almost all of them coming in under $3 and most servings coming in under $2.

We live in Brooklyn, New York, which a study by The Council for Community and Economic Research in 2013 named the second most expensive city in the United States in which to live. So we felt this would bode well for how our calculations per serving would translate to readers in other communities (i.e., it'll probably cost you less to make these meals in your own neighborhood).

We also wanted to reinforce the fact that eating vegan and healthy is not notably more expensive than eating junk food or including meat in your diet. The idea that it's wildly more expensive to eat healthy is based on several flawed studies done more than ten years ago that measured the cost of foods per calorie. Yes, you read that right. The studies that told us eating a meat- and dairy-based diet full of prepackaged meals and junk food was remarkably cheaper than eating a fruit- and vegetable-based diet were *measuring by calorie*

---

* Although I'd like to point out that according to an article in *The New York Times* by Mark Bittman, an average family of four eating at McDonald's will pay between $20 and $35 for a meal.

content—not serving size or amount of food. But a new study done in 2012 by economists at the USDA took another look at this—and even with farm subsidies factored in, when food is measured by *price per average amount consumed* (i.e., per serving size), vegetables came out in a strong lead for the most economical.

And this makes perfect sense. Fire up your search engine and ask the Internet how to save money at the grocery store. Almost every article you find will say the same thing: Reduce or eliminate meat from your diet.

But for many people this raises the question: "If I don't eat animals, where will I get my protein?" The answer, of course, is that beans, quinoa, tofu, tempeh, and vegan products like mock meat are good, healthier alternatives. But how does this translate into saving money?

Let's look at one of the most commonly eaten meats in the United States: chicken.

According to PBS, the average meat-eating American eats more than 50 pounds of chicken in a year. While price points can go as low as Walmart's modest $2.09/pound, using the Bureau of Labor Statistics' average of $3.70/pound for non-organic or free-range poultry comes out to around $185 a year for one person. The price of tofu, on the other hand, can range from $1.00 to $2.50/pound depending on organic and non-GMO certification, making the same amount per year around $125 per person for organic, non-GMO tofu. And then there are beans. A can of black beans averages about a pound, and can cost anywhere from $1 to $2.79 a can, depending again on organic and non-GMO certification—making a grand total of around $140 per person per year for organic and non-GMO beans.

This might not be a huge savings you can appreciate every day, but over the course of weeks and months, it can start to show in your bank account. Plus, you're eating better, kinder, organic, non-GMO food instead of factory-farmed chicken!

KEEPING IT REAL WITH FAUX

Vegan products like mock meat and vegan cheeses were where our goal of saving money got tricky. Those products can unfortunately cost about as much as cheap meat options and are often cited as the financial excuse many use for not eating vegan. So we had a choice: We could eliminate those options from our diet and produce yet another book that stripped recipes down to the bones to meet a low price point; or we could do something else…something new. We decided to continue using the amazing vegan options available on the market today, but move them into a supporting role where they could still be enjoyed in moderation. We also included recipes for how to create large batches of mock meat from scratch, for those who are more the DIY type. We've tried to create recipes that save money but don't require you to sacrifice to the point where you lose interest or feel unsatisfied. That's not a sustainable lifestyle and won't save money in the long run.

We'd been vegan for years and years before starting this project to fine-tune our kitchen finances, so we were already reaping the monetary benefits from eliminating meat from our diets.[†] The real work for us was in eliminating waste (i.e., throwing away food that has expired or otherwise gone bad), and we're not the only people who have this problem.

According to a paper released by the Natural Resources Defense Council in 2012 citing USDA research, the average American household ends up throwing out 25 percent of the food it purchases. That translates to the average family of four losing between $1,365 and $2,275 worth of food to waste each year. There's a lot of speculation as to why so much food is being wasted, ranging from more people eating out, larger packages of food with shorter expiration dates, lack of meal planning in the home, or just a general lack of awareness and undervaluing of food leading to spoilage.

This is a vicious cycle, much bigger than just our kitchen and wallets. So we set out to create a shopping strategy that would allow us to maximize every purchase into multiple meals.

[†] As well as the health benefits and sense that we're making a positive difference in the world.

Beans, Beans Are Good For Your Wallet...

Cooking dry beans unfortunately takes a lot longer than opening a can; but when you're talking money, dry beans are your best friend. You can make 2 cups of dry beans for 34 cents—that's more than you'd get from a 15-ounce can for $2. You can make large batches, too, and keep extras in the freezer to use later. Cooking with dry beans also improves the texture and flavor of your food, while having the added benefit of not being soaked in salt, sugar, corn syrup, or animal fat before being canned. Do I even need to mention that eating BPA- and aluminum-free beans is better for you and the planet? Didn't think so. They really are a magical fruit.

PREPARING DRY BEANS IN FOUR STEPS

Step 1: Spread dry beans out on a cookie sheet and pick through them, tossing any small rocks or shriveled beans you find. This is when you have to be tough—not every bean will make the cut, so you need to have high standards and stick to them.

Step 2: Pour all your finest beans into a wire-mesh colander and rinse them under cool water.

Step 3: Move the beans to a large pot or bowl. Add enough cold water to cover the beans by at least 3 inches. Set aside and let soak overnight (at least 8 hours). Drain in the morning.

Step 4: Now your beans are ready to cook. Put them in a large pot and add enough water to cover them by 2 inches. Cover and slowly bring to a boil over low heat. Keep an eye on the pot and skim off any foam or yuckiness that starts to form on the top. While the beans are simmering, stir them occasionally and add more water, ¼ cup at a time, if needed. Beans are done once they're tender enough to stab with a fork. This can take 1 to 2 hours, or up to 3 hours if you got a stubborn batch. You know who you are, you jerky garbanzo beans.

PREPARING DRY BEANS: QUICK-SOAK METHOD

If you're one of those "time equals money" folks, you might want to try what's called a quick-soak method to prepare dry beans. After sorting and rinsing the beans, put them in a large pot with 3 cups water for every cup of beans. Bring to a boil over high heat. Continue to boil for 5 minutes, then cover the pot and remove it from the heat. Let the beans soak for 1 hour and 30 minutes. Then drain and rinse the beans, and use them as you like.

PEAS AND LENTILS IN JUST TWO STEPS

Peas and lentils aren't just ridiculously cheap, convenient, and good for you—they're also good for the animals. I can confidently say that lentils have probably saved more animals over the years than Superman has rescued kittens from trees, by replacing meat in numerous meals and recipes with ease. They're packed with both fiber and protein, and versatile enough to be used in almost every type of cuisine and recipe—except maybe cupcakes and smoothies.

Step 1: Sort and rinse dry peas or lentils to weed out any weirdos—but skip the presoak you'd do for larger beans.

Step 2: In a large stockpot, pour 1½ cups water for every 1 cup dry peas or lentils you'll be cooking (don't add them to the pot yet). Bring the water to a rolling boil over high heat, then add the dry peas or lentils, cover, and reduce the heat to maintain a simmer. Cook the peas or lentils for 30 to 45 minutes, stirring them occasionally to make sure they're cooking evenly. They're ready to use in a recipe when tender enough to squish with your fingers. You can also just rinse them and toss them directly in a soup or sauce recipe to cook; just make sure to have some extra broth or water ready to keep your dish from reducing too much.

This method works better for smaller beans and legumes rather than larger ones. Garbanzos and lima beans, for example, don't usually yield the best results when quick-soaked.

THE MOST DANGEROUS BEANS

Be careful when working with dry kidney beans. They contain a toxin that can cause food poisoning if they are undercooked, making them one of the bad boys of beans. Of course, they're overshadowed by castor beans, which you might remember from Walt's science/crime lessons on *Breaking Bad*. They're where the deadly poison ricin comes from. So, you know, not so good in a hummus or chili.

Using Coupons and Club Cards

When we decided to be more mindful of our spending and reduce waste in our home, we started by looking at our grocery receipts. We made a note of what stores we went to the most and looked up info on their discount clubs online. We made a spreadsheet of what kind of points we had racked up and asked at the customer service desk what we could actually do with these points.

We did what they don't actually want you to do: We got to know the little card on our key chains. We trashed the ones that were just decoys to encourage us to buy things

we didn't need with point systems going toward things we didn't want…like a free frozen turkey on Thanksgiving. The ones that actually saved us money on produce, juices, pastas, etc., and included items like spices rather than just instant meals became our go-to cards—and ultimately our go-to stores, in addition to shopping at our local farmers' markets, which you can read more about on page 83.

Then we took our card program analysis a step further. See, we have a credit card that offers a cash-back program—you know, you spend X dollars and get Y percent back toward other purchases or paying your bill. Well, it turns out those same cards have deals every month or quarter where you can earn extra cash back—one month it'll be for purchases at gas stations, and the next month, drugstores. After a period of strategically stocking up on environmentally friendly toilet paper when we earned more cash back from drugstores and waiting to see movies during months when that'd rack up extra points…it actually added up. I can be a cynical person, and no one was more shocked than me to find that discount clubs actually *could* lead to discounts, and that cash-back programs could actually pay out.

And then there were coupons. Now, anyone who has ever worked from home or had any kind of extended bout with daytime TV knows there are a lot of shows out there that sing the praises of extreme couponing. They tell the tales of families all over the United States who are buying gallons of mayo and pallets of paper towels for pennies. Okay, I'm exaggerating. But seriously, there are people stocking basements and pantries like an atomic bomb will drop any day now. This style of shopping just didn't fit with how we wanted to live, but couponing can still be useful even if it's not "extreme."

To me, good couponing comes down to one thing: getting a discount on something I need or want to buy anyway. According to an NCH Marketing report, there was a 17 percent drop in coupon redemption in 2012 and 2013. When asked why American consumers were using fewer coupons, the most popular explanation was: "I can't find coupons for the products I want to buy."

So we went to the websites of products and brands we were already buying, signed up for their newsletters, and sent e-mails asking how to get coupons. In a few weeks, we had all the coupons for mock meats and vegan cheeses we would need for the year. Most were good for at least a year, but the few that had upcoming expiration dates encouraged us to stock our freezer with vegan goodies. And if we used our coupons in combination with sales, well, all the better!

Then we looked into phone apps that offered coupons and discounts. Some have deals that pop up when you "check in"

somewhere, and others list coupons or sales in your area. Either way, they can save you time and money by giving you savings at your fingertips.

The next step was keeping track of which of the stores at which we shopped accepted coupons and what they charged for the products we liked to buy. Some local stores or co-ops don't accept coupons, but their prices on items like soy milk are more reasonable than the bigger chains, even with a coupon!

Ultimately, a lot of this information came out during the weekly and monthly review of our receipts. It took about two months to fine-tune a shopping strategy where we visited three stores once or twice a week with coupons and joined programs where we were saving up points for things we actually needed.

How to Read a Price Tag

Few of us can honestly say that we took a class in high school that taught us skills that we still use every day and that helped put us on the track to being a successful human on this planet. I can say this.

My senior year of high school, I took a class called Single Survival. It was presented as a home economics class to help us silly kids go into the world with a good understanding of what it was going to take to stay alive. Okay, I'm being dramatic, but it taught me good life skills: how to write a résumé, how to do taxes, how to budget for a car and rent, what classes to take in college, how to be a good roommate, what it legally meant to get married, some sex ed stuff, and a dose of reality from guest speakers who had gotten DUIs, become single parents, or experienced the dangers of binge drinking and drugs. I can name more than a few moments from my twenties when I avoided doing something remarkably dumb specifically because I remembered something from that class.

When I go grocery shopping, I know how to read a price tag because of that class. Over the years I've been surprised by how many people don't know how to do this, so I'm sharing.

The first step is to look at the unit price. It's usually labeled, and the number is usually written in the second-largest font on the left-hand side of the shelf tag. Most products calculate it in ounces or liters, and you can tell just by looking at it how much you can save per ounce/liter by buying a larger package or bottle. But if your store doesn't clearly indicate the unit price on their tags, you can divide the total price of the item by how it's measured and get the number yourself.

Looking at the unit price is also how you can determine the amount of money you save by buying generic or store brands instead of the better-known, schmancier brands.

Buying Seasonal Produce

These days we live in a world with refrigerated semi-trucks, cargo planes, and ships that bring us any kind of fruit or vegetable our hearts desire. The days when *Poor Richard's Almanac* was the last word on what we got to eat every month are long since past. But even with all these modern conveniences, there are some cold, hard facts we can't avoid:

1. A fruit or vegetable that is bought in season will have a superior texture and flavor.
2. Fruits and vegetables in season will always be cheaper than those not in season.
3. Buying fruits and vegetables that have been shipped around the world is bad for the environment, as well as expensive. The cost of this practice always ends up trickling down to consumers in one way or another.

We're including a little chart of what fruits and vegetables are generally in season during what months in the northern hemisphere (where we live) to help you plan your meals.

MONTH	FRUIT	VEGETABLE
January	Apples, Oranges, Grapefruit, Lemons	Broccoli, Cabbage, Kale, Leeks, Cauliflower
February	Apples, Oranges, Grapefruit, Lemons, Pears	Broccoli, Cauliflower, Kale, Winter squash
March	Apples, Mangoes, Pears, Pineapples	Broccoli, Kale, Lettuce, Winter squash
April	Mangoes, Pears, Pineapples	Artichokes, Asparagus, Broccoli, Cauliflower, Lettuce, Spinach, Rhubarb, Zucchini
May	Apricots, Cherries, Pears, Pineapples	Artichokes, Arugula, Asparagus, Broccoli, Cauliflower, Lettuce, Radishes, Rhubarb, Spinach, Zucchini
June	Apricots, Blueberries, Cherries, Peaches, Pears, Watermelon	Asparagus, Beets, Broccoli, Cabbage, Cauliflower, Corn, Lettuce, Radishes, Rhubarb, Spinach
July	Apples, Apricots, Berries, Peaches, Pears, Plums, Watermelon	Beets, Broccoli, Cabbage, Cauliflower, Corn, Cucumbers, Green beans, Lettuce, Peppers, Spinach, Summer squash, Tomatoes, Zucchini
August	Apples, Apricots, Berries, Cherries, Kiwi, Peaches, Pears, Plums, Watermelon	Beets, Broccoli, Cabbage, Cauliflower, Corn, Cucumbers, Eggplant, Green beans, Lettuce, Leeks, Peppers, Radishes, Spinach, Summer squash, Tomatoes, Winter squash, Zucchini
September	Apples, Grapes, Peaches, Pears, Plums, Raspberries, Watermelon	Beets, Broccoli, Brussels sprouts, Cabbage, Cauliflower, Cucumber, Eggplant, Green beans, Leeks, Lettuce, Peppers, Pumpkins, Radishes, Spinach, Summer squash, Tomatoes, Winter squash, Zucchini
October	Apples, Cranberries, Grapes, Pears, Watermelon	Beets, Broccoli, Brussels sprouts, Cabbage, Cauliflower, Cucumber, Eggplant, Leeks, Lettuce, Peppers, Pumpkins, Winter squash
November	Cranberries, Pears	Beets, Broccoli, Brussels sprouts, Cauliflower, Cucumber, Leeks, Pumpkins, Winter squash
December	Cranberries, Pears	Beets, Broccoli, Leeks, Winter squash

Victory Gardens

During World War II, growing food became the patriotic duty of every American left behind on the home front. Everyone was encouraged to "make do" in any way possible, and that meant growing your own vegetables.

In May 1941, the Office of Civilian Defense was founded to help with this effort. This mostly female, volunteer-based program was created to help organize projects that civilians could participate in to assist the war effort abroad. It's mostly known for training air raid marshals who patrolled suburbs looking for surprise attacks from Japanese bombers, but they did other less comical (in hindsight) stuff, too, like organizing scrap metal drops for salvaging and recycling, and childcare services for soldiers' wives who wanted to work in factories. They also reintroduced the concept of the victory garden.

Victory gardens had been quite popular during World War I. The concept was for any citizen with access to land—on their personal property or a communal plot—to grow food to feed their family and neighbors, thus reducing the amount of food large-scale commercial farmers would need to grow to feed the civilian population, plus reducing the demand for related resources, like fuel for transporting food.

During World War II, victory gardens popped up everywhere from Golden Gate Park to rooftops in Queens. It's estimated that in 1944 there were more than 18 million victory gardens in the United States. By 1945, there were more than 30 million. Even First Lady Eleanor Roosevelt had her own victory garden at the White House. The USDA estimated that between 9 and 10 million tons of food came from those gardens during World War II.

These days, Dan and I don't have access to an apartment rooftop to grow our own vegetables, but I did when I lived in Seattle and Atlanta, and I can tell you that if you have the ability to at least try to grow your own food, you should! It'll save you a little money in the long run, but it'll also provide you with a sense of accomplishment and hours of cheap entertainment on the weekends.

Here are some things to take into consideration when getting started:

- Make sure the dirt on your plot of land is not contaminated with pollutants like asphalt runoff, and check how much sun your garden will get throughout the day. These problems can be fixed with raised soil boxes and maybe a little tree trimming.
- Research what edible plants are native to your area. They'll be easier to grow and produce more.
- Be realistic about how much time you have to dedicate to your garden. If you're a busy person who isn't home much, you'll need low-maintenance crops.

If you're like us and have no land to speak of, you can always join a community garden or a CSA (community supported agriculture) program. CSAs let people who can't farm their own food buy into a local farm or cooperative that will in turn deliver fresh, seasonal, and often organic produce to their homes. The downside to CSAs is that sometimes you end up with 10 pounds of organic and locally grown zucchini—but the upside to that much zucchini is you'll be able to freeze and enjoy zucchini bread for the next ten months. Bottom line, you get a lot of produce for very little money. I think Eleanor Roosevelt would agree that that, too, is a victory.

CHAPTER 3

BREAKFAST

Breakfast is universally accepted as awesome, and yet it's a meal people often take for granted. It's not uncommon for people to trade in a good breakfast for a chance to hit the snooze button a few times. They either grab a granola bar, microwave instant oatmeal, or skip the meal altogether, only to regret it the second they get to work. All this adds up to breakfast being both beloved and misunderstood. The recipes in this section range from the simple and speedy to the momentous, without the extravagant grocery bills.

> Ginger-Plum Oatmeal 26
> Emily Dickinson Porridge 27
> PB&J Granola Bars 28
> Granola Grrrl Bars 29
> Green Tea and Pear Smoothie 30
> Clementine and Coconut Smoothie 31
> Cinnamon Roll Pancakes 32
> Sweet Potato Pancakes 34
> BLT Pancake Stacks 36
> Roasted Red Flannel Hash 38
> Virgin Crêpes Suzette 39
> Savory Crêpes with Easy "Hollandaise" Sauce 42
> Banana Churro Waffles 44

> Easy Mixed Berry Muffins 45
> Pumpkin Pie Muffins 46
> Cinnamon Peach Skillet Rolls 47
> Orange Drop Doughnuts 49
> Fresh Blueberry Blintzes 51
> Baked Strapatsada—Greek Baked "Egg" Cups 53
> Vegan Bacon and "Egg" Enchiladas 55
> Smoky Butternut Squash Scramble 57
> Vegan Bacon and Broccoli Quiche 59
> Rosemary Potato Frittata 60
> Tofu à la Goldenrod 61
> Mexican Coffee 63
> Pumpkin Spice Latte 64

Ginger-Plum Oatmeal

Oatmeal gets a bad rap because, to be honest, it can look a little like the gruel they serve orphans in Oliver Twist. But oatmeal is one of the healthiest and easiest breakfasts a person can eat. Even if you don't use instant oatmeal, it cooks rather quickly. And it has a lot of the soluble fiber that lowers cholesterol, as well as those good slow-burning carbs that provide energy for your body over a long period of time. We started combining our oatmeal with some spices and seasonal fruit and found that this ginger-plum combination is our favorite by far.

MAKES 4 TO 6 BOWLS   **$1.15 PER SERVING**

1 cup steel-cut oats

2 plums

2 to 3 teaspoons packed brown sugar (you may want more for topping)

1 teaspoon ginger paste (less if you prefer a more subtle flavor)

1 teaspoon ground cinnamon

Bring 4 cups water to a rolling boil over medium heat. Add the oats, then reduce the heat to maintain a simmer. Stir occasionally to prevent the oats from sticking to the pot. While the oats are cooking, in a blender, combine one of the plums, the brown sugar, ginger paste, and cinnamon, and puree. Stir this puree into the oats and continue to simmer until the oatmeal is tender to your liking.

Slice the remaining plum. Serve the oatmeal hot, with a few plum slices and a pinch of brown sugar on top of each bowl, if you like.

> **You can use any leftover brown sugar to make:**
>
> Emily Dickinson Porridge on page 27
>
> Granola Grrrl Bars on page 29
>
> Jerk "Chicken" Pasta Salad on page 98
>
> Spiced Pear Cupcakes with Maple Frosting on page 256
>
> Monkey Bread on page 274
>
> Molasses Crinkle Cookies on page 280
>
> Carrot Cake Cookies on page 282

Emily Dickinson Porridge

Many people don't know that during her lifetime, Emily Dickinson was more famous for her baking than her poetry. In fact, if you ever visit her house in Amherst, Massachusetts, you can see the pulley she would use to lower cookies down to the neighborhood children from her bedroom window. Although she's now famous for being a recluse, she was known among friends and family for being generous with care packages of homemade baked goods. One of her most beloved recipes was called Cocoanut Cake. The recipe was found scribbled on the back of one of her poems. This porridge was inspired by her recipe, and combines warm vanilla with toasted coconut to make a rich, sweet treat.

MAKES 4 TO 6 BOWLS   **$0.65 PER SERVING**

1 cup steel-cut oats

½ cup coconut milk, from a carton, not a can

½ teaspoon vanilla extract

1 teaspoon packed brown sugar (you may want more for topping)

1 cup shredded coconut, toasted (see Note, below)

Bring 4 cups water to a rolling boil over medium heat. Add the oats, then reduce the heat to maintain a simmer. Stir occasionally to prevent the oats from sticking to the pot. Stir in the coconut milk, vanilla, brown sugar, and ½ cup of the toasted coconut. Let cook, stirring occasionally, until the oats are tender to your liking.

Serve hot, with some of the remaining toasted coconut and some brown sugar sprinkled over the top of each bowl.

You can use any leftover shredded coconut to make:

Granola Grrrl Bars on page 29

Mango Coconut Pie on page 269

Snowball Cupcakes on page 258

White Wedding Cupcakes on page 310

TOASTING COCONUT

Toasting coconut is an easy process that can level up any dessert or dish in about 10 minutes.

Start by preheating the oven to 325°F. Line a cookie sheet with aluminum foil.

Spread raw coconut flakes on the lined cookie sheet in a thin layer and put it in the oven. The thinner or smaller the flakes, the faster the coconut will toast, so keep an eye on it. Within 5 to 10 minutes, the edges should turn a golden brown. You may want to flip the coconut with a spatula halfway through so it toasts evenly. Once the coconut is toasted, add it to any recipe!

PB&J Granola Bars

Oh, peanut butter and jelly. You're soul mates that have graced many an elementary school lunch and late-night dorm snack. You're both a comfort and an everyday treasure. Now you are also a delicious granola bar.

MAKES 24 BARS   **$0.49 PER SERVING**

1 cup old-fashioned rolled oats

2 cups brown rice cereal

½ cup dry-roasted peanuts

½ cup raisins or dried cherries

2 tablespoons ground flaxseed

¾ cup creamy peanut butter

¼ cup agave nectar

1 teaspoon vanilla extract

Preheat the oven to 350°F. Line a cookie sheet with aluminum foil.

Spread the oats in a thin, even layer on the lined cookie sheet and toast them in the oven for 5 to 10 minutes. Remove the oats from the oven when they are a light golden brown and transfer them to a large bowl.

Add the rice cereal, peanuts, and raisins to the bowl and gently mix with a large spoon.

In a separate bowl, whisk the flaxseed, peanut butter, agave nectar, and vanilla together until blended. Pour the flaxseed mixture into the oat mixture and stir gently until completely blended. Be careful not to crush the cereal while doing this.

Line a cookie sheet with parchment paper, then pour the granola bar mix onto the sheet. Gently press it into an even layer and form it into a rectangle with your hands.

Cover with plastic wrap and let set for 15 minutes. Uncover and cut into bars with a pizza cutter or a large, sharp knife.

> *You can use any leftover old-fashioned rolled oats to make:*
>
> Granola Grrrl Bars on page 29
> Humble Apple Pie on page 267
> Betty's Wartime Walnut Burger on
>   page 189

Granola Grrrl Bars

Living in Olympia, Washington, in the nineties was an experience I wouldn't change for the world. Sure, there were ups and downs, but ultimately it's the place that helped me become who I am today. The women I met while working at Safeplace, a domestic violence support and rape crisis center, are still some of the most inspirational people I have ever known. This recipe celebrates those crunchy hippies, creative and unique proto-hipsters, and sweet-hearted amazons.

MAKES 24 BARS   **$0.39 PER SERVING**

2 cups old-fashioned rolled oats

¾ cup shredded coconut

⅓ cup sliced almonds

1 cup brown rice cereal

½ cup vegan chocolate chips

¼ cup coconut oil

¾ cup peanut butter or almond butter

½ teaspoon vanilla extract

⅓ cup packed brown sugar

Preheat the oven to 350°F. Line two cookie sheets with parchment paper.

In a large bowl, toss together the oats, coconut, and almonds. Spread the mixture over one of the lined cookie sheets and bake for 3 to 5 minutes, or until the oats and coconut are lightly toasted. Set aside to cool.

Once the oat mixture has cooled, pour it into a large bowl and gently mix in the rice cereal and chocolate chips.

In a separate bowl, whisk together the coconut oil, peanut butter, vanilla, and brown sugar until smooth. Pour the coconut oil mixture into the oat mixture and gently mix with a large spoon until the oats are completely coated. Be careful not to crush the rice cereal.

Pour the granola bar mixture onto the remaining lined cookie sheet. Using your hands, gently press the mixture into an even rectangle. Let it set for 15 minutes, then use a pizza cutter or large knife to cut it into bars. Cover the pan with plastic wrap and refrigerate for 10 minutes.

Wrap each bar individually in waxed paper. You can eat these at room temperature, but store them in the fridge to keep the coconut oil from getting too soft.

> **You can use any leftover coconut oil to make:**
>
> Cinnamon Peach Skillet Rolls on page 47
> Snowball Cupcakes on page 258
> Mango Coconut Pie on page 269
> Salted Caramel Skillet Cake on page 250

Green Tea and Pear Smoothie

This smoothie has the mild caffeine boost of green tea mixed with the sweetness of pears. It's a great big bright green way to add a little boost to your morning.

MAKES 4 TO 6 SERVINGS   **$0.43 PER SERVING**

2 ripe Bartlett pears

1 banana

1 teaspoon matcha green tea powder (can be found at most Whole Foods)

2 cups almond milk

1 to 2 teaspoons agave nectar

Slice the pears, clean out any seeds, and cut off the stems. Do not peel them. In a blender, combine the pears, banana, matcha, and almond milk and puree until smooth. Add 1 or 2 teaspoons of agave nectar, depending how sweet you like your breakfast, and pulse just to combine.

> *You can use any leftover almond milk to make:*
>
> Banana Churro Waffles on page 44
>
> Pumpkin Spice Latte on page 64
>
> Parsnip and Peppercorn Soup on page 95
>
> S'mores Cookie Bars on page 260
>
> Chai Spice Cheesecake on page 272
>
> Butternut Squash and Beer Poutine Party on page 288

Clementine and Coconut Smoothie

I won't lie: This smoothie was inspired by those cheap orange sherbet and vanilla ice cream cups they always handed out at the Knights of Columbus ice cream socials when I was a kid. No, not classy or fancy, but still special. This recipe is much healthier, but I think it captures the spirit of those frozen treats quite nicely.

MAKES 4 TO 6 SERVINGS   **$0.42 PER SERVING**

2 bananas

1 cup coconut milk, from a carton, not a can

4 clementines, peeled and separated

1 cup orange juice with pulp

Toss all the ingredients into a blender and puree.

Serve cold.

You can use any leftover coconut milk to make:

Vegan Bacon Ranch Dipping Sauce on page 165

Pumpkin Curry Soup on page 216

Salted Caramel Skillet Cake on page 250

Peanut Butter Cup Pie on page 264

Cinnamon Roll Pancakes

This recipe has existed since the 1940s in many forms. It was a clever trick that evolved into a pretty decadent breakfast, perfect for special days like birthdays, Valentine's Day, Mother's and Father's Day, or those days when you just want to show someone how fancy the humble pancake can be.

MAKES 12 PANCAKES   **$0.45 PER SERVING**

. . . .

Cinnamon Swirl

¾ cup packed brown sugar

½ cup vegan margarine

1 tablespoon plus 1 teaspoon ground cinnamon

Pancakes

2 cups all-purpose flour

1 tablespoon baking powder

1 teaspoon sea salt

2 tablespoons vegan margarine

1 cup soy milk

1 tablespoon applesauce

Olive oil cooking spray

Cream Cheese Drizzle

½ (8-ounce) package vegan cream cheese

½ cup powdered sugar

1 cup soy milk

. . . .

Preheat the oven to 200°F.

Make the cinnamon swirl: In a bowl, combine all the cinnamon swirl ingredients and blend together with an electric handheld mixer until creamy. Fit an icing gun with the smallest tip and fill it with the cinnamon swirl mixture.

Make the pancakes: In a large bowl combine all the pancake ingredients and blend together with an electric handheld mixer.

Spray a cast-iron skillet with olive oil cooking spray and set it over medium heat. Once the skillet is hot, use a ladle to pour a ⅓-cup portion of the batter into the skillet. While the pancake cooks, use the icing gun to make a wide swirl of the cinnamon mixture on the top. Be careful not to get too close to the pancake's edges. Let the pancake cook until the edges begin to get brown and crispy. Very quickly flip the pancake so you don't smear the swirl.

Let the pancake cook until both sides are a light golden brown. Move the cooked pancake to an oven-safe plate and keep warm in the oven while you make the other pancakes.

Repeat the process until you have used all the pancake batter.

Make the cream cheese drizzle: In a large bowl, combine the cream cheese drizzle ingredients and beat with an electric hand-held mixer until smooth.

Serve the warm pancakes stacked, with the vegan cream cheese drizzle swirled over the top.

You can use any leftover vegan cream cheese to make:

Pumpkin Pie Muffins on page 46

Fresh Blueberry Blintzes on page 51

Chocolate Strawberry Cheesecake Cups on page 306

Sweet Potato Pancakes

By using sweet potatoes to replace the eggs in this classic dish, we've transformed an iconic breakfast into a hearty, everyday meal. Bake your sweet potato the night before so you can quickly scoop it out in the morning and make your pancakes without skipping a beat.

MAKES 12 PANCAKES   **$0.22 PER SERVING**

. . . .

1 large sweet potato

2 cups vegan Bisquick mix

1 cup coconut milk, from a carton, not a can

1 tablespoon applesauce

½ teaspoon ground cinnamon

Pinch of grated nutmeg

1 tablespoon packed brown sugar

Olive oil cooking spray

Vegan margarine, melted, and maple syrup, for serving

. . . .

Preheat the oven to 400°F.

Bake the sweet potato until tender, about 30 minutes, then remove it from the oven and reduce the oven temperature to 200°F.

Scrape the soft flesh from the sweet potato into a large bowl. Add the Bisquick, coconut milk, applesauce, cinnamon, nutmeg, and brown sugar and mix with an electric handheld mixer until smooth.

Spray a cast-iron skillet with a heavy coating of olive oil cooking spray and set it over medium heat. Once the skillet is hot, use a ladle to carefully pour ¼ cup of the batter into the skillet. Cook the pancake until it begins to bubble and the bottom is golden brown, then flip and cook on the second side until golden brown. Transfer the pancake to an oven-safe plate and keep warm in the oven.

Repeat until you have used all the pancake batter.

Serve the pancakes warm, with some melted margarine and maple syrup.

> *You can use your leftover vegan Bisquick mix to make:*
>
> BLT Pancake Stacks on page 36
> Easy Mixed Berry Muffins on page 45
> Sloppy Joel Pie on page 171
> Mac and Cheez Pie on page 173

SECOND BREAKFAST!

You can't really save leftover pancake batter, but you can make a batch of pancakes that'll feed you for days!

Stack the leftover pancakes, placing a piece of waxed paper between each one. Then, wrap the stack in aluminum foil, put it in a freezer bag, and refrigerate. Your pancakes can hang out in the fridge for at least a week before you'll have to toss them.

To Reheat:

Preheat the oven to 375°F. Unwrap the pancakes and place them in a single layer on a pizza stone or a cookie sheet and bake for 5 minutes, or until warm in the center.

BLT Pancake Stacks

During World War II, when meat was being rationed, housewives were always on the lookout for new and creative ways to make their meals "go further." Shepherd's pie and other recipes that combined a whole meal into a single dish became a great way to do that. These creative combos led to some of America's most famous (or, perhaps, infamous) dishes, like cheeseburger pie and taco casserole. This next recipe was inspired by both my desire to eat sandwiches for breakfast and the ingenuity behind some of those thrifty meals.

MAKES 4 TO 6 SERVINGS   **$0.83 PER SERVING**

Pancakes

1½ cups vegan Bisquick mix

1 cup soy milk

1 teaspoon ground flaxseed

Olive oil cooking spray

BLT

4 to 6 slices tempeh bacon (we recommend Lightlife Smart Bacon)

½ avocado, peeled and sliced

1 large tomato, sliced

1 cup arugula

Vegan mayonnaise (we recommend Vegenaise or Just Mayo; optional)

Make the pancakes: In a large bowl, combine the Bisquick, soy milk, and flaxseed and blend together with an electric handheld mixer until smooth.

Spray a cast-iron skillet with a heavy coating of olive oil cooking spray and set it over medium heat. Once the skillet is hot, use a ladle to pour ¼ cup of the batter into the skillet. Cook the pancake until the edges are light brown and slightly crispy, then flip and cook the other side until light brown.

Transfer to a plate while you make the remaining pancakes.

Repeat until you have used all the pancake batter.

Assemble the BLT: Spray the same skillet with another coating of olive oil cooking spray and return to the stovetop over medium heat. Cook the tempeh bacon until crispy, then transfer to a plate. Using a spatula, break the tempeh bacon into bite-size pieces.

For each BLT, place one pancake on a plate, top with a few pieces of the tempeh bacon, slices of avocado and tomato, and some arugula, and finally top with a second pancake. If you like vegan mayo, you might want to spread a little on the top pancake before closing the sandwich.

You can use your leftover avocado to make:

Avocado and Grapefruit Salad with Cilantro Dressing on page 81

Roasted Red Flannel Hash

Red Flannel Hash is a classic New England dish that came into its own during the Great Depression. It traditionally combines a lot of "odds and ends" and inexpensive ingredients like potatoes and beets, which are cubed and fried up in a skillet. Our recipe is inspired by this classic American fare, but is roasted in the oven rather than fried to make it a bit healthier.

MAKES 4 TO 6 SERVINGS   **$1.02 PER SERVING**

¼ cup olive oil

2 teaspoons vegan Worcestershire sauce

1 clove garlic, minced

¼ teaspoon vegan liquid smoke

1 teaspoon dried thyme

½ teaspoon dried oregano

Pinch of celery seed

1 red onion, diced

4 small beets, trimmed, peeled, and cut into small cubes

1 pound new potatoes, cut into small cubes

⅓ cup chopped raw kale leaves

Preheat the oven to 400°F.

In a small bowl, whisk together the olive oil, vegan Worcestershire sauce, garlic, vegan liquid smoke, thyme, oregano, and celery seed. Toss in the onion, beets, and potatoes and mix with a large spoon.

Transfer the vegetable mixture to a cast-iron skillet and bake for 15 minutes. Remove from the oven, flip the vegetable mixture with a spatula, and bake for another 15 minutes. Once the vegetables are tender, stir in the kale and bake for another 5 minutes.

Once the kale is slightly wilted, remove the skillet from the oven and let cool. Serve the hash warm.

> *You can use the rest of your vegan Worcestershire sauce to make:*
>
> Blackstrap Vegan Bangers and Mash with Onion Gravy on page 125
>
> Sloppy Joel Pie on page 171
>
> Beefless Brussels Sprout Shepherd's Pie on page 183
>
> Yankee Pot Roast Dinner on page 144
>
> Beet "Boudin" Balls with Garlic Aioli on page 206
>
> Vegan Gyros on page 219

Virgin Crêpes Suzette

Unlike in the movies, there are no music montages that kick in to help someone overcome a tragedy in the span of a pop song. There are good days, when you think you just might be yourself again someday, and then there are the other kind of days. It was on one of those bad days that I rediscovered the comfort that comes with the ritual of breakfast. There is a lyrical routine to a good morning, and once I had the breakthrough I mentioned in the introduction (see page 1), I found my rhythm again in the book Julia's Kitchen Wisdom.

It began with Julia Child's crêpes suzette. It was one of those Sundays when I didn't have any plans but chores, and something told me that making flaming dessert crêpes for breakfast was going to save the day from just being whiled away doing laundry. Plus, we had a dusty bottle of orange liqueur that we'd brought back from a trip to Rome, and I had been trying to figure out what to do with it for ages. The morning ended up being kind of frightening—literally filled with fireballs* and fighting smoke alarms with broomsticks—but the crêpes were pretty delicious, and it was the first time I can remember laughing again. We've reworked this recipe since then, so you don't need to buy a ticket to Italy to pick up some booze or burn down your house to enjoy this classic French treat for breakfast.

MAKES 12 CRÊPES   **$0.42 PER SERVING**

Olive oil cooking spray

2 firm sweet oranges

2 tablespoons agave nectar

3 tablespoons packed brown sugar

½ cup plus 2 tablespoons vegan margarine, plus more for cooking

½ cup orange juice with pulp

1½ cups all-purpose flour

1 tablespoon granulated sugar

½ teaspoon baking powder

½ teaspoon sea salt

2 cups soy milk

½ teaspoon vanilla extract

2 tablespoons applesauce

Powdered sugar, for topping (optional)

Preheat the oven to 300°F. Lightly coat an oven-safe lasagna dish with olive oil cooking spray and place it in the oven to warm.

Using a Microplane or a box grater, zest the peel of one orange. Peel the other orange and

cut it in half. Slice one half of the orange into thin slices. Make sure you have one slice of orange per crêpe. Toss the remaining orange half in a food processor with the orange zest, agave nectar, brown sugar, ½ cup of the vegan margarine, and the orange juice. Blend until creamy. Set the orange mixture aside.

(continued)

---

* This is not a joke.

In a bowl, combine the flour, granulated sugar, baking powder, salt, and soy milk and blend with an electric handheld mixer until smooth. We suggest using a whisk attachment to get the best batter. Add the remaining 2 tablespoons vegan margarine, the vanilla, and the applesauce and blend for 2 to 3 minutes with the bowl tilted so the mixture gets smooth and creamy.

Heat your deepest cast-iron skillet over medium heat and lightly coat it with vegan margarine. (You'll have to coat the skillet between each crêpe, so keep the margarine out.) Once the margarine begins to bubble, you're ready to make crêpes.

To make each crêpe, pour ⅓ cup of the batter into the skillet. Immediately rotate the skillet by rolling your wrist while holding the handle until a thin layer of batter covers the bottom. If your skillet is heavy, use a potholder to hold the other side of the skillet and use both hands to rotate the skillet. Cook until the edges of the crêpe begin to turn light brown. Run a wide spatula along the edge to loosen the crêpe, then flip and cook the other side until light brown. Transfer the finished crêpe to a plate, top it with a piece of waxed paper, and cover with a clean kitchen towel. Repeat until you have used all the crêpe batter.

Pour the orange mixture into the hot skillet and cook over medium heat, stirring gently, until it begins to bubble and become syrupy.

Working with one crêpe at a time, carefully drop them into the orange mixture. Flip them once to lightly coat both sides of each crêpe. Remove the crêpe from the orange mixture and fold it in half once, then in half again to make a wedge shape using tongs or a rubber tipped spatula so you don't burn your fingers. Place folded crêpe in the warm lasagna dish in the oven with an orange slice on top. Repeat with the remaining crêpes making a single layer that barely overlaps until all have been coated, folded, and transferred to the lasagna pan.

Pour 1 to 2 tablespoons of the orange mixture over the top of the folded crêpes. Bake for 5 minutes or until all of the orange mixture has melted and the orange slices topping the crêpes are lightly baked.

Serve hot, dusted with some powdered sugar if you have a sweet tooth.

> *You can use your leftover agave nectar to make:*
>
> Green Tea and Pear Smoothie on
>   page 30
> Pumpkin Spice Latte on page 64
> Thai Vegan Chicken Slaw on page 69
> Avocado and Grapefruit Salad with
>   Cilantro Dressing on page 81
> Tofu Spring Rolls with Agave Chili Sauce
>   on page 121

Julia's Blue Kitchen

Last September, Dan and I had the honor of speaking at D.C. Vegfest. I won't lie, I was pretty nervous about the whole thing—not just because I have what I'm pretty sure is an undiagnosed form of social anxiety disorder, but because so many of our readers and fans of our first book had written to tell me they would be there to see us present. I felt this looming pressure not to disappoint our readers, the organizers of the event, and Dan. For weeks, I couldn't sleep.

We had an extra day in D.C. before the event, so I took a trip—a pilgrimage—to the Smithsonian to see Julia Child's kitchen.

I've never been one for hero worship, so I didn't go in with the rose-colored glasses you'd expect a cookbook author to have. Instead, I peeked through the Plexiglas panels into her re-created robin's-egg-blue kitchen with peg boards full of copper pots and pans and found a calm solace I hadn't felt in weeks, and I had a moment of what can only be described as respect. Not for her cooking—the lady used whole cream, eggs, and meat in everything—but for her real craft: teaching.

Julia Child was undoubtedly a master of cooking. But more important, she was a teacher whose inviting nature inspired others to approach their kitchens with a fearless confidence. No, she wasn't perfect; she was, like all of us, a product of her time and the limitations of her experiences. But her ability to inspire others to embrace a different way of cooking, and to look at food in new ways, is what I aspire to more than anything, and I have so much respect for that.

Julia was once quoted in *People* magazine as saying, "Personally, I don't think pure vegetarianism is a healthy lifestyle. It's more fear of food—that whole thing that red meat is bad for you. And then there are people who don't eat meat because it's against their morals. Well, there's nothing you can do with people like that. I've often wondered to myself: Does a vegetarian look forward to dinner, ever?" Understandably, most vegetarians and vegans can never forgive her for it.

But the part of me that tries to see the best in people wants to believe she felt that way because her first exposure to vegetarianism was in the 1960s, when a cruelty-free lifestyle was labeled a "health-food fad" and a weight-loss diet—two things she had notoriously little patience for. She also never had our Apple-Sage Tempeh Sausage over Savory Polenta (page 133) or our Yankee Pot Roast Dinner (page 144). The world Julia lived in was much different than ours. In just the past ten years, technology has come so far that anything can be made vegan with little to no sacrifice in taste or texture. All of her friends and colleagues remember Julia as being a very kind and compassionate person, so I'd like to think that although she would probably never go vegan (the woman basically bathed in butter), I hope she'd be intrigued by today's vegans and at least recognize our shared passion for food. She was a sincere believer in her mantra: "Life itself is the proper binge." And like I've said before, *no one loves food like a vegan.*

As I walked away from Julia's kitchen, I thought back to my ultimate goal when I started our blog and food projects back in 2009: to help people fall in love with a compassionate lifestyle in an accessible and fun way, not unlike Julia and her passion for French cuisine. The next day, I took the stage with Dan and channeled a little Julia.

Savory Crêpes with Easy "Hollandaise" Sauce

This recipe was first conceived of when I wrote a feature for the blog Our Hen House about what led me to work for PETA back in 2004. It was a piece about how I've always felt a duty to advocate for animals because they can't speak for themselves. Or as I so ineloquently put it in the feature: Bunnies can't type, so I need to.

When people ask why we're vegans, we always answer: "Because we love animals and don't want to contribute to a system that is built on their suffering." And that's always true, but we don't care why you're enjoying a vegan meal. You can enjoy the health and financial benefits, while doing something good for the environment and saving animals all at the same time—just by choosing to leave the eggs and dairy out of your crêpes.

MAKES 6 TO 8 SERVINGS   **$0.66 PER SERVING**

Easy "Hollandaise" Sauce

⅓ cup vegan mayonnaise (we recommend Vegenaise or Just Mayo)

1 tablespoon nutritional yeast

1½ teaspoons fresh lemon juice

Crêpes

1½ cups white flour

½ teaspoon baking powder

½ teaspoon salt

Pinch of ground black pepper

¼ teaspoon nutritional yeast

2 cups soy milk

2 tablespoons vegan margarine, softened

2 tablespoons applesauce

Olive oil cooking spray

Filling

4 teaspoons olive oil (you may need a little more if your vegetables are large)

12 asparagus spears

4 mushrooms, sliced

1 shallot, sliced

1 tablespoon plus 1 teaspoon balsamic vinegar

Chopped fresh chives and smoked paprika, for garnish (optional)

Make the easy "hollandaise" sauce: In a small bowl, whisk together the vegan mayo, nutritional yeast, and lemon juice until completely blended. Cover and refrigerate until needed.

Make the crêpes: In a large bowl, combine the flour, baking powder, salt, pepper, nutritional yeast, soy milk, vegan margarine, and applesauce and blend until smooth using an electric handheld mixer.

Lightly coat a cast-iron skillet with cooking spray and set it over medium heat. Once the skillet is hot, use a ladle to pour ¼ cup of the batter into the skillet. Immediately rotate the skillet by rolling your wrist while holding the handle until a thin layer of batter covers the bottom. If your skillet is heavy, use a potholder to hold the other side of the skillet and use both hands to rotate the skillet. Cook until the batter begins to look dry and a light brown edge forms. Run a wide spatula along the edge to loosen the crepe, then flip it and cook the other side until light brown. Transfer the crepe to a plate, top with a piece of waxed paper, and cover with a clean kitchen towel. Repeat until you have used all the crepe batter.

Make the filling: In the same skillet, heat 2 teaspoons of the olive oil over medium heat, rotating the skillet to coat the bottom with the hot oil. Place some asparagus in a single layer in the pan; you'll probably have to cook the vegetables in batches, so don't worry if they don't all fit. Roll the asparagus with a spatula until coated in the hot oil, cover, and cook for 30 seconds. Toss in the mushrooms, shallots, and 2 teaspoons of the balsamic vinegar. Toss the vegetables lightly so they get an even coating of the oil and vinegar. Cover and cook for another minute. Once the asparagus is tender, remove the vegetables from the heat and use a fork to check if the asparagus is done. Repeat, using more olive oil and vinegar as needed, until all of the vegetables are cooked.

To serve, place a flat crepe on a plate and set 2 or 3 spears of asparagus in the center, along with some shallots and mushrooms. Fold the sides of the crepe up over the vegetables and pour some "hollandaise" sauce over the top to secure the fold. Sprinkle some chives and smoked paprika over the sauce, if desired, for a little color and flavor. Repeat until all the crepes have been filled.

You can use any leftover mushrooms to make:

Smoky Butternut Squash Scramble on page 57

Sriracha and Sweet Onion Stew on page 104

Chickpea à la King Skillet on page 123

Chop Suey Noodles on page 178

Angel Hair Pasta with Garlic and Rosemary Mushrooms on page 202

Banana Churro Waffles

When we were in Mexico, we saw churro stands just hanging out on the corner, beckoning us with the sweet scent of cinnamon like a siren's call. But we never got a chance to try any, because, honestly, it was so hot all I wanted was shaved ice. I will always regret that decision, and I try to make up for it with these freakin' awesome waffles. Seriously, this recipe combines banana waffles and churros...it's heaven.

MAKES 12 WAFFLES   **$0.32 PER SERVING**

. . . .

Waffles

2 cups all-purpose flour

1 tablespoon plus 2 teaspoons baking powder

1 teaspoon salt

2 teaspoons sugar

1 tablespoon ground flaxseed

1 ripe banana, lightly mashed

1½ cups almond milk

⅓ cup vegan margarine

1 teaspoon vanilla extract

¼ teaspoon ground cinnamon

Topping

⅓ cup sugar

2 tablespoons ground cinnamon

1 to 2 bananas

. . . .

Make the waffles: Preheat and prepare a waffle iron following the manufacturer's instructions.

In a large bowl, whisk together the flour, baking powder, salt, and sugar.

In a separate bowl, combine the flaxseed, banana, almond milk, vegan margarine, vanilla, and cinnamon and beat with an electric handheld mixer. Add the flour mixture and beat until smooth.

Make the topping: In a shallow bowl, combine the sugar and cinnamon. Set aside.

Make waffles following the manufacturer's instructions. As soon as you remove the waffles from the iron, place them in the dish with the cinnamon-sugar topping and flip a few times to get an even coating.

Serve the waffles hot with sliced bananas over the top. You'll want to slice the bananas as you serve your waffles to keep them from browning.

You can use your leftover almond milk to make:

Pumpkin Spice Latte on page 64

Parsnip and Peppercorn Soup on page 95

S'mores Cookie Bars on page 260

Chai Spice Cheesecake on page 272

Butternut Squash and Beer Poutine Party
on page 288

Easy Mixed Berry Muffins

Bake a batch of these on Sunday night and enjoy them for breakfast for days. They'll make you look forward to Monday morning.

MAKES 24 MUFFINS   **$0.09 PER SERVING**

. . . .

2 cups vegan Bisquick mix

⅔ cup soy milk

¼ cup sugar

2 tablespoons olive oil

1 tablespoon applesauce

1 teaspoon ground flaxseed

½ cup frozen mixed berries

. . . .

Preheat the oven to 400°F. Line two 12-cup muffin tins with paper liners.

In a large bowl, combine the Bisquick, soy milk, sugar, olive oil, applesauce, and flaxseed and beat with an electric hand-held mixer until smooth. Fold in the frozen berries.

Divide the batter evenly among the lined muffin cups. Bake the muffins for 10 to 15 minutes, or until a bamboo skewer inserted into the center of a muffin comes out clean.

You can use your leftover flaxseed to make:

PB&J Granola Bars on page 28

Banana Churro Waffles on page 44

Pumpkin Pie Muffins on page 46

Carrot Cake Cookies on page 282

Lavender and Vanilla Cupcakes on page 308

Pumpkin Pie Muffins

Every fall I would see the non-vegan version of these muffins pop up in bakery cases all over Brooklyn. They always looked so good, with their dollop of cream cheese inside a pumpkin pie–spiced muffin. Veganizing them was the easy part; not eating them all in one sitting was harder.

MAKES 24 MUFFINS   **$0.19 PER SERVING**

Muffins

1½ cups all-purpose flour

2 teaspoons baking powder

2 teaspoons pumpkin pie spice

½ teaspoon salt

1 tablespoon applesauce

1 tablespoon ground flaxseed

½ (15-ounce) can pure pumpkin puree

½ cup coconut milk, from a carton, not a can

½ cup packed brown sugar

¼ teaspoon vanilla extract

Cream Cheese Topping

½ (8-ounce) container vegan cream cheese

1 tablespoon powdered sugar

1 tablespoon coconut milk, from a carton, not a can

Make the muffins: Preheat the oven to 375°F. Line two 12-cup muffin tins with paper liners.

In a large bowl, whisk together the flour, baking powder, pumpkin pie spice, and salt.

In a separate large bowl, combine the applesauce, flaxseed, pumpkin puree, coconut milk, brown sugar, and vanilla and beat with an electric handheld mixer. Add the flour mixture to the applesauce mixture and beat until creamy.

Make the topping: In a medium bowl, combine the vegan cream cheese, powdered sugar, and coconut milk and beat with an electric handheld mixer until well blended.

Fill each muffin cup two-thirds full with batter, then top with a dollop of the topping. Gently push the dollop of topping into the batter.

Bake for 25 minutes, or until the muffins are a light golden brown.

> *You can use your leftover pumpkin puree to make:*
>
> Pumpkin Spice Latte on page 64
> Pumpkin Curry Soup on page 216

Cinnamon Peach Skillet Rolls

If you want to make friends and influence people without spending a lot of cash, make cinnamon rolls. Baked together in a skillet all pioneer woman–style, this recipe more closely resembles a Finnish Bostonkakku or Boston cake than the enormous rolls you find at your local mall—but they are just as delicious and crowd-pleasing.

MAKES 12 ROLLS   **$0.74 PER SERVING**

Rolls

1 cup warm water

1 package active dry yeast

2 tablespoons granulated sugar

4 cups all-purpose flour, plus more for dusting

1½ teaspoons sea salt

½ cup olive oil

1 tablespoon applesauce

1 teaspoon ground flaxseed

1 teaspoon vanilla extract

Coconut oil, for the pan

½ cup vegan margarine, melted

1 cup packed brown sugar

1 tablespoon plus 2 teaspoons ground cinnamon

1½ cups frozen peaches, defrosted

Peach Glaze

Juice from the frozen peaches

1 to 2 cups powdered sugar

Make the rolls: In a small bowl, whisk together the water, yeast, and granulated sugar. Let sit for 5 minutes.

Meanwhile, in a large bowl, combine the flour, salt, olive oil, applesauce, flaxseed, and vanilla and beat with an electric handheld mixer using the bread hook attachments. Pour the yeast mixture into the flour mixture and blend until smooth. Use a spatula to scrape the sides of the bowl. Cover and let rise in a warm spot for 1 hour.

Grease a cast-iron skillet with coconut oil.

Roll out the dough on a floured work surface into a 10 x 18-inch rectangle. Brush the dough with the melted margarine and sprinkle with the brown sugar and cinnamon. Place the peach slices in a single layer over the dough. Roll the dough into a tube and use a knife with a serrated blade or a cheese wire to cut it crosswise into 1- to ½-inch-thick slices. Gently tuck the loose end under the roll. Place each roll in the greased skillet so they are touching. Roll any leftover dough into little balls that you can tuck into any open spots between the rolls.

(continued)

Bake for 30 to 45 minutes, or until the rolls are golden brown.

Meanwhile, make the peach glaze: In a small bowl, whisk together the peach juice and 1 cup of powdered sugar until smooth. Then gradually add more powdered sugar a tablespoon at a time until your glaze gets the desired thickness. Set aside.

Let the rolls cool for 15 minutes in the pan, then drizzle with the peach glaze. Let cool for another 5 minutes. Serve warm.

Warning/Promise: These are sticky.

You can use any leftover flaxseed to make:

Betty's Wartime Walnut Burger on page 189

Beet "Boudin" Balls with Garlic Aioli on page 206

Cuba Libre Cake on page 248

Salted Caramel Skillet Cake on page 250

Chocolate Chip and Banana Brownie Cookies on page 281

Lavender and Vanilla Cupcakes on page 308

Orange Drop Doughnuts

During World War I, young women volunteering with the Salvation Army went out into the trenches of war-torn France with artillery helmets, thermoses of coffee, and large buckets of these simple orange doughnuts to deliver a little kindness to some very grateful soldiers. They were called "Doughnut Girls," and their efforts improved morale so much that the Red Cross began to join in as well. At one point these doughnuts became so popular that the girls were rumored to be giving out more than four hundred doughnuts a minute—not just to the troops, but to everyone affected by the war. Because of the high demand, they began just dropping the dough straight into vats of oil, rather than taking the time to form the traditional doughnut ring. Thus, the Orange Drop Doughnut was born.

MAKES 24 DOUGHNUTS   **$0.22 PER SERVING**

1 to 2 quarts vegetable oil, for frying

1 cup sugar

2 cups all-purpose flour

2 teaspoons baking powder

¼ teaspoon salt

1 tablespoon applesauce

1½ teaspoons Ener-G egg replacer

1 tablespoon grated orange zest

½ cup orange juice with pulp

2 tablespoons vegan margarine

Pour the oil into a large soup pot or Dutch oven that can hold all of the oil without being more than halfway full, so you don't have to worry about overflowing. Heat the oil over high heat. If you have a deep-fry thermometer, use it to check your oil. When it hits around 350 degrees your oil is the perfect temperature to fry your doughnuts.

Place ½ cup of the sugar in a shallow dish. Place a few paper towels on a plate so you have a place for your doughnuts to drain after they're done.

In a large bowl, whisk together the flour, baking powder, and salt.

In a separate large bowl, combine the applesauce, egg replacer, remaining ½ cup sugar, the orange zest, orange juice, and vegan margarine and mix until smooth. Gradually stir in the flour mixture until you have a creamy batter.

Using a large soup spoon, drop a few large dollops of the batter into the hot oil, being careful not to crowd the pan. Fry the doughnuts until lightly crispy and dark brown on all sides. Use a slotted spoon to transfer the

(continued)

doughnuts to the paper towel–lined plate to drain.

Once the doughnuts are cool enough to handle, roll them gently in the dish of sugar to coat.

Enjoy at room temperature.

You can use the rest of your Ener-G egg replacer to make:

Pink Lemonade Cupcakes on page 254

Chai Spice Cheesecake on page 272

Cookie Pizza on page 276

Spiced Pear Cupcakes with Maple
    Frosting on page 256

Chocolate Strawberry Cheesecake Cups
    on page 306

SAVING FRYING OIL

When it comes to making doughnuts, one of the greatest expenses is actually the oil used to deep-fry them. The good news is that for generations, kitchens all around the world have saved and reused kitchen oil. Here's how they do it.

The first thing to figure out is if you're going to be deep-frying again in the next 24 hours. If not, you should really just toss your used oil, or you run the risk of it going rancid or just being gross and ruining your future meal.

If you are going to fry again soon, wait for your oil to cool significantly, then use a slotted spoon or fork to remove any particles of whatever you last deep-fried. Then, use a rubber band to secure a piece of cheesecloth over the open mouth of a glass mason jar large enough to hold all your oil. This will filter out any food particles too small for your slotted spoon. Now, wait for the frying oil to cool to room temperature before moving to this next step to avoid burning yourself. Once oil is cool, *very* slowly and carefully pour it through the cheesecloth into the jar.

Remove the rubber band and cheesecloth. Screw the jar lid as tightly as you can and put your oil in the fridge to use the next time you deep-fry.

Fresh Blueberry Blintzes

Blintzes are a New York institution, like the Empire State Building and Yellow Cabs. A blintz is basically a crepe filled with slightly sweet and lemony ricotta filling (in our case, vegan cream cheese and tofu in place of ricotta) and often topped with a fruit compote. We decided to use fresh blueberries to make it a little healthier.

MAKES 6 TO 8 SERVINGS   **$1.54 PER SERVING**

Filling
½ (8-ounce) package vegan cream cheese
½ (16-ounce) package extra-firm tofu
¼ cup powdered sugar
1 teaspoon vanilla extract
Zest of 1 lemon

Crêpes
1½ cups white flour
1 tablespoon granulated sugar
½ teaspoon baking powder
½ teaspoon salt

2 cups soy milk
½ cup plus 2 tablespoons vegan margarine, plus more for cooking
½ teaspoon vanilla extract
2 tablespoons applesauce

To Assemble
Olive oil cooking spray
¼ cup vegan margarine, melted
1½ to 2 cups fresh blueberries
Powdered sugar, for dusting

Make the filling: In a food processor, combine the vegan cream cheese, tofu, powdered sugar, vanilla, and lemon zest and blend until creamy. Refrigerate until ready to use.

Make the crêpes: In a large bowl, combine the flour, granulated sugar, baking powder, salt, and soy milk and beat together with an electric handheld mixer. Once the batter is completely blended, add 2 tablespoons of the vegan margarine, the vanilla, and the applesauce. Blend for 2 to 3 minutes with

the bowl tilted so the batter gets light and creamy.

Heat your deepest cast-iron skillet over medium heat and lightly coat it with vegan margarine. (You'll have to coat the skillet between each crêpe, so keep the margarine out.) Once the margarine begins to bubble, you're ready to make crêpes.

Using a ladle, pour ⅓ cup of the crêpe batter into the skillet. Immediately rotate the skillet by rolling your wrist while holding

(continued)

the handle until a thin layer of batter covers the bottom. If your skillet is heavy, use a potholder to hold the other side of the skillet and use both hands to rotate the skillet. Cook until the edges of the crêpe begin to turn light brown. Run a wide spatula along the edge to loosen the crêpe, then flip it and cook the other side until light brown. Transfer the crêpe to a plate, top with a piece of waxed paper, and cover with a clean kitchen towel. Repeat until you have used all the crêpe batter.

Assemble the blintzes: Preheat the oven to 400°F. Coat a baking dish with olive oil cooking spray.

Place one crêpe on a flat surface and spoon 3 tablespoons of the filling into the center in a straight line. Fold one edge of the crêpe over the filling and gently press it into the filling, then fold the other sides over and tuck them underneath. Place the blintz on a plate with the seam side up. Repeat until you have filled all the crêpes.

Brush the same skillet in which you cooked the crêpes with some of the melted vegan margarine and set it over medium heat. Once the skillet is hot, place the blintzes in the skillet, seam-side down, and brush with more melted margarine. You may need to work in batches.

Cook the blintzes for about 30 seconds to seal them. Using a spatula, gently roll the blintzes in the skillet and cook them evenly until they are a golden brown and have lightly crispy edges. Try not to brown the blintzes for more than 2 minutes.

Transfer the browned blintzes to the prepared baking dish. Bake the blintzes for 10 to 15 minutes. Remove from the oven and let cool in the dish for 5 minutes.

Serve warm, topped with some blueberries and a pinch or two of powdered sugar.

You can use the rest of your vegan cream cheese to make:

Cinnamon Roll Pancakes on page 32
Chocolate Strawberry Cheesecake Cups
    on page 306
Pumpkin Pie Muffins on page 46

Baked Strapatsada—Greek Baked "Egg" Cups

When we were in Athens, strapatsada was a dish we saw on menus all over the city, but we had to wait until we got home to veganize it. It's a simple, inexpensive dish that consists of fresh tomatoes, scrambled eggs, and olive oil. But once we started to learn more about Greek food, we found versions of strapatsada that included artichoke hearts, leeks, spinach, and ground lamb. So we experimented with different vegan versions and this one, made with red peppers and spinach, was our favorite. It makes a great breakfast alongside coffee and fresh fruit.

MAKES 4 TO 6 SERVINGS   **$1.33 PER SERVING**

Olive oil cooking spray

1 (16-ounce) package extra-firm tofu, drained

2 tablespoons nutritional yeast

2 teaspoons ground cumin

¼ teaspoon smoked paprika

1 teaspoon dried marjoram

½ teaspoon dried oregano

¼ teaspoon ground turmeric

1 teaspoon onion powder

½ teaspoon dried thyme

1 clove garlic, minced

1 teaspoon capers, drained

⅓ cup pitted kalamata olives

¼ cup roasted red peppers in oil

½ cup chopped spinach

Salt and black pepper

Preheat the oven to 400°F. Coat four 6-ounce or six 4-ounce ramekins with olive oil cooking spray.

In a large bowl, use a fork to gently mash the tofu into bite-size pieces—not into a paste. Then, using a large spoon, mix in the nutritional yeast, cumin, paprika, marjoram, oregano, turmeric, onion powder, and thyme. Adding one ingredient at a time, gently mix in the garlic, capers, olives, red peppers, and spinach, until completely blended. Season with salt and black pepper to taste.

Fill the ramekins evenly with the tofu mixture. Make sure to get some roasted red peppers in every ramekin.

Bake for 20 to 25 minutes, or until the top of the mixture is a light golden brown. Remove from the oven and let cool for 2 to 3 minutes.

Serve warm.

(continued)

You can use your leftover nutritional yeast to make:

Vegan Bacon and "Egg" Enchiladas on
  page 55

Smoky Butternut Squash Scramble on
  page 57

Kale Caesar Salad on page 78

Chef's Pasta Salad on page 97

Vegan Bacon, White Bean, and Spinach
  Risotto on page 155

Yankee Doodle Macaroni on page 191

Vegan Bacon and "Egg" Enchiladas

Fact: Very few meals sound as fun and appetizing as enchiladas. Just the word can make even the grumpiest of grumpasauruses smile. Don't believe me? Go ask any grumpasaurus if they like enchiladas. We'll wait here.

MAKES 6 TO 8 SERVINGS   **$1.60 PER SERVING**

Enchilada Sauce

1 (28-ounce) can crushed tomatoes

2 small tomatoes

1 (4-ounce) can green chilies

2 cloves garlic, minced

1 tablespoon chili powder

½ teaspoon dried oregano

1 teaspoon ground cumin

1 teaspoon soy sauce or Bragg's Liquid Aminos

Enchilada Filling

1 (16-ounce) package extra-firm tofu, drained

2 tablespoons nutritional yeast

1 teaspoon garlic powder

1 teaspoon onion powder

1 teaspoon ground cumin

½ teaspoon ground turmeric

¼ teaspoon smoked paprika

¼ cup vegan bacon bits

¾ cup raw baby spinach leaves

To Assemble

6 to 8 6.5-inch flour tortillas

¼ cup vegan cheddar or pepper Jack cheese, shredded (we recommend Daiya)

Preheat the oven to 350°F.

Make the enchilada sauce: In a saucepan, combine the tomatoes, chilies, garlic, chili powder, oregano, cumin, and soy sauce. Bring to a boil over medium heat, then reduce the heat to maintain a simmer.

Make the enchilada filling: In a large bowl, gently mash the tofu with a fork into bite-size pieces—not into a paste. Then, with a large spoon, mix in the nutritional yeast, garlic powder, onion powder, cumin, turmeric, and paprika. Mix in the vegan bacon bits and spinach.

Assemble the enchiladas: Ladle ¼ cup of the enchilada sauce into a baking dish.

Pour the remaining enchilada sauce into a separate shallow dish. Place one tortilla in the dish with the sauce and flip it a few times to coat evenly. Spoon some of the filling into the tortilla and gently roll it into a

(continued)

loose cigar. Place the rolled enchilada in the baking dish, seam-side down. Repeat until you have coated, filled, and rolled all the tortillas, placing them in the baking dish so they are snug and tucking any loose edges underneath to prevent them from unrolling.

Pour the remaining sauce from the shallow dish over the enchiladas and sprinkle the top evenly with the vegan cheese.

Bake for 20 minutes, or until the vegan cheese has melted and the tortilla edges are crispy.

You can use the rest of your bottle of Bragg's Liquid Aminos to make:

Blackstrap Vegan Bangers and Mash with Onion Gravy on page 125
Wild Mushroom Risotto on page 135
Sloppy Joel Pie on page 171
Chili-Stuffed Sweet Potatoes on page 167

You can use any leftover tortillas to make:

Sweet Potato and Black Bean Tacos on page 182
Roasted Pear, Walnut, and Brussels Sprout Tacos on page 197

Smoky Butternut Squash Scramble

Oh, butternut squash, you're a winter squash packed with beta-carotene and lots of vitamin C—making you not only the perfect way to thicken a sauce or gravy, but also a healthy addition to a tofu scramble when roasted and fried up in a cast-iron skillet. You're like little globs of sunshine.

For this dish, you'll need to prepare the squash the night before, so be sure to plan ahead.

MAKES 4 TO 6 SERVINGS   **$1.49 PER SERVING**

1 butternut squash, peeled, seeded, and cubed

1 tablespoon olive oil

Dash of vegan liquid smoke

1 (16-ounce) package extra-firm tofu, drained

2 tablespoons nutritional yeast

2 teaspoons ground cumin

½ teaspoon smoked paprika

½ teaspoon ground turmeric

1 teaspoon garlic powder

½ teaspoon onion powder

1 red onion, diced

¼ teaspoon rubbed sage

5 or 6 mushrooms, sliced

Olive oil cooking spray

½ cup chopped kale leaves

Hot sauce, for serving (optional)

Preheat the oven to 400°F.

In a baking dish, toss the squash with the olive oil and liquid smoke until evenly coated. Bake for 20 minutes, or until tender. Cover the baking dish with aluminum foil and refrigerate overnight.

In the morning, place the tofu in a bowl and use a fork to mash it into bite-size pieces—not into a paste. Mix in the nutritional yeast, cumin, paprika, turmeric, garlic powder, and onion powder. Use a large spoon to mix in the cooked squash, red onion, sage, and mushrooms.

Spray a cast-iron skillet with olive oil cooking spray and set it over medium heat.

Add the squash and tofu mixture and use a spatula to spread it into an even layer in the skillet. Cook for 3 minutes, then flip the mixture a few times so it cooks evenly. Be sure to scrape up any bits of tofu or squash that stick to the skillet with the spatula to keep them from burning.

Once the tofu begins to get slightly crispy edges, mix in the kale.

The scramble is ready once the tofu is a light golden brown and the kale is slightly wilted.

Serve hot—and if you're feeling spicy, add a few dashes of hot sauce.

(continued)

SMOKED PAPRIKA

The first international trip Dan and I ever took together was to Budapest, Hungary, back in 2008. We ate vegan goulash, drank huge beers, and learned firsthand how much Hungarians love paprika (a lot). Before that trip, I wouldn't have thought I'd have such strong feelings for this neglected spice—but I do. Made from ground peppers, paprika comes in almost as many different flavors and colors as there are snowflakes. Some are sweet, others are smoky, and some bring the heat. We've found we get the most use out of smoked paprika, which is more of a Spanish style and is often labeled pimentón. If you're wondering what else you can do with smoked paprika, we recommend making some Cajun Nachos on page 129, Chimichurri Rice Casserole on page 148, or Hungarian Goulash Stew on page 229.

Vegan Bacon and Broccoli Quiche

Real men don't just eat vegan quiche—they make it. This is one of Dan's favorite recipes in the book.

MAKES 1 9-INCH QUICHE   **$1.60 PER SERVING**

1 vegan piecrust, store-bought or homemade (see page 262)

Filling

1 (16-ounce) package extra-firm tofu, drained

¼ cup nutritional yeast

2 tablespoons olive oil

1 clove garlic, minced

1 teaspoon onion powder

1 teaspoon garlic powder

1 teaspoon ground turmeric

1 teaspoon ground cumin

1 teaspoon smoked paprika

¼ teaspoon vegan liquid smoke

1 tablespoon soy sauce or Bragg's Liquid Aminos

1 teaspoon salt

¼ cup raw walnuts

½ red onion, diced

1 cup broccoli florets

⅓ cup vegan bacon bits

Hot sauce (optional)

Preheat the oven to 425°F.

Prebake your vegan piecrust following the directions on the package or according to the recipe on page 262.

Meanwhile, make your filling: In a food processor, combine the tofu, nutritional yeast, olive oil, garlic, onion powder, garlic powder, turmeric, cumin, paprika, vegan liquid smoke, soy sauce, salt, and walnuts and process into a creamy paste.

In a large bowl, mix the tofu mixture with the red onion, broccoli, and vegan bacon bits. Pour the tofu-vegetable mixture into the crust and use a spatula to smooth the filling into an even layer.

Bake for 20 to 30 minutes, or until the crust is a light golden brown and the filling is firm.

Slice like a pie and serve warm with hot sauce, if desired.

> *You can use your leftover walnuts to make:*
>
> Betty's Wartime Walnut Burger on page 189
>
> Kale Caesar Salad on page 78
>
> Cookie Pizza on page 276
>
> Roasted Pear, Walnut, and Brussels Sprout Tacos on page 197

Rosemary Potato Frittata

When we were in Italy, we saw frittatas on every breakfast menu. This crustless, quiche-like dish is easy and inexpensive to make but has the showmanship and flair of a much more complicated dish.

MAKES 1 FRITTATA   **$0.90 PER SERVING**

1 (16-ounce) package extra-firm tofu, drained

2 tablespoons nutritional yeast

1 teaspoon ground turmeric

½ teaspoon smoked paprika

1 teaspoon garlic powder

1 teaspoon ground cumin

½ teaspoon onion powder

1½ teaspoons dried rosemary, crushed

1 teaspoon whole black peppercorns, crushed

2 tablespoons soy milk

2 tablespoons chopped fresh parsley

3 new potatoes, cut into very thin slices

¼ cup shredded vegan cheddar cheese (we recommend Daiya)

Olive oil cooking spray

Preheat the oven to 425°F.

In a food processor, combine the tofu, nutritional yeast, turmeric, paprika, garlic powder, cumin, onion powder, rosemary, peppercorns, and soy milk and process until well combined.

Transfer the tofu mixture to a large bowl and stir in the parsley, potatoes, and vegan cheese.

Spray a cast-iron skillet with olive oil cooking spray, then fill it with the tofu mixture. Use a spatula to get all the tofu from the bowl and smooth the tofu mixture into an even layer.

Bake the frittata for 20 to 25 minutes, or until a light golden brown crust forms on top. When a bamboo skewer into the center of the frittata comes out clean, the frittata is done.

You can use any leftover vegan cheddar cheese to make:

Mexican Stuffed Zucchini on page 146

Quinoa Taco Casserole on page 152

Brinner Lasagna on page 169

Cajun Nachos on page 129

Mac and Cheez Pie on page 173

Cincinnati Chili on page 177

Tofu à la Goldenrod

Eggs à la Goldenrod is a Depression-era classic that was once a popular item on diner menus all over the United States. It was a basic meal composed of scrambled eggs over an egg-based gravy served with toast points. I admit we took liberties when veganizing this recipe, but I think the result is a hearty, flavorful meal that goes great with a cup o' joe.

MAKES 2 TO 4 LARGE SERVINGS   **$1.49 PER SERVING**

. . . .

Scramble

1 (16-ounce) package extra-firm tofu, drained

2 tablespoons nutritional yeast

1 teaspoon ground turmeric

1 teaspoon smoked paprika

½ teaspoon garlic powder

¼ teaspoon onion powder

1 teaspoon ground cumin

½ teaspoon lemon pepper

Olive oil cooking spray

Simple Gravy

4 tablespoons vegan margarine

2 teaspoons soy sauce or Bragg's Liquid Aminos

4 tablespoons whole wheat flour

1½ teaspoons ground black pepper, plus more as needed

1 teaspoon onion powder

1 cup soy milk

Salt

To Assemble

2 to 4 slices of your favorite bread

. . . .

Make the scramble: In a large bowl, use a fork to gently mash the tofu into bite-size pieces—not into a paste. Using a large spoon, mix the nutritional yeast, turmeric, paprika, garlic powder, onion powder, cumin, and lemon pepper with the tofu.

Spray a cast-iron skillet with a heavy coating of olive oil cooking spray and set it over medium heat. Transfer the tofu mixture to the hot skillet and cook for 2 minutes. Use a spatula to flip the tofu occasionally to make sure it cooks evenly and scrape up any bits of tofu that stick to the skillet to keep them from burning. Flip the tofu a few times to help the moisture cook off, but don't overflip—you want the tofu to have contact with the pan so it gets lightly crispy edges.

(continued)

Meanwhile, make the simple gravy: In a saucepan, melt the vegan margarine over medium heat. Whisk in the soy sauce, flour, pepper, onion powder, soy milk, and salt to taste until creamy. Taste and add more salt and pepper as needed. Reduce the heat to low to keep the gravy warm while the scramble is cooking.

Assemble the dish: Once the scramble is cooked to the desired texture and the gravy is lightly bubbling, toast the bread. We recommend cutting your toast diagonally into toast points.

To serve, place a few pieces of toast on a plate, cover with gravy, and top with the scramble.

TURMERIC

For most of my adult life, I thought of turmeric as a spice that didn't do much more than add a little color and a mild flavor. Little did I know that this often-overlooked spice is currently being studied for medicinal properties and preventive applications for diseases ranging from Alzheimer's to cancer. While scientists are still researching this spice, we've come to appreciate turmeric more. If you're wondering what else you can use turmeric in, try making the Samosa Pizza on page 161, Vegan BLT Mac and Cheez on page 193, and The Six Million Dollar Tofu "Egg" Salad on page 67.

For the Price of a Cup of Coffee...

When making a monthly food budget, there's one item many folks tend to overlook: coffee.

It might be a legitimate mistake, because some would categorize coffee as a necessity—like deodorant and toothpaste. Some take a more honest approach and list coffee mentally with their addictions, like cigarettes or cable TV. This way of thinking might account for the long lines at coffee shops and the (debatable) need for said shops to be located only blocks from one another.

It might also account for the findings of a 2012 survey that said the average American spends more than $1,000 a year on coffee from coffee shops. Yahoo! Business broke it down like this: If you buy one $4 latte each day, that habit will set you back $28 a week, about $120 a month, and $1,460 per year. A writer at TheSimpleDollar.com researched what it would cost to make a "good" cup of coffee at home, and after contacting the Specialty Coffee Association of America found that the cost of a 16-ounce cup of coffee made with high-quality beans came out to about 44 cents—including water, the "start-up cost" of a coffee machine, filters, cups, and even electricity. When you add soy creamer or nondairy milk to the coffee and sugar, that comes out to around 80 cents.

A grande or 16-ounce cup of black coffee at Starbucks will run you about $2—the savings of $1.20 may not seem that huge, but over a year it can equal many hundreds of dollars. It's no wonder that every year one of the most popular New Year's resolutions is to stop buying coffee from coffee shops.

Mexican Coffee

Mexico has a well-deserved reputation for having some of the most delicious chocolate and coffee in the world. While we were there, Dan enjoyed several cups of traditionally brewed Mexican coffee served in little clay pots with his breakfast. This recipe is inspired by that rich, flavorful drink—but you can make it on your stovetop, no plane tickets required.

MAKES 4 SERVINGS   **$0.27 PER SERVING**

6 cups strong brewed coffee

⅓ cup packed brown sugar (you may want more if you like sweeter coffee)

½ teaspoon ground cloves

1½ teaspoons ground cinnamon

In a saucepan, combine the coffee, brown sugar, cloves, and cinnamon and bring to a boil over medium heat while whisking continuously. Once the coffee begins to bubble, remove the pan from the heat and divide the coffee evenly among four mugs.

Give it a taste test, and if you like it sweeter, add more brown sugar. Enjoy warm.

Pumpkin Spice Latte

The Pumpkin Spice Latte is the darling of the fall food season. People all over the United States wait eagerly all September for the first glimpses of it to appear on the chalkboards of their favorite coffee shops. But much to the disappointment of vegans everywhere, major coffee retailer Starbucks changed their Pumpkin Spice formula in 2013, making it no longer vegan. So we made our own, using actual pumpkin and agave nectar instead of just a bunch of chemical nonsense.

MAKES 4 SERVINGS   **$0.70 PER SERVING**

- 3 cups strong brewed coffee
- 3 to 4 cups almond milk (depending on how strong you like your coffee)
- 2 teaspoons pumpkin pie spice
- 1 tablespoon pumpkin puree
- 3 tablespoons agave nectar

In a saucepan, combine the coffee, 3 cups of almond milk, pumpkin pie spice, pumpkin puree, and agave nectar and bring to a boil over medium heat while whisking continuously. Use a spoon to give it a taste test and add more almond milk if desired. Once the coffee begins to bubble, remove it from the heat and divide it among four mugs.

Enjoy warm.

CHAPTER 4

LUNCH

A 2012 survey found that 66 percent of Americans spend more than $2,000 a year eating out for lunch, and that around 19 percent skipped lunch altogether. When you take into account that there aren't usually leftovers from lunch, lunch is America's most expensive meal per serving—even though a bunch of us aren't even eating it. This chapter is all about how to doll up, pack up, and fall back in love with your midday meal.

› The Six Million Dollar Tofu "Egg" Salad 67

› Thai Vegan Chicken Slaw 69

› Lemon-Tahini Fattoush 71

› Groove Is in the Artichoke Heart Salad 72

› Roasted Beet and Lentil Salad 73

› Red Beans and Rice Salad 75

› Pan-Seared Corn and Quinoa Salad . . . 76

› Kale Caesar Salad 78

› Club Sandwich Salad with Dijon Mustard Dressing 80

› Avocado and Grapefruit Salad with Cilantro Dressing 81

› Mason Jar Farmers' Market Salad 82

› Roasted Garlicky Garbanzos 84

› Cheezy Croutons 85

› Green Bean, Olive, and Roasted Potato Salad 86

› French Potato Salad 88

› Tom Kha Gai—Spicy Coconut
  Soup.............................. 89

› Roasted Red Pepper and Lentil
  Soup.............................. 91

› Green Shchi—Russian Cabbage
  Soup.............................. 92

› Caldo Verde—Portuguese Soup 93

› Parsnip and Peppercorn Soup 95

› Chef's Pasta Salad.................. 97

› Jerk "Chicken" Pasta Salad 98

› Simple Soba Noodles 100

› Sesame Peanut Noodles 101

› Ribollita Soup 103

› Sriracha and Sweet Onion Stew 104

› Chipotle Avocado Sandwiches...... 106

› Lasagna Sandwiches featuring
  Italian Tempeh Sausage 107

› Greek Garbanzo Bean
  Salad Pitas 109

› Tuscan Eggplant and White Bean
  Sandwiches 110

› Sesame Miso Kale Chips........... 111

› Baked Creole Carrot Chips 112

› Sweet Beet Mix 113

The Six Million Dollar Tofu "Egg" Salad

Deciding that something isn't going to kill you is only the first step. The next is deciding it'll make you stronger. Better. Faster. Yes. The first day I walked back into my kitchen after the weeks of seclusion I mentioned in the introduction to this book (see page 1), I had the intro to The Six Million Dollar Man *in my head.*

"Gentlemen, can we rebuild her?"
"Yes. We have the technology... and the tofu."

It started with a very special block of tofu that Dan had taken out of the freezer and mentioned in passing as he was leaving for work. It was a trap he'd set to lure me back into the kitchen, and I knew it; but I was helpless to resist. See, freezing and unfreezing tofu is an old Chinese cooking trick called Thousand-Year-Old Tofu that you can read about on page 68, and it also is the first step to making a perfect tofu "egg" salad.

A tofu "egg" salad might not seem like that big of a deal in the grand scheme of things. But after I posted a photo of it on our Facebook page, the first comment was from a vegan baker at the Hannah Banana Bakery in the U.K. She posted a single heart. In about an hour and a half, my simple tofu "egg" salad with toast points had forty-three "likes" and I had more than 130 messages from people all over the world welcoming me back to the kitchen.

MAKES 4 TO 6 SERVINGS   **$1.16 PER SERVING**

. . . .

1 (16-ounce) package extra-firm tofu, drained

⅓ cup vegan mayonnaise (we recommend Vegenaise or Just Mayo)

2 medium dill pickles, diced

¼ cup chopped kale leaves

2 stalks celery, diced

1½ teaspoons chopped fresh dill

¼ red onion, diced

2½ teaspoons Dijon mustard

¼ cup nutritional yeast

½ teaspoon ground cumin

½ teaspoon onion powder

¼ teaspoon garlic powder

¼ teaspoon ground turmeric

¼ teaspoon celery seed

1 teaspoon tahini

½ teaspoon lemon juice

½ teaspoon grated lemon zest

Toast, for serving

. . . .

(continued)

If you want to use frozen tofu, cut the drained tofu block into 4 pieces, put them in a plastic bag, then put it in the freezer. Once the tofu is frozen solid, remove it from the freezer and defrost it overnight in the fridge. Make sure the tofu is completely defrosted before using. You'll notice even more water has drained from the tofu while it was defrosting. Pour that water out of the bag and gently squeeze the tofu between paper towels to remove any remaining water.

In a large bowl, use a fork to gently mash the tofu into bite-size pieces—not into a paste. Using a large spoon, stir in the vegan mayo, pickle, kale, celery, dill, and red onion.

In a separate bowl, whisk together the mustard, nutritional yeast, cumin, onion powder, garlic powder, turmeric, celery seed, tahini, lemon juice, and lemon zest. Add the mustard mixture to the tofu mixture and stir gently to combine. Cover with aluminum foil and refrigerate for 3 hours.

Enjoy with toast and some fierce Lee Majors sideburns if you got 'em.

WHAT'S THE DEAL WITH FREEZING TOFU?

Freezing tofu is an old vegan trick that's common in parts of China and Taiwan, but if you haven't been adventurous with your soy-based friend, you may not have tried it. Give it a shot!

Drain your tofu, then lightly press out as much of the moisture as you can. When you freeze it overnight, whatever water is left will form small ice crystals; and when the ice melts, those crystals will leave little air pockets behind, making your tofu chewier. It'll also turn a little yellow. In my opinion, the resulting texture reinvents boring old tofu. But if that's not enough to win you over, how about this: The Chinese call tofu prepared this way Thousand-Year-Old Tofu. I'm not sure why this name sounds so downright romantic to me, but it just does.

Thai Vegan Chicken Slaw

This is one of those recipes you make the night before, and when you eat it the next day at lunch you feel the tangible rewards of being a proper grown-up who planned ahead.

MAKES 4 TO 6 SERVINGS   **$2.31 PER SERVING**

Vegan Chicken

1 package vegan chicken, defrosted (we recommend Beyond Meat Chicken-Free Strips or Gardein Chick'n Scallopini)

1 tablespoon sesame oil

1½ teaspoons soy sauce or Bragg's Liquid Aminos

Dash of vegan liquid smoke

Ginger-Miso Dressing

¼ cup miso broth, at room temperature

¼ cup agave nectar

¼ cup rice vinegar

⅓ cup sesame oil

1 teaspoon Sriracha or Thai chili sauce

2 tablespoons soy sauce or Bragg's Liquid Aminos

2 cloves garlic, minced

1½ teaspoons ginger paste

½ teaspoon sesame seeds

To Assemble

2 cups shredded green cabbage

1 large carrot, grated

½ red bell pepper, thinly sliced

2 stalks celery, diced

½ cup fresh cilantro leaves

2 green onions, diced

⅓ cup dry-roasted peanuts

1 lime, cut into wedges

Sriracha sauce

Make the vegan chicken: In a large bowl, toss the vegan chicken with the sesame oil, soy sauce, and vegan liquid smoke.

Heat a cast-iron skillet over medium heat. Once the skillet is hot, pour in the vegan chicken with any liquid left in the bowl. Cook the vegan chicken, flipping it a few times to make sure it cooks evenly, until it is light golden brown and has crispy edges. Transfer the vegan chicken to an airtight container and refrigerate overnight.

About 20 minutes before you're ready to eat, remove the vegan chicken from the fridge and dice it into bite-size pieces.

Make the ginger-miso dressing: In a food processor, combine the miso broth, agave nectar, vinegar, sesame oil, Sriracha, soy sauce, garlic, ginger paste, and sesame seeds

(continued)

and process until well combined. Transfer to a lidded container and refrigerate until ready to use.

Assemble the dish: In a large bowl, combine the vegan chicken, dressing, cabbage, carrot, bell pepper, celery, cilantro, green onions, and peanuts and toss with a large spoon until blended. Serve cold with a lime wedge and more Sriracha sauce alongside.

You can use any leftover rice vinegar to make:

Tofu Spring Rolls with Agave Chili Sauce on page 121

Steamed Sesame Seitan Dim Sum on page 141

Sesame Peanut Noodles on page 101

Lemon-Tahini Fattoush

This is not your traditional fattoush. Although it does combine toasted pita bread with mixed vegetables like the original Middle Eastern salad, we decided to use a lemon- and tahini-based dressing to make the dish a little more filling. But if you're more comfortable keeping it old school, you can drizzle some olive oil and lemon juice over your salad and call it a day!

MAKES 4 TO 6 SERVINGS　　　　　　　　　**$1.73 PER SERVING**

Salad

2 (8-inch) pitas

3 green onions, diced

1 head romaine lettuce, chopped

4 or 5 cherry tomatoes, quartered

¼ cup pitted kalamata olives

½ red onion, sliced

1 cucumber, sliced

½ cup chopped fresh parsley leaves

½ cup chopped fresh mint leaves

Lemon-Tahini Dressing

½ cup tahini

2 tablespoons olive oil

Juice of 1 lemon

2 tablespoons fresh dill, chopped

1 clove garlic, minced

Make the salad: Toast the pitas and set them aside to cool, then break them into bite-size pieces. In a large bowl, toss together the salad ingredients. Add the toasted pita pieces once they are completely cool.

Make the dressing: In a small bowl, whisk together the tahini, olive oil, lemon juice, dill, and garlic until combined.

Mix the dressing into the salad with a large spoon right before serving and toss to make sure the salad is evenly dressed.

FRESH MINT

If you've read the section on Fresh Herbs on page 14, you already know that mint is one of the easiest-to-grow, and therefore cheapest, herbs in the United States. It's also one of the most versatile. You can put fresh mint leaves in your tea or water to add some flavor, or you can toss them in a salad like the Strawberry Salad on page 300 or the Groove Is in the Artichoke Heart Salad on page 72. You can also use them to make the Turkish Pizza— Lahmacun on page 163 or the Vegan Gyros on page 219.

Groove Is in the Artichoke Heart Salad

This faux-fancy lunch is easy and delicious. It might be a little grown-up for your kid's school cafeteria, but it's a perfect addition to any significant other's lunch. It says "I love you" without the embarrassing sticky note.

MAKES 4 TO 6 SERVINGS   **$1.65 PER SERVING**

Salad

1 (14-ounce) can artichoke hearts, drained and quartered

1 (15-ounce) can garbanzo beans, drained and rinsed, or 1½ cups cooked dry garbanzo beans

½ cup pitted kalamata olives

½ red bell pepper, diced

¼ cup chopped fresh parsley leaves

¼ cup fresh mint leaves, chopped

Balsamic and Black Pepper Dressing

¼ cup balsamic vinegar

½ cup olive oil

2 teaspoons Italian seasoning

Juice of 1 lemon

¼ teaspoon crushed black peppercorns

Make the salad: In a large bowl, combine the artichoke hearts, garbanzos, olives, bell pepper, parsley, and mint and toss to combine.

Make the dressing: In an airtight container, combine the vinegar, olive oil, Italian seasoning, lemon juice, and peppercorns. Shake to emulsify.

Add the dressing to the salad and toss with a large spoon. Cover the bowl with plastic wrap and let marinate in the refrigerator overnight.

Serve cold.

You can use the other half of that red bell pepper to make:

Thai Vegan Chicken Slaw on page 69

Tom Kha Gai—Spicy Coconut Soup on page 89

Greek Garbanzo Bean Salad Pitas on page 109

Sesame Peanut Noodles on page 101

Pasta Primavera on page 239

Chickpea à la King Skillet on page 123

Roasted Beet and Lentil Salad

Beets. I know I should love you. You're full of fiber, iron, and folic acid while still being low calorie. I just have such a hard time with your earthy flavor. Which is why, when I say this incredibly nutritious, French-inspired salad makes a wonderful lunch with some sparkling water and a baguette, please listen to me. I'm not someone who recommends beets often, so when I do, I really mean it. Comprenez-vous?

MAKES 4 TO 6 SERVINGS   **$1.14 PER SERVING**

Salad

1 large red beet

2 tablespoons olive oil

¼ teaspoon sea salt

¼ teaspoon crushed black peppercorns

1½ cups cooked dry lentils or canned lentils

3 tablespoons raw hulled pumpkin seeds

2 stalks celery, diced

3 green onions, diced

Dill Dressing

1 cup chopped fresh dill

¼ cup olive oil

3 tablespoons white wine

2 tablespoons soy sauce or Bragg's Liquid Aminos

½ teaspoon onion powder

2 cloves garlic, minced

Make the salad: Preheat the oven to 400°F.

Cut the stem off and peel the beet. Place the beet on a piece of aluminum foil large enough to encase it. Drizzle the beet with olive oil and sprinkle a pinch of salt and a pinch of ground pepper over the top. Wrap the beet up in foil. Roast for 30 to 45 minutes.

Once the beet is tender, remove it from the oven and carefully unwrap it. Let it cool until it's just cool enough to handle. Then thinly slice the peeled beet.

In a large bowl, toss the warm beet with the lentils, pumpkin seeds, celery, green onions, the remaining olive oil, sea salt, and crushed pepper. Cover and refrigerate for 1 hour.

Make the dill vinaigrette: In a food processor, combine the dill, olive oil, white wine, soy sauce, onion powder, and garlic and process until well combined. Drizzle the dressing over the salad and relax.

(continued)

> **You can use the rest of your green onions to make:**
>
> Thai Vegan Chicken Slaw on page 69
>
> Lemon-Tahini Fattoush on page 71
>
> Pan-Seared Corn and Quinoa Salad on
> page 76
>
> Pasta with Asparagus and Green Onion
> Pesto on page 200
>
> Fresh Herb and Heirloom Tomato Salad
> on page 304

Red Beans and Rice Salad

Red beans and rice is one of the signature dishes of New Orleans. Traditionally made for lunch on Monday out of leftovers from Sunday dinner, it has a long, proud tradition of saving people money and reducing waste in the kitchen.

MAKES 4 TO 6 SERVINGS   **$0.94 PER SERVING**

2 (15-ounce) cans red beans, drained and rinsed, or 1½ cups cooked dry red beans

1 clove garlic, minced

½ red onion, diced

3 stalks celery, diced

1 green bell pepper, diced

2 cups white rice, cooked

¼ cup chopped fresh parsley

2 green onions, diced

2 tablespoons soy sauce or Bragg's Liquid Aminos

Dash of vegan liquid smoke

½ cup olive oil

1 teaspoon smoked paprika

2 pinches of cayenne pepper

Toss all the ingredients in a large bowl with a wooden spoon. Cover with plastic wrap and refrigerate overnight.

Serve cold.

> **You can use the other half of that red onion to make:**
>
> Vegan Bacon and Broccoli Quiche on page 59
>
> The Six Million Dollar Tofu "Egg" Salad on page 67
>
> Lemon-Tahini Fattoush on page 71
>
> Greek Garbanzo Bean Salad Pitas on page 109
>
> Fajita Pizza on page 160
>
> Tabbouleh Salad on page 294

Pan-Seared Corn and Quinoa Salad

We're not going to tell you how to live your life or eat your lunch—but if you toast your quinoa while you're pan-searing your corn, it will increase your enjoyment of this recipe by at least 75 percent.* You can find instructions for how to do this on page 77.

MAKES 4 TO 6 SERVINGS   **$1.44 PER SERVING**

. . . .

Lime and Pepper Dressing

⅓ cup olive oil

Juice of 3 limes

2 cloves garlic, minced

1 teaspoon ground cumin

1 teaspoon soy sauce or Bragg's
Liquid Aminos

1 teaspoon dried oregano

¼ teaspoon crushed black peppercorns

½ teaspoon chili powder

Pinch of paprika

Salad

1 tablespoon olive oil

2 ears corn, husked

1 cup quinoa, cooked

½ cup fresh cilantro

2 stalks celery, chopped

½ red bell pepper, diced

3 green onions, chopped

¼ cup raw hulled pumpkin seeds

1 jalapeño, seeded and diced

1 lime, cut into wedges

. . . .

Make the lime and pepper dressing: In an airtight container, whisk together the dressing ingredients. Cover and set aside for 15 to 20 minutes to help the flavors mingle.

Make the salad: Brush a cast-iron skillet with olive oil and set it over medium heat. Once the skillet is hot, add the corn and brush the ears with olive oil. Using a fork, gently roll the corn to evenly sear. It should take about 3 minutes for the corn to be

lightly browned. Transfer the corn to a plate and place in the fridge to cool.

In a large bowl, toss together the quinoa, cilantro, celery, bell pepper, green onions, and pumpkin seeds. Add as much of the jalapeño as you like, ½ teaspoon at a time, depending on how hot you want the salad to be.

Remove the corn from the fridge. Set the stalk end of one ear of corn in a large bowl and hold the top by the narrow end. Gently run a large, sharp knife down the cob to remove the kernels, letting them fall into the bowl. Rotating the corn is less awkward

---

* This is a guesstimate based on no real scientific data besides our own anecdotal research.

than moving the knife and will get you larger kernels.

Toss the corn kernels into the quinoa salad and mix with a large spoon. Mix in the dressing, transfer the salad to an airtight container, and refrigerate for at least 15 minutes.

Serve cold, with a wedge of lime to squeeze over the top.

You can use your leftover jalapeño to make:

Tom Kha Gai—Spicy Coconut Soup on page 89

Quinoa Taco Casserole on page 152

Aloha Dogs on page 175

Check out the section on page 176 on how to handle jalapeños so you don't burn your fingers.

TOASTED QUINOA IS ABOUT TO STEAL YOUR HEART

The first time I took the extra time to toast my quinoa, I was furious with myself for not doing it sooner. I cursed "Past Me" for being so impatient and stubborn. See, prior to that night I thought I knew everything. I thought I knew more than my fellow vegans, who swore that toasting quinoa was an invaluable step. Then I tried it, and—like a scene out of some rom-com starring one of the blond women from *Grey's Anatomy*—I got it, immediately changed my ways, and ran through the streets in search of more quinoa, vowing never again to take this little wonder grain for granted. End Scene.

To toast your quinoa:

Use 1 tablespoon olive oil for every 1½ cups quinoa you'll be toasting. Heat the oil in a skillet over medium heat. Once the oil is hot, toss in rinsed quinoa and let it toast while continuously flipping with a spatula. Let the little grains toast to a very light golden brown; it should take about 5 minutes. Your quinoa isn't *cooked* yet—it's ready to cook. You've just leveled it up.

Kale Caesar Salad

I guess it wouldn't be a vegan cookbook without a recipe for kale salad. This one combines omega-3–rich walnuts, vitamin B–packed nutritional yeast, and nutritional superfood kale to make an easy meal that's remarkably good for you.

MAKES 4 SERVINGS   **$1.68 PER SERVING**

Lemon and Caper Caesar Dressing

1 teaspoon grated lemon zest

Juice of 2 lemons

2 tablespoons capers with their brine

1 tablespoon plus ½ teaspoon Dijon mustard

½ teaspoon dried oregano

¼ teaspoon nutritional yeast

⅓ cup olive oil

½ teaspoon soy sauce or Bragg's Liquid Aminos

1½ teaspoons crushed black peppercorns

Salad

2 cups kale leaves, chopped into bite-size pieces

¾ cup vegan croutons, such as Cheezy Croutons (page 85)

¼ cup crushed walnuts

Make the lemon and caper Caesar dressing: In a food processor, combine all the dressing ingredients and process into a thin, smooth sauce. Pour the dressing into an airtight container and refrigerate while you prepare the salad.

Make the salad: In a large bowl, gently massage the kale leaves, rubbing them between your hands until they're soft. Toss the massaged kale leaves with as much of the chilled dressing as you like. We like a lot of dressing, but you might be more conservative and that's okay.

Once the kale is dressed, toss in the croutons and walnuts and serve immediately.

> **You can use the rest of your jar of capers to make:**
>
> Angel Hair Pasta with Garlic and Rosemary Mushrooms on page 202
>
> Cajun Nachos on page 129
>
> Pan-Seared Tofu with Arugula, Capers, and Tomatoes on page 210

You can use your leftover walnuts to make:

Betty's Wartime Walnut Burger on
   page 189

Roasted Pear, Walnut, and Brussels
   Sprout Tacos on page 197

Vegan Bacon and Broccoli Quiche on
   page 59

Cookie Pizza on page 276

Club Sandwich Salad with Dijon Mustard Dressing

The club sandwich's origin story is shrouded in mystery. Some say it was invented in a Saratoga Springs resort in the 1800s. Some say it's been an American staple since long before that. No matter where you stand on the great club sandwich creation debate, let's all agree on this: This sandwich-inspired salad is frakking good!

MAKES 4 TO 6 SERVINGS   **$1.42 PER SERVING**

Dijon Mustard Dressing

2 tablespoons Dijon mustard

½ cup tahini

¼ cup apple cider vinegar

1 tablespoon agave nectar

1 teaspoon soy sauce or Bragg's Liquid Aminos

2 tablespoons chopped fresh parsley

1 clove garlic, minced

¼ teaspoon crushed black peppercorns

½ teaspoon dried thyme

Salad

½ package Hickory Smoked Tofurky Deli Slices

1 head romaine lettuce, chopped

6 or 7 cherry tomatoes

1 large carrot, shredded

2 tablespoons vegan bacon bits

¾ cup vegan croutons, such as Cheezy Croutons (page 85)

Make the Dijon mustard dressing: In a food processor, combine all the dressing ingredients and process until creamy. Set aside.

Make the salad: Without separating the slices, chop the Tofurky into bite-size pieces and place them in a large bowl. Add the remaining salad ingredients and toss together.

Drizzle the desired amount of dressing over the top right before serving.

> *You can use the rest of your Dijon mustard to make:*
>
> Green Bean, Olive, and Roasted Potato Salad on page 86
>
> The Six Million Dollar Tofu "Egg" Salad on page 67
>
> Vegan BLT Mac and Cheez on page 193
>
> Beet "Boudin" Balls with Garlic Aioli on page 206
>
> Kale Caesar Salad on page 78

Avocado and Grapefruit Salad with Cilantro Dressing

This bright and beautiful salad is an easy lunch that you can pack and bring to work or enjoy on a Sunday afternoon while watching a marathon of your favorite TV show. Either way, this salad brings joy to all.

MAKES 2 TO 4 SERVINGS **$0.63 PER SERVING**

Cilantro Dressing

3 tablespoons fresh cilantro, diced

1 green onion, diced

2 tablespoons grapefruit juice or lemon juice

1 teaspoon agave nectar

¼ teaspoon black pepper

2 dashes of hot sauce

1 ruby red grapefruit

1½ ripe avocado

Make the cilantro dressing: In an airtight container, combine all the dressing ingredients and shake until emulsified. Refrigerate until ready to use, to allow the flavors to mingle.

Cut one end off the grapefruit so it sits flat. Using a sharp knife, cut along the side of the grapefruit to remove the peel and the bitter white pith. Holding the peeled grapefruit over a large bowl, carefully cut the fruit segments out from between the membranes and let them fall in the bowl.

Halve the avocado and remove the pit and peel. Cut the flesh into slices and add them to the bowl with the grapefruit segments.

Toss the grapefruit segments and avocado slices with the cilantro dressing, cover, and refrigerate until well chilled.

Serve cold.

AGAVE NECTAR

When we were in Mexico, we got the chance to drive through the agave cactus fields near Valladolid. It gave us a new sense of respect, not just for an ingredient that has been sweetening food in the Americas since before Columbus was born, but for the people who grow it. This is where we remind you to check to see if your agave nectar—and anything else you buy, for that matter—is fair trade. It may cost a few pennies more, but the difference the increased income makes for these farmers and their families is significant.

Wondering what else to enjoy with your agave nectar? Try making the PB&J Granola Bars on page 28, Strawberry Salad on page 300, or Tofu Spring Rolls with Agave Chili Sauce on page 121.

Mason Jar Farmers' Market Salad

Mason jars were originally created for canning fruits and vegetables and foods made from them so they would keep through the winter. But as we moved from an agrarian society to an industrial one, refrigeration, freezing, and metal cans or "tins" replaced cellars full of glass jars. Making homemade jams and sauces became a hobby for most people, rather than a necessity. These days you're more likely to find mason jars full of Pabst Blue Ribbon in Brooklyn bars than holding pickles in people's basements.

One popular way to repurpose a mason jar is to use it as a lunchbox. It seals up good and tight to prevent leaking and is environmentally friendly—it's reusable and isn't made from BPA-riddled plastics. It's also the perfect size for bringing a salad to work. People all over the world have started doing this, and there are numerous Pinterest boards to prove it!

MAKES 2 TO 4 SERVINGS   **$0.96 PER SERVING**

- 1¼ cups arugula leaves or spring mix
- 1¼ cups baby spinach leaves
- 1 recipe salad dressing (we recommend using the Greek Lemon Dressing on page 109)
- 6 to 8 cherry tomatoes
- ½ cucumber, sliced
- 1 carrot, sliced
- ¼ cup garbanzo beans (we recommend using the Roasted Garlicky Garbanzos on page 84)
- ⅓ cup pearl barley, cooked and chilled

If you're making two salads, use two 1-quart mason jars; if you're making four salads, use four 1-pint mason jars.

In a large bowl, combine the arugula and spinach leaves and set aside.

Pour 4 tablespoons of salad dressing into each of your two mason jars (or 2 tablespoons each if you're using four jars). Then, divide the remaining ingredients evenly among the jars, adding the cherry tomatoes first, then the cucumber slices, carrot, garbanzo beans, and chilled barley. Finally, top each jar off with the mixed arugula and spinach leaves.

Put lids on each jar and seal tight. Refrigerate until ready to eat.

When you're ready to eat, shake the jar lightly so that the veggies are mixed together and the salad is well coated with the dressing, then pour it into a bowl and enjoy.

Farmers' Markets

There is some debate about how economical it really is to shop at your local farmers' market rather than large commercial grocery chains. We think it comes down to where you live.

In Los Angeles, our friend Anjali Prasertong, who writes for the blog *The Kitchn*, knows all the best markets in the city. When we visit, we load up on everything from reasonably priced locally made pomegranate jams and olive oil to cheap, gorgeous avocados and colorful heirloom tomatoes, because, let's be honest, California is a produce wonderland. When I lived in Georgia, I had to drive for over an hour to get to the nearest fruit stand, which was worth it for the downright mythical apples and peaches they sold. Sometimes if I was lucky they'd have cabbages, green beans, and huge pallets of some kind of berry; but they were priced a little higher than what I could get at the local grocery store. In Brooklyn, the farmers' market is usually full of local wines, baked goods, and pickles, as well as tons of inexpensive produce from New Jersey.

Beyond saving you money, farmers' markets also support small businesses, local farmers, and local workers, and they help to reduce the environmental footprint of your diet, because the food is often grown organically, transported fewer miles, and sold with less packaging. However, we encourage you to confirm at your local farmers' market information booth that the vendors follow these practices—don't just assume they do.

If you're new to the farmers' market scene, we recommend that you do some research to see what kind of local markets are available in your area, then check them out. You might be surprised by how much you can save while contributing to your community.

Roasted Garlicky Garbanzos

These roasted garbanzo beans add a nice crunch to any salad, or you can just toss them in a small container and eat them as a snack throughout the day. You should be warned, however, that while delicious, they are garlicky, so you might want to invest in some breath mints.

MAKES 6 TO 8 SERVINGS   **$0.26 PER SERVING**

1 teaspoon garlic powder

1 clove garlic, minced

1 tablespoon vegan Parmesan cheese

2 tablespoons olive oil

Pinch of smoked paprika

2 (15-ounce) cans garbanzo beans, drained and rinsed, or 1½ cups cooked dry garbanzo beans

Preheat the oven to 425°F. Line a rimmed cookie sheet with parchment paper.

In a bowl, whisk together the garlic powder, garlic, vegan Parmesan cheese, olive oil, and paprika. Then toss in the garbanzos and mix with a large spoon. Once the garbanzos are coated, spread them out on the lined cookie sheet.

Bake for 45 minutes to 1 hour, keeping an eye on them so that they don't burn. Once they've turned golden brown and have begun to split, remove from the oven and let cool slightly on the pan.

Serve at room temperature, either over a salad or by the handful as a snack.

You can use your leftover vegan Parmesan to make:

Spinach and Tempeh Pastitsio on page 180

Hermes' Pizza on page 221

Ribollita Soup on page 103

Angel Hair Pasta with Garlic and Rosemary Mushrooms on page 202

Vegan Cheese Party Pizza on page 278

Pasta with DIY Marinara on page 226

Cheezy Croutons

Using day-old bread to make croutons before it gets stale is a great way to eliminate waste in the kitchen. We make a lot of croutons because, I admit, I adore freshly baked bread. We live close to several bakeries in Brooklyn, and there are only two of us, so there's usually more bread around our kitchen than there are opportunities to eat it. We also love salads.

You can use these croutons on any mixed green salad, like the Club Sandwich Salad on page 80, or in any soup, like the Ribollita on page 103.

MAKES 6 TO 8 SERVINGS **$0.24 PER SERVING**

½ baguette, or 6 to 8 slices of your favorite bread

¼ cup olive oil

2½ teaspoons nutritional yeast

¼ teaspoon smoked paprika

Preheat the oven to 300°F. Line a rimmed cookie sheet with aluminum foil.

Using a serrated knife, cut the bread into cubes and place them in a large bowl. In a small bowl, whisk together the olive oil, nutritional yeast, and paprika.

Add the oil mixture to the bread cubes and toss until they are lightly coated, then arrange them on the lined cookie sheet, spreading them out so they aren't touching.

Bake for 10 to 15 minutes, until the croutons are lightly toasted and have crispy edges. Let cool to room temperature before serving.

Store in an airtight container in the fridge.

> *You can use your leftover nutritional yeast to make:*
>
> Vegan Gyros on page 219
>
> Pan-Fried Artichoke Hearts and Sauce on page 227
>
> Rosemary Chicklins and Dumplins Stew on page 127
>
> Savory Crêpes with Easy "Hollandaise" Sauce on page 42

Green Bean, Olive, and Roasted Potato Salad

Bistros were originally small restaurants offering modestly priced Parisian-style midday meals. Their menus were usually full of fresh baked goods, salads, and simple meat-and-cheese sandwiches on baguettes. This recipe is designed to bring the rustic charm of a bistro to your desk or potluck without the heavier prices that come with the modern day bistro.

MAKES 4 TO 6 SERVINGS   **$1.18 PER SERVING**

1 pound new potatoes, quartered

4 tablespoons olive oil

¼ teaspoon sea salt, plus more as needed

1 pound green beans, trimmed

1½ teaspoons dried oregano

½ teaspoon smoked paprika

2 teaspoons Dijon mustard

1 tablespoon grated lemon zest

1 tablespoon lemon juice

3 tablespoons balsamic vinegar

½ red onion, cut into rings and separated

3 radishes, thinly sliced

3 stalks celery, chopped

⅓ cup mixed pitted Greek olives

3 tablespoons chopped fresh parsley

Salt and ground black pepper

Preheat the oven to 400°F.

In a casserole dish, toss the potatoes with 2 tablespoons of the olive oil and salt and roast for 20 minutes, or until the potatoes are tender and have golden, crispy edges.

In a saucepan, bring 4 cups water to a boil, then toss in the green beans. Cook until tender, then drain.

Place the roasted potatoes and cooked green beans in an airtight container and refrigerate.

Twenty minutes before serving, make the dressing by whisking together the remaining 2 tablespoons olive oil, the oregano, paprika, Dijon mustard, lemon zest, lemon juice, and vinegar.

Transfer the chilled potatoes and green beans to a large bowl, add the red onion, radishes, celery, olives, parsley, and the dressing, and toss until the salad is evenly coated. Season with salt and pepper to taste. Cover the bowl with aluminum foil and refrigerate for 15 minutes.

Serve cold.

You can use any leftover olives to make:

Mezze Platter on page 292

Baked Strapatsada—Greek Baked "Egg" Cups on page 53

Cajun Nachos on page 129

A Guide to Lunch Boxes

Sure, bringing a healthy and delicious meal to enjoy during the workday seems like a great idea…until you start thinking about actually doing it. Whether you drive or walk, take the train or ride the bus, lugging your lunch to work every day is no simple matter. And as cute as that old-school Wonder Woman tin lunch box looks on the Internet, it's not going to cut it in the real world. Here are some tips for making sure you've got a delicious daily meal at work, without a daily hassle.

- A thermos isn't just for coffee anymore. Sure, bringing soup to work in a thermos isn't the most original idea in the world—but how often do you actually do it? I bet you've never done it. It's okay—we all have to have a first time, and there's nothing to be embarrassed about. But what are you waiting for? Most of the soups in this book are perfect for this—and you can find all sorts of "vacuum flasks" (the nonbranded name for a Thermos—who knew?) for sale on the Internet that are specifically designed for soup.

- A small Tupperware set is your friend. One of the downsides of prepping a meal ahead of time is that all the ingredients have to hang out together for hours before you actually eat them—which can be particularly problematic with wet and dry combos like tomato slices and bread. You can get around this by packing your lunch piecemeal, with separate containers for dry (like bread and Tofurky slices) and wet (like lettuce and tomato) ingredients.

- One *giant* Tupperware will be your other BFF. A classic lunch maneuver is to prep a big pot of chili or some other massive meal and then dole it out into small containers for lunch each week. Why not bring a whole mess of it into work in one big container on Monday morning, and then eat with a proper plate and silverware like a civilized person, rather than out of your single-serving Tupperware? Admittedly, this works a lot better if you drive to work (and have enough room in the fridge).

- You don't have to make your lunch at home—you can just bring the ingredients with you and make it at work! This works great with salads—just bring a whole mess of veggies and fixins' in with you on Monday, and then assemble your delicious lunch in the office kitchen every day throughout the week. Since your food is vegan, no need to worry about it spoiling in the fridge between Monday and Friday. Of course, you *do* have to worry about your coworkers stealing your food…

French Potato Salad

French potato salad doesn't usually have mayonnaise in it (or in our case, Vegenaise) but while we were cooking our way through Julia Child's Kitchen Wisdom, *we were impressed with her five different types of potato salads. We weren't sure we needed that many potato salads at once, though—so we created this vegan hybrid of them all.*

MAKES 4 TO 6 SERVINGS   **$0.90 PER SERVING**

- 2 pounds small red potatoes, cut into ¼-inch-thick slices
- 1 tablespoon sea salt
- 2 cloves garlic, minced
- 2 teaspoons Dijon mustard
- 2 tablespoons vegan mayonnaise (we recommend Vegenaise or Just Mayo)
- 1 tablespoon plus 1 teaspoon white wine vinegar
- ¼ cup olive oil

- Zest and juice of 1 lemon
- 1 teaspoon crushed black peppercorns, plus more for serving
- 1 small shallot or ¼ red onion, diced very small
- 1 tablespoon plus 2 teaspoons chopped fresh chives, plus more for sprinkling
- 1 tablespoon dried oregano
- 1 tablespoon fresh parsley leaves
- 1 tablespoon fresh tarragon leaves (optional)

In your largest Dutch oven or stew pot, combine 6 cups water, the potatoes, and the salt and bring to a boil over high heat. Reduce the heat to maintain a simmer and cook, uncovered, until the potatoes are tender but still firm. Drain, but don't rinse.

In a small bowl, whisk together the garlic, mustard, vegan mayo, vinegar, olive oil, lemon zest, lemon juice, and pepper. Set aside.

In your largest mixing bowl, gently toss together the potatoes, shallot, chives, oregano, parsley, and tarragon (if using). Drizzle the dressing over the potatoes and gently mix it in.

Serve immediately for the warm European style salad or put in the fridge for an hour if you prefer your potato salad chilled, with a few pinches of fresh chives and crushed pepper over the top.

Emily Dickinson Porridge, page 27

Roasted Red Flannel Hash, page 38

Virgin Crêpes Suzette, page 39

Ginger Plum Oatmeal, page 26

Savory Crêpes with Easy "Hollandaise" Sauce, page 42

Banana Churro Waffles, page 44

Easy Mixed Berry Muffins, page 45

Pumpkin Pie Muffins, page 46

Cinnamon Peach Skillet Rolls, page 47

Orange Drop Doughnuts, page 49

Fresh Blueberry Blintzes, page 51

Strapatsada – Greek Baked "Egg" Cups, page 53

Smoky Butternut Squash Scramble, page 57

BLT Pancake Stacks, page 36

Tofu à l a Goldenrod, page 61

Pan-Seared Corn and Quinoa Salad, page 76

Lemon-Tahini Fattoush, page 71

Club Sandwich Salad with
Dijon Mustard Dressing, page 80

Cheezy Croutons, page 85

Tom Kha Gai – Spicy Coconut Soup, page 89

Green Shchi – Russian Cabbage Soup, page 92

Roasted Red Pepper and Lentil Soup, page 91

Simple Soba Noodles, page 100

Sesame Peanut Noodles, page 101

Ribollita Soup, page 103

The Sweet Beet Mix, page 113

Rustic Pesto and Heirloom Tomato Tart, page 117

Chickpea à la King Skillet, page 123

Rosemary Chicklins and Dumplins Stew, page 127

Cajun Nachos, page 129

Apple-Sage Tempeh Sausage over Savory Polenta, page 133

Swiss Chard Rolls with Domestic Goddess Sauce, page 139

Yankee Doodle Macaroni, page 191

Yankee Pot Roast Dinner, page 144

Ratatouille Rice Bake, page 153

Green Bean, Olive, and
Roasted Potato Salad, page 86

Vegan Bacon, White Bean, and Spinach Risotto, page 155

Chili-Stuffed Sweet Potatoes, page 167

Brinner Lasagna, page 169

Tom Kha Gai—Spicy Coconut Soup

There are few pleasures in this world that compare to a bowl of Thai coconut soup. Creamy yet spicy, with a touch of lime juice, this soup has a unique flavor more exotic than any weeknight dinner has the right to be. The tofu needs to be baked the night before serving, so plan ahead.

MAKES 4 SERVINGS　　　　　　　　　　　　　　　　**$2.55 PER SERVING**

1 (16-ounce) package extra-firm tofu, drained

2 tablespoons sesame oil

3 cups vegan chicken broth or vegetable broth

1 (14-ounce) can coconut milk

2 teaspoons ginger paste

2 cloves garlic, minced

3 white mushrooms, sliced

Juice of 1 lime

3 tablespoons soy sauce or Bragg's Liquid Aminos

2/3 cup frozen peas

1/2 red bell pepper, sliced

1 jalapeño, seeded and sliced

1 lime, cut into wedges

1/3 cup fresh cilantro leaves

Preheat the oven to 400°F.

Brush the tofu with the sesame oil and place it in a baking dish. Bake for 15 to 20 minutes. Once the tofu is a light golden brown, flip it with a spatula and bake for another 10 minutes. Remove from the oven, cover, and refrigerate overnight.

Fifteen minutes before serving, in a large soup pot or Dutch oven, whisk together the broth, coconut milk, ginger paste, garlic, mushrooms, lime juice, soy sauce, peas, and bell pepper and bring to a boil over medium heat. Use a wooden spoon to stir the soup occasionally. Once it begins to bubble, reduce the heat to maintain a simmer and cook for 10 minutes. Give it a taste, then add jalapeño slices a few at a time until you like the heat and flavor. We recommend stopping at four slices, but you might like it hotter.

While the soup is cooking, cut the tofu into 8 to 10 pieces

Serve the soup hot, with a lime wedge, 2 to 3 pieces of tofu, and some fresh cilantro on top.

(continued)

You can use the other half of your red bell pepper to make:

Pan-Seared Corn and Quinoa Salad on
    page 76

Sesame Peanut Noodles on page 101

Greek Garbanzo Bean Salad Pitas on
    page 109

Groove Is in the Artichoke Heart Salad
    on page 72

You can use the rest of your bottle of sesame oil to make:

Thai Vegan Chicken Slaw on page 69

Tofu Spring Rolls with Agave Chili Sauce
    on page 121

Tofu, Green Beans, and Cashews on
    page 185

Sesame Miso Kale Chips on page 111

Roasted Red Pepper and Lentil Soup

We travel. We don't eat out much or go to a lot of movies just so we can take a long flight to some exotic or rainy or ruined location once a year. No matter where we've been, we've found exceptional vegan food. Like the soy cheese pizza we had at Napfényes Ízek in Budapest, or the mezze platter we shared in Istanbul. But no matter where we've been, there's always been one constant: lentil soup. We've had red lentil soup in Brussels and green lentil soup in Valladolid. We've had French lentil soup with beets in Paris (obviously) and a yellow dal-like soup in Athens. Lentils are a true constant. Lucky for us, we love lentils. This soup is an homage to all the soups we've loved before.

MAKES 6 SERVINGS   **$1.09 PER SERVING**

- 3 tablespoons olive oil
- 1 red onion, diced
- 1 large sweet potato, diced
- 1 large carrot, sliced
- 5 cups vegetable broth
- 3 cloves garlic, minced
- 1 tablespoon soy sauce or Bragg's Liquid Aminos

- ½ teaspoon red pepper flakes
- 1½ cups dry red lentils
- ¼ teaspoon vegan liquid smoke
- 1 cup jarred roasted red peppers with juices
- ¼ teaspoon celery seed
- 1 teaspoon ground black pepper

In a Dutch oven or large stew pot, heat the olive oil over medium heat. Add the onion, sweet potato, and carrot and cook until tender. Reduce the heat to low. Add the broth, garlic, soy sauce, red pepper flakes, lentils, and vegan liquid smoke. Cover and simmer, stirring occasionally to make sure the soup cooks evenly, for 30 minutes, or until the lentils are tender. Add the red peppers, celery seed, and black pepper and blend the soup directly in the pot using an immersion blender, or, working in batches, transfer to a food processor and process until smooth.

LIQUID SMOKE

Not sure what you're going to do with that left-over liquid smoke? Make some Simple Korean Kimchi BBQ Burgers (page 187). Once you've had a veggie burger made with vegan liquid smoke, it's pretty hard to go back to the original. This little bottle of ingenious wizardry is usually made using real wood smoke-infused steam, so it's a surprisingly natural way to flavor your food without adding salt, and will give your food that certain something so many mock meats have lacked over the years.

Green Shchi—Russian Cabbage Soup

Say what you will about the Russians—they know how to boil a cabbage. Shchi is one of the national soups of Russia, and much like pasta in Italy or cheese in France, it can vary greatly from region to region. Some regions use sauerkraut, some use a ton of sour cream; this recipe is a healthy vegan hybrid of them all that'll keep you so warm all winter, you won't even need a fur hat. Seriously, please don't wear fur. It's super mean.

MAKES 4 TO 6 SERVINGS   **$0.97 PER SERVING**

3 tablespoons olive oil

1 red onion, chopped

1 cabbage, cored and sliced

4 or 5 new potatoes, quartered

2 large carrots, sliced

2 stalks celery, chopped

2 bay leaves

½ teaspoon crushed black peppercorns

8 cups vegan chicken broth or vegetable broth

3 tablespoons chopped fresh parsley

1 tablespoon chopped fresh dill

Bread, for serving

In a large soup pot or Dutch oven, heat the olive oil over medium heat. Add the onion and use a wooden spoon to move the onion around a bit to make sure it cooks evenly. Once the onion is tender, add the remaining ingredients, except the bread, to the pot, stir, and cover. Once the soup begins to bubble, reduce the heat to maintain a simmer.

Let the soup simmer until the potatoes are tender, about 20 minutes.

Serve hot, with some bread for dipping.

You can use any leftover vegetable broth to make:

Tom Kha Gai—Spicy Coconut Soup on page 89

Parsnip and Peppercorn Soup on page 95

Pumpkin Curry Soup on page 216

Hungarian Goulash Stew on page 229

Chickpea à la King Skillet on page 123

Yankee Pot Roast Dinner on page 144

Vegan Gyros on page 219

Caldo Verde—Portuguese Soup

2013 was a tough year for us, full of a lot of adult stuff like deciding if we should buy a house, trying to start a family, and promoting our first book. So we did what any adults with way too many adult decisions to make would do: We cashed in all our frequent-flyer miles and went to Portugal—a country full of castles, ornately tiled walkways, and an amazing amount of delicious vegan food.

This potato-based soup is known as the national soup of Portugal. We enjoyed vegan caldo verde at a masterful vegan restaurant called Casa da Horta in Porto during our visit. Yes, in Portugal, even the sleepy little towns like Porto have kick-ass vegan restaurants.

MAKES 4 LARGE SERVINGS   **$2.04 PER SERVING**

2 red onions, diced

4 Yukon Gold potatoes, diced

1 large carrot, diced

2 stalks celery, diced

3 tablespoons olive oil (you'll want a little more to drizzle over the top)

3 cloves garlic, minced

Pinch of celery seed

2 teaspoons nutritional yeast

5½ cups vegan chicken broth or vegetable broth

½ cup white wine

¾ pound Swiss chard, kale, or collard greens

Olive oil cooking spray

1 cup vegan chorizo sausage (we recommend Upton's Naturals Chorizo Seitan, or Tofurky Chorizo Style Grounds), sliced or crumbled

Crushed black peppercorns

Red pepper flakes

In a Dutch oven or large stew pot, combine the red onions, potatoes, carrot, celery, olive oil, garlic, celery seed, nutritional yeast, broth, and wine. Bring to a boil over medium heat. When the soup begins to bubble, reduce the heat to maintain a simmer.

While the soup is heating, working with one leaf at a time, roll the greens into a cigar shape. Cut the rolled greens crosswise into thin strips. Set aside.

Spray your favorite cast-iron skillet with cooking spray and set it over medium heat. Add the vegan chorizo and brown it on all sides. Remove from the heat and set aside.

Check the soup—when the potatoes are tender, puree the soup directly in the pot using an immersion blender until it's smooth and creamy; alternatively, working in batches, transfer the soup to a food processor and process until smooth, then return the soup to the pot. Toss the greens into the soup, cover, and cook for 2 to 3 minutes.

(continued)

Serve the soup with a drizzle of olive oil and some vegan chorizo, black peppercorns, and red pepper flakes on top.

CARROTS

During World War II in Europe, when food was scarce, parents would give their children carrots on sticks. No joke. You can look it up. You'll find dozens of black-and-white photos of excited children gnawing on carrots like they're ice cream cones. Food rationing posters and cookbooks sang the praises of carrots as the perfect vegetable. And why not? They're nutritious, cheap, and great in everything from cakes to stews. Since then, their popularity has waned a bit, but they still remain one of the most versatile, healthy, and budget-friendly vegetables you can eat. If you're wondering what to make with leftover carrots, we recommend trying Green Shchi—Russian Cabbage Soup (page 92), Baked Creole Carrot Chips (page 112), Rosemary Chicklins and Dumplins Stew (page 127), or Pasta Primavera (page 239). Or you can always just enjoy them raw with the Vegan Bacon Ranch Dipping Sauce on page 165.

Parsnip and Peppercorn Soup

Oh, forgotten parsnips, you're so much more than just "white carrots." In medieval Europe, you were all the culinary rage, because you were sweet when all the other vegetables available were not. In the colonial United States, you were treasured as a delicious mashed meal—until those Peruvian potatoes returned to the New World via Spanish and English traders. But to us, you'll always be treasured as the base of this wonderful soup.

MAKES 4 TO 6 SERVINGS **$1.07 PER SERVING**

2 large leeks, white and pale green parts only, halved and cut into ¼-inch-thick half-moons

2 tablespoons plus 1½ teaspoons olive oil

1 clove garlic, minced

1 pound parsnips, cut crosswise into ¼-inch-thick pieces

1 pound Yukon Gold potatoes, cut into ¼-inch-thick slices

5 cups vegan chicken broth or vegetable broth

½ cup almond milk

2 teaspoons nutritional yeast

1½ teaspoons onion powder

½ teaspoon rubbed sage

¼ teaspoon celery seed

2 bay leaves

Sea salt

Crushed black peppercorns

Red pepper flakes

Whole wheat bread, toasted, for serving

Put the leeks in a colander and rinse them well under cold running water to get the grit and dirt off them.

In your largest Dutch oven or stew pot, heat the olive oil over medium heat. Add the leeks and garlic and cook until the leeks are tender. Add the parsnips, potatoes, broth, almond milk, nutritional yeast, onion powder, sage, celery seed, and bay leaves. Cover, bring the soup to a rolling boil, then reduce the heat to maintain a simmer.

Uncover and simmer for 5 to 10 minutes, frequently checking the parsnips and potatoes to see if they are tender yet. Once the parsnips are soft enough that they can be easily smushed against the side of the pot, remove the soup from the heat.

Use a spoon to remove the bay leaves. Then blend the soup directly in the pot using an immersion blender until smooth and creamy, or, working in batches, transfer the soup to a food processor and process until smooth. Season with salt and black pepper to taste.

Serve the soup hot, with a pinch of red pepper flakes and black pepper sprinkled over the top and whole wheat toast alongside.

(continued)

You can use any leftover almond milk to make:

Green Tea and Pear Smoothie on page 30

Banana Churro Waffles on page 44

Pumpkin Spice Latte on page 64

S'mores Cookie Bars on page 260

Chai Spice Cheesecake on page 272

Butternut Squash and Beer Poutine Party
   on page 288

Chef's Pasta Salad

This is a lunch for the old-school ethical vegan. The vegan who celebrates the modern world with its vegan Swiss cheese and plant-based pepperoni. A vegan who can appreciate how easy it is to live a cruelty-free life these days and wants to revel in it by eating all the mock-stars they can find. God bless you, everyone!

You'll need to cook the pasta the night before, so plan ahead.

MAKES 4 TO 6 SERVINGS   **$1.93 PER SERVING**

1 (1-pound) package bow-tie pasta

½ (16-ounce) package extra-firm tofu, drained

1 tablespoon nutritional yeast

½ package Hickory Smoked Tofurky Deli Slices, diced

3 tablespoons vegan bacon bits (we recommend Bac-Os)

3 tablespoons shredded vegan cheddar cheese (we recommend Daiya)

3 slices vegan Swiss cheese, diced (we recommend Daiya)

5 or 6 pieces vegan pepperoni, diced (we recommend Lightlife Smart Deli Pepperoni)

2 tablespoons chopped fresh parsley

2 carrots, sliced

1 cucumber

⅔ cup baby spinach leaves

1 recipe Dijon Mustard Dressing (page 80), chilled

Bring a large pot of salted water to a boil. Cook the pasta according to the directions on the package, drain, then transfer to an airtight container and refrigerate overnight.

In a small bowl, toss the tofu pieces with the nutritional yeast until the tofu is well coated.

In a large bowl, toss the pasta, tofu, vegan meats and cheeses, parsley, carrots, cucumber, and spinach. Add the dressing and toss until the salad is mixed and well coated.

Cover and refrigerate for no more than 15 minutes. Serve cold.

Jerk "Chicken" Pasta Salad

This recipe may have a lot of ingredients, but if you take a closer look you'll see we've re-created what you'd find in a "jerk" flavor packet in a healthier, non-sodium-based way. And if you look through this book you'll see every ingredient except the pineapple can be reused in multiple recipes. You could say this recipe is the embodiment of what we strived to do with our entire kitchen.

MAKES 4 TO 6 SERVINGS   **$2.41 PER SERVING**

1 (1-pound) package bow-tie pasta

2 cups vegan chicken, defrosted (we recommend Beyond Meat Chicken-Free Strips or Gardein Chick'n Scallopini)

2 tablespoons olive oil

3 tablespoons soy sauce or Bragg's Liquid Aminos

1 tablespoon packed brown sugar

1 tablespoon molasses

1 teaspoon ginger paste

1 tablespoon white wine

2 teaspoons ground cinnamon

½ teaspoon grated nutmeg

½ teaspoon ground cloves

½ teaspoon ground allspice

1 teaspoon ground cumin

½ teaspoon smoked paprika

¼ to 1 teaspoon cayenne pepper (you may want to add more or less)

1 teaspoon dried thyme

Dash of vegan liquid smoke

½ cup pineapple juice

1 cup vegan mayonnaise (we recommend Vegenaise or Just Mayo)

Juice of 1 lime

1 red bell pepper, diced

½ cup fresh pineapple pieces

3 green onions, diced

¼ cup fresh cilantro leaves

Preheat the oven to 400°F.

Bring a large pot of salted water to a boil. Cook the pasta according to the instructions on the package, drain, then transfer to an airtight container and refrigerate while you prepare the vegan chicken.

Cut the vegan chicken into bite-size pieces and place them in a baking dish. In a small bowl, make a marinade by whisking together the olive oil, soy sauce, brown sugar, molasses, ginger paste, white wine, cinnamon, nutmeg, cloves, allspice, ½ teaspoon of the cumin, the paprika, cayenne pepper to taste, the thyme, vegan liquid smoke, and ¼ cup of the pineapple juice. Pour the marinade over the vegan chicken and flip it a few times until completely coated. Let it sit for 5 minutes. (If you're using Beyond Meat, let the vegan chicken marinate for another 10 minutes, since it's a much denser product.)

Bake the vegan chicken for 10 minutes, then flip with a spatula so it'll brown evenly and bake for another 5 minutes.

In a bowl, whisk together the vegan mayo, remaining ½ teaspoon cumin, the lime juice, and remaining 1/4 cup pineapple juice.

In your largest mixing bowl, toss together the chilled pasta, cooked chicken with any extra marinade, vegan mayo mixture, bell pepper, pineapple pieces, green onions, and fresh cilantro. Cover the bowl with plastic wrap and refrigerate for 20 minutes before serving.

BLACKSTRAP MOLASSES

You can usually find a good-size bottle of blackstrap molasses for between $5 and $7, and it can last for about a year if you store it in your fridge. As a sweetener, blackstrap molasses is also better for you than agave nectar or sugar because it's a great source of iron and calcium—things vegans are sometimes concerned about having enough of in their diet. Looking for other ways to use your blackstrap molasses? Try making Blackstrap Vegan Bangers and Mash with Onion Gravy (page 125), Simple Korean Kimchi BBQ Burgers (page 187), or Molasses Crinkle Cookies (page 280).

Simple Soba Noodles

If you follow me on any of the various social networks out there, you know I live my life by a few mottos. One is this: You can never have enough noodles.

MAKES 4 TO 6 SERVINGS   **$1.75 PER SERVING**

1 (8-ounce) package soba noodles

5 cups vegetable broth

1 tablespoon diced fresh lemongrass (optional)

1 carrot, shredded

⅔ cup snow peas

¼ cup frozen corn

⅔ cup cremini, shiitake, or enoki mushrooms

⅔ cup baby spinach leaves

½ cup broccoli florets, cut small

1 clove garlic, minced

In a large soup pot or Dutch oven, combine all the ingredients. Bring to a boil over medium heat, then reduce the heat to maintain a simmer and simmer until the noodles are tender. This should take about 5 minutes. We recommend following the instructions on your package of soba noodles.

Serve hot.

> **You can use any leftover frozen corn to make:**
>
> Cowboy Quinoa Chili on page 241
>
> Simple Spanish Rice Bake on page 232
>
> Chili-Stuffed Sweet Potatoes on page 167

Sesame Peanut Noodles

There's an Asian restaurant near where we live that makes the most divine[†] sesame peanut noodles to ever grace a Brooklyn takeout box. And if money were no object, I'd gladly pay for them to be delivered to my eager arms every day—but alas, this is not my reality, so I had to make my own. This recipe is inspired by those tasty noodles and is just as good, in my opinion,[‡] but I bet way healthier.

MAKES 4 TO 6 SERVINGS   **$1.67 PER SERVING**

Peanut Sauce

⅓ cup peanut butter (the natural kind, made with real peanuts)

¼ cup tahini

2 tablespoons Sriracha or Thai chili sauce

2 tablespoons rice vinegar

2 tablespoons soy sauce or Bragg's Liquid Aminos

1 teaspoon garlic paste

2 cloves garlic, minced

Pinch of red pepper flakes

Noodles

4 to 6 servings of soba or udon noodles (measure out a bundle ¾ inch in diameter per serving)

1 tablespoon sesame oil

½ green bell pepper, sliced

½ red bell pepper, sliced

3 to 4 green onions, diced

¼ cup dry-roasted peanuts

2 tablespoons sesame seeds

Make the peanut sauce: In a bowl, whisk together the peanut sauce ingredients until completely blended. Set aside.

Make the noodles: Cook the noodles according to the directions on the package. Drain and set aside.

In a wok or large cast-iron skillet, heat the sesame oil over medium heat. Toss in the noodles and bell peppers. Cook, tossing continuously with a spatula or wooden paddle, until the peppers are tender. Add 2 green onions, the peanuts, and the sesame seeds, then mix in the peanut sauce (give it a stir first if it looks like it's starting to separate). Once the noodles are coated, remove from the heat.

Serve hot or cold, with a pinch of green onions over the top.

[†] That's right—I said it. They're *divine!*

[‡] Sorry if that's braggy.

(continued)

SRIRACHA

For some, 2013 will be remembered by The Great Sriracha Scare. When Huy Fong Foods, makers of the most popular Vietnamese hot sauce in the world, was ordered to cease production in their California factory for thirty days due to complaints from neighbors, spiciness enthusiasts everywhere let out a collective gasp. They rushed to their markets to load up on that rooster sauce[§] like a hurricane was coming. Some began exploring other Asian chili sauces, and that one person who likes their food with just a pinch of pepper scratched his head and shrugged. If you're one of those folks who love a little Sriracha in their food, you may want to try the Chop Suey Noodles on page 178, the Sriracha and Sweet Onion Stew on page 104, or the Simple Korean Kimchi BBQ Burgers on page 187.

[§] It's called this because of the iconic rooster on the label, not because it actually includes any poultry products. Sriracha sauce is, in fact, vegan.

Ribollita Soup

Ribollita soup is a Tuscan peasant soup traditionally made with bits of bread, cannellini beans, and a variety of cheaper vegetables like onions, tomatoes, and carrots. Sometimes it is made by reheating leftover minestrone with stale bread from dinner the night before. Hence the name, ribollita, which means "boiled twice." This is a great recipe for when you've got leftover bread kicking around.

MAKES 4 TO 6 SERVINGS　　　　　　　　**$1.36 PER SERVING**

- 2 tablespoons olive oil
- 1 large red onion, diced
- 3 cloves garlic, minced
- 2 (15-ounce) cans cannellini beans, drained and rinsed, or 1½ cups cooked dry cannellini beans
- 1 (28-ounce) can diced tomatoes
- Dash of vegan liquid smoke
- 2 carrots, sliced
- 3 stalks celery, chopped
- 1 cup chopped kale leaves
- ½ cup fresh basil leaves
- 3 cups vegetable broth
- 2 teaspoons Italian seasoning
- ½ teaspoon fennel seed
- ½ teaspoon red pepper flakes
- 1 bay leaf
- ½ stale baguette, cubed
- Vegan Parmesan cheese (optional)

In a large soup pot with a lid or a Dutch oven, heat the olive oil over medium heat. Add the red onion and garlic and cook, flipping with a spatula so they cook evenly, until the onion is tender. Toss in all the remaining ingredients except the bread and vegan Parmesan and bring to a boil. Cover and reduce the heat to maintain a simmer, and cook for 10 minutes.

Remove from the heat and gently mix in the bread cubes. Serve hot, with some vegan Parmesan sprinkled over the top.

FRESH BASIL

Fresh basil is an investment. Buying basil is making a promise to yourself that you're going to cook your meals this week and you're going to love it. It's a promise you can keep and feel good about. If you're wondering what to make with your leftover basil, try baking the Rustic Pesto and Heirloom Tomato Tart on page 117 or making the Tuesday Night Dinner on page 203 or the Spinach and Broccoli Stuffed Shells on page 205.

Check out some tips for making your basil last longer on page 14.

Sriracha and Sweet Onion Stew

Unfortunately, I didn't grow up in a house where we ever had Sriracha sauce hibernating in the back of the fridge, so I didn't fall under the spell of the "rooster sauce" until I was in college. I blame my current dependence on this red stuff on my former roommate Libbe, who you may remember from the Hot and Sour Soup adventure in our book Betty Goes Vegan. Without the rooster sauce, this is just a lovely onion-based stew. But with it, it's a rock star you can reheat for lunch all week and look forward to all day.

MAKES 4 TO 6 SERVINGS   **$0.98 PER SERVING**

- 4 tablespoons olive oil
- 3½ large sweet onions, thinly sliced
- 2 cloves garlic, minced
- 4 cups vegetable broth
- 1 large Yukon Gold potato, cut into bite-size pieces
- 1 teaspoon dried thyme
- 8 to 10 mushrooms, sliced
- 4 tablespoons white wine

- 1 tablespoon soy sauce or Bragg's Liquid Aminos
- ½ cup coconut milk
- 1 tablespoon lemon juice
- ½ teaspoon crushed black peppercorns
- ¼ teaspoon red pepper flakes
- 3 large Swiss chard leaves, chopped
- 1 to 2 teaspoons Sriracha or Thai chili sauce (depending how much heat you can handle)

In your favorite Dutch oven or stew pot, heat 3 tablespoons of the olive oil over medium heat. Once the oil is hot, add the onions and toss a few times until they're coated in the hot oil. Sauté the onions until tender. Add the garlic, vegetable broth, half the potato pieces, and the thyme and reduce the heat to maintain a simmer.

In a cast-iron skillet or frying pan, heat the remaining 1 tablespoon olive oil over medium heat. Toss in the mushrooms and 2 tablespoons of the white wine. Cook until the mushrooms are tender, then remove from the

heat. Add two-thirds of the mushrooms to the pot with the stew.

Add the remaining 2 tablespoons white wine, the soy sauce, coconut milk, lemon juice, black pepper, and red pepper flakes to the stew and stir until blended. Cover and simmer for 2 minutes. Then, directly in the pot using an immersion blender, blend the stew until creamy and smooth, or, working in batches, transfer the stew to a food processor and process until creamy and smooth, then return to the pot.

Toss the remaining potato pieces and

reserved mushrooms into the stew. Cover and simmer for 10 minutes, or until the potatoes are tender. Add your Swiss chard leaves. Give it a taste test, then stir in 1 teaspoon of Sriracha sauce at a time until the stew is as spicy as you want. We went with 2 teaspoons, but maybe you're braver and will make it to 3. Just remember: You're making stew, not winning a bet, so don't go crazy.

You can use the other half of your sweet onion to make:

Tofu Vindaloo on page 195

Rosie the Riveter and Her Lunch Pail

Many people are shocked when they learn that Rosie the Riveter can be a controversial figure. This American cultural icon is often thought of as an empowering figure of femininity that celebrates women joining the workforce and contributing to the United States's efforts in World War II. Rosie is the perfect combination of beauty—dolled-up with red lipstick and chestnut curls—and strength—with her flexed biceps and healthy physique. But to some, she's just part of the propaganda machine that was way too active during those years and manipulated women into taking jobs in factories where they were paid less than their male peers because it was their patriotic responsibility to do so. To some, Rosie contributed to the problem of gender inequality in the workplace that still exists today by reinforcing the notion that it was okay to pay women less—in many cases, a lot less—because they were just working out of a sense of patriotic duty, not for a steady paycheck.

But there's another layer to Rosie that I think is overlooked, and is best captured in Norman Rockwell's *Saturday Evening Post* cover in 1943. It was one of the most popular covers on one of the most popular publications of the time. Rockwell's Rosie is no scowling pinup. She's a cheery, Rubenesque woman painted in Rockwell's cheerful palette with somewhat Herculean arms, an enormous rivet gun across her lap, and a copy of Hitler's manifesto under her heel. And she's enjoying a great big sandwich. You could say that she was the America we were fighting for and people may not have even known they cherished: America's *gosh-darn* abundance.

Women could look at Rosie and see nobility in their struggle to maintain normalcy despite rationing, the difficulty of working outside the home for the first time while still acting as homemakers, and an escape from the loneliness many expressed feeling. Men could look at Rosie and see the girl they left back home, the job that was waiting for them, and the prosperity that was returning in the wake of the Great Depression (i.e., that great big sandwich).

That's the Rosie I choose to see.

Chipotle Avocado Sandwiches

Unless you live in California, where avocados literally grow in your backyard, you're like us and live for the few times a year they go on sale. You snatch them up and have green feasts that can only be described as jubilant. These sandwiches are a way for you to bring that joy with you to work—where you need it most.

MAKES 4 TO 6 SERVINGS   **$1.22 PER SERVING**

⅔ cup shredded vegan cheddar or pepper Jack cheese (we recommend Daiya)

1 baguette, halved horizontally

2 ripe avocados, halved, pitted, and peeled

1 chipotle pepper in adobo sauce, diced

3 cherry tomatoes, quartered

Set the oven to broil.

Sprinkle the vegan cheese over the cut sides of the baguette and put the baguette on the oven rack to toast, vegan-cheese-side up. Broil for 5 minutes, or until the vegan cheese has melted. Keep an eye on it, though; broiling can be dangerous and quickly escalate to burning.

While the bread is toasting, in a large bowl, mash the avocados with the chipotle peppers, then use a large spoon to fold in the tomatoes.

Spoon the chipotle-avocado mix onto the bread, close the sandwich, and cut it crosswise into 4 to 6 individual sandwiches.

Serve hot, if you can, or wrap in aluminum foil to bring to work.

> *You can use any leftover vegan cheddar cheese to make:*
>
> Rosemary Potato Frittata on page 60
> Mexican Stuffed Zucchini on page 146
> Brinner Lasagna on page 169
> Cajun Nachos on page 129
> Mac and Cheez Pie on page 173
> Cincinnati Chili on page 177

Lasagna Sandwiches featuring Italian Tempeh Sausage

We love lasagna. We make it all the time. It's an always-adapting love that changes depending on the seasonal vegetables available to us and how many people we're feeding. Our love for all things lasagna has also come to include this sandwich.

MAKES 4 TO 6 SANDWICHES   **$1.90 PER SERVING**

Italian Tempeh Sausage

- 1 (8-ounce) package tempeh
- 1 tablespoon plus 1 teaspoon soy sauce or Braggs Liquid Aminos
- 1½ teaspoons fennel seed
- ¼ teaspoon ground black pepper
- 1 teaspoon red pepper flakes
- 1½ teaspoons Italian seasoning
- ¼ teaspoon celery seed
- ½ teaspoon smoked paprika
- 2 dashes of vegan liquid smoke
- 1 clove garlic, minced

Sandwich

- 2 tablespoons red wine
- 1 (6-ounce) can tomato paste
- ⅔ cup shredded vegan mozzarella cheese (we recommend Daiya)
- 1 baguette, halved horizontally
- 4 cherry tomatoes, quartered
- ¼ cup roasted red peppers
- Vegan Parmesan cheese (optional)

Make the Italian tempeh sausage: Crumble the tempeh into a bowl, then mix in all the remaining sausage ingredients and stir with a wooden spoon until combined. Set aside to marinate, mixing it a few times while it marinates to make sure the flavors are evenly distributed.

Make the sandwich: In a small saucepan, heat the red wine and tomato paste over medium heat, stirring, until the mixture begins to bubble, then remove from the heat and set aside.

Set the oven to broil.

Sprinkle the vegan cheese over the cut sides of the baguette and put the baguette on the oven rack to toast, vegan-cheese-side up. Broil for 5 minutes, or until the vegan cheese has melted. Keep an eye on it, though; broiling can be dangerous and quickly escalate to burning. I don't think I have to tell you any time fire is involved, it is serious business. Remove the baguette from the oven and set aside to cool a bit. Switch the oven to the bake setting and preheat it to 400°F.

(continued)

Meanwhile, add the wine-tomato sauce, cherry tomatoes, and roasted red peppers to the bowl with the tempeh sausage and mix with a large spoon.

Top the baguette with tempeh sausage and sauce, close the sandwich, then cut it crosswise into 4 to 6 individual sandwiches.

Heat each sandwich in the oven for 5 minutes before serving.

Serve with some vegan Parmesan cheese sprinkled over the top, if desired.

You can use any leftover vegan mozzarella cheese to make:

Spinach and Broccoli Stuffed Shells on page 205

Pocket Calzones on page 228

Vegan Cheese Party Pizza on page 278

Greek Garbanzo Bean Salad Pitas

The Greek lemon dressing in this recipe is so frakking good, it'll make you reconsider ever buying another bottle of the premade stuff again.

MAKES 4 TO 6 SANDWICHES   **$1.19 PER SERVING**

Greek Lemon Dressing

Juice of 1 lemon

¼ cup olive oil

1 clove garlic, minced

1 teaspoon Dijon mustard

1 teaspoon dried oregano

¼ teaspoon crushed black peppercorns

Pitas

1 (15-ounce) can garbanzo beans, drained and rinsed, or 1½ cups cooked dry garbanzo beans

1 cucumber, diced

½ red onion, diced

2 to 3 cherry tomatoes, quartered

¼ cup pitted kalamata olives

½ red bell pepper, diced

2 tablespoons fresh mint leaves, chopped

¾ cup baby spinach leaves

2 to 3 whole wheat pitas, warmed

Make the Greek lemon dressing: Combine all the dressing ingredients in an airtight container and shake until blended.

Make the pitas: In a large bowl, toss together the garbanzo beans, cucumber, red onion, tomatoes, olives, bell pepper, mint, spinach, and the dressing. Mix with a large spoon until all the ingredients are coated with the dressing.

Cut the pitas in half and open them gently. Then, fill the pitas with the salad and enjoy with some lemonade or iced tea.

KALAMATA OLIVES

Kalamata olives are usually cheapest to buy from your grocery store's olive bar, where you can measure out how much you'll need without paying for lots of brine. (Just be sure to get *some* brine in the container, or the olives will dry out.) Other recipes that feature these dark purple jewels of Mediterranean cuisine are the Lemon-Tahini Fattoush on page 71, the Groove Is in the Artichoke Heart Salad on page 72, and the Baked Strapatsada—Greek Baked "Egg" Cups on page 53.

Tuscan Eggplant and White Bean Sandwiches

Let's get real—we're not fans of eggplant. We've tried for years and years to find the perfect eggplant recipe, and it's been a struggle. Yet I can honestly say one of my favorite parts of this sandwich is how the baked marinated eggplant makes inexpensive and delicious "deli slices." You can use these eggplant slices in numerous recipes: on sandwiches and pizzas or chopped up in a salad or tofu scramble. They're good in pretty much everything, and as someone who isn't a fan of eggplant, that's saying a lot.

MAKES 6 TO 8 SANDWICHES   **$1.15 PER SERVING**

White Bean Spread

2 (15-ounce) cans cannellini beans, drained and rinsed, or 3 cups cooked dry cannellini beans

3 cloves garlic

Juice of 1 lemon

1½ teaspoons ground black pepper

1 teaspoon dried oregano

1 tablespoon olive oil

Salt

Eggplant

1 large eggplant, thinly sliced crosswise to make round "deli slices"

1 cup vegan beef broth (we recommend Better Than Bouillon)

1 to 2 tablespoons olive oil

To Assemble

1 loaf whole wheat bread

1 red bell pepper, sliced

⅓ cup fresh basil leaves

Make the white bean spread: In a food processor, combine all the white bean spread ingredients except the salt and process until creamy. Give it a taste test, and then add the desired amount of salt. Set aside until ready to use.

Make the eggplant: In a shallow dish, marinate the eggplant slices in the vegan beef broth for 10 minutes.

In a cast-iron skillet, heat 1 tablespoon of the olive oil over medium heat. Working in batches, fry the eggplant slices on both sides until the edges are crisp. Add more oil as needed and have a plate ready for the finished eggplant slices.

Assemble the sandwiches: For each sandwich, place a few slices of eggplant on one piece of bread, then top with some bell pepper slices and a few fresh basil leaves. Use a butter knife to smear the white bean spread over another piece of bread. Put the two together and ta-da! Sandwich!

Sesame Miso Kale Chips

It breaks my heart to tell you this, but I'm going to give it to you straight: Those prepackaged kale chips we all love so much are not your friend. They can cost anywhere from $6 to $8 for two servings, but can be made at home for around 72 cents per serving. Yes, you'll have to make them yourself and even put them in a container with your own hands. But in the end, even when you add in your own labor, you still come out way ahead.

MAKES 4 TO 6 SERVINGS　　　　　　　　　　　　**$0.72 PER SERVING**

1 pound kale leaves

1 tablespoon nutritional yeast

3 tablespoons white miso

Juice of 1 lemon

2 tablespoons sesame oil

2 tablespoons sesame seeds

Preheat the oven to 300°F. Line a cookie sheet with parchment paper.

Cut the kale leaves into pieces smaller than your palm. Set aside.

In a food processor or blender, combine the nutritional yeast, white miso, lemon juice, sesame oil, and 2 tablespoons water and process into a smooth paste. Pour the miso sauce into a shallow dish.

Dip the kale leaves into the miso sauce and place them on the lined cookie sheet, arranging them so they aren't touching. Sprinkle the sesame seeds over the top.

Bake until crisp, no more than 20 minutes, checking frequently to make sure they don't burn. Remove from the oven as soon as they become crisp.

Let cool to room temperature before serving.

Baked Creole Carrot Chips

The first time I made carrot chips, I thought I was so smart. I was an arrogant twentysomething who assumed no one had ever thought to make these crispy orange snacks before. Fifteen years later, I have to laugh at my former bravado. I may not have invented carrot chips, but at least this particular recipe is one that I've put many years into perfecting.

MAKES 4 TO 6 SERVINGS   **$0.22 PER SERVING**

6 large carrots

¼ cup olive oil

2 tablespoons Tony Chachere's Original Creole Seasoning

Preheat the oven to 300°F. Line a cookie sheet with parchment paper.

Cut the carrots crosswise into very thin coins, using a mandoline, if you have one, to get even slices.

In a bowl, whisk together the olive oil and Creole seasoning. Then, gently toss the carrots in the oil mixture until lightly coated. Place the carrots on the lined cookie sheet, arranging the slices so they aren't touching.

Bake for 20 to 25 minutes, or until crispy, keeping an eye on them while they bake so they don't burn. The thinner ones will be done first. Move fully baked chips to a plate lined with a paper towel to soak up any extra oil.

Let cool to room temperature before serving.

> **You can use the rest of your Tony Chachere's Original Creole Seasoning to make:**
>
> Green Gunpowder Gumbo Skillet on
>   page 131
> Slow-Cooker Tempeh Jambalaya on
>   page 213
> Cajun Nachos on page 129

Sweet Beet Mix

Fact: Russet potatoes aren't the only root vegetable that can make a nice chip. Beets work beautifully, too.

MAKES 4 TO 6 SERVINGS $0.62 PER SERVING

2 large beets, scrubbed and *very* thinly sliced

2 large sweet potatoes, scrubbed and *very* thinly sliced

2 tablespoons olive oil

½ teaspoon sea salt

¼ teaspoon ground cumin

¼ teaspoon curry powder

Preheat the oven to 400°F. Line a cookie sheet with aluminum foil.

Toss the beets and sweet potato slices in a large bowl with the olive oil until they are lightly coated.

Spread the beets and sweet potatoes out in a single layer on the lined cookie sheet. You may need to bake them in batches or on two sheets.

Bake for 20 to 25 minutes. Keep an eye on them; depending on how thin the vegetables are cut, some may bake faster than others. Halfway through baking, flip the chips with a spatula so both sides bake evenly. Once the edges are crispy, the chips are ready to take out of the oven. Don't worry if the center is still a little tender. Move them to a large plate lined with a paper towel to soak up any extra oil.

Sprinkle the chips with salt, cumin, and curry powder and let cool to room temperature before eating.

CURRY POWDER

It can be frustrating trying to figure out which curry powder to buy. Some brands are very specific, using proper names like garam masala or ras el hanout, but often you'll just see descriptive terms like "mild" or "hot" on two different bottles that appear to hold a relatively similar golden powder. But while each blend is unique in its own way, they usually share the same key flavors. We kept it pretty generic in our recipes so that you can use whichever curry powder you prefer or have access to. If you're wondering what else you can use your curry powder in, try making the Pumpkin Curry Soup on page 216, Aloo Saag on page 235, or Samosa Pizza on page 161.

CHAPTER 5

DINNER

After all the work we put into perfecting our pantry and developing our shopping strategy, there was one fact we couldn't escape: We needed a collection of exciting dinner recipes that were easy enough that people would want to make them after a long day at work, and also provided left-overs to bring for lunch the next day. And because there's more to life than money, we wanted recipes that would be nice for date nights or fun for kids—so you and your family can enjoy your more frugal lifestyle.

› Rustic Pesto and Heirloom Tomato Tart.....................117

› Lasagna Bolognese................119

› Tofu Spring Rolls with Agave Chili Sauce........................121

› Chickpea à la King Skillet..........123

› Blackstrap Vegan Bangers and Mash with Onion Gravy...........125

› Rosemary Chicklins and Dumplins Stew...................127

› Cajun Nachos.....................129

› Green Gunpowder Gumbo Skillet...........................131

› Apple-Sage Tempeh Sausage over Savory Polenta...................133

› Wild Mushroom Risotto...........135

› Bubbie's Polish Potato Pierogies.....137

› Swiss Chard Rolls with Domestic Goddess Sauce...................139

› Steamed Sesame Seitan Dim Sum...141

> Yankee Pot Roast Dinner. 144

> Mexican Stuffed Zucchini. 146

> Chimichurri Rice Casserole 148

> Tater Tot Pie 150

> Quinoa Taco Casserole 152

> Ratatouille Rice Bake 153

> Vegan Bacon, White Bean, and
Spinach Risotto. 155

> Irish Stout Stew 157

> Pizza Dough. 159

> Fajita Pizza. 160

> Samosa Pizza. 161

> Turkish Pizza—Lahmacun. 163

> Buffalo Cauliflower Calzones
with Vegan Bacon Ranch
Dipping Sauce. 165

> Chili-Stuffed Sweet Potatoes 167

> Brinner Lasagna 169

> Sloppy Joel Pie. 171

> Mac and Cheez Pie 173

> Aloha Dogs. 175

> Cincinnati Chili. 177

> Chop Suey Noodles. 178

> Spinach and Tempeh Pastitsio. 180

> Sweet Potato and Black
Bean Tacos. 182

> Beefless Brussels Sprout
Shepherd's Pie 183

> Tofu, Green Beans, and
Cashews 185

> Pan-Seared Black Tea and
Pepper Tofu 186

> Simple Korean Kimchi
BBQ Burgers. 187

> Betty's Wartime Walnut Burger. 189

> Yankee Doodle Macaroni 191

> Vegan BLT Mac and Cheez 193

> Tofu Vindaloo 195

> Roasted Pear, Walnut, and
Brussels Sprout Tacos 197

> Sesame and Soy Marinated
Mushroom Steaks. 198

> Pasta with Asparagus and
Green Onion Pesto 200

> Angel Hair Pasta with Garlic and
Rosemary Mushrooms. 202

> Tuesday Night Dinner 203

> Spinach and Broccoli Stuffed
Shells. 205

> Beet "Boudin" Balls with Garlic
Aioli. 206

> Chipotle Chicken Chilaquiles. 208

> Pan-Seared Tofu with Arugula,
Capers, and Tomatoes 210

Rustic Pesto and Heirloom Tomato Tart

Heirloom tomatoes are some of the most impressively colorful vegetables out there. They range from dark purple to sunshine yellow, and can be as small as a Roma tomato or as big as a navel orange. You'll find the best ones at the best prices in July and August when they're in season, but no matter when you get them, use them quickly. Their shelf life is shorter than that of their classic red brethren. If you can't find heirloom tomatoes in your area, you can make this recipe with Roma or plum tomatoes instead.

MAKES 1 TART   **$1.26 PER SERVING**

Dough

1 cup all-purpose flour
1 cup whole wheat flour
¼ teaspoon salt
¼ cup olive oil

Pesto

3 tablespoons olive oil
1 cup fresh basil leaves
½ cup fresh spinach leaves

3 cloves garlic
¼ cup sun-dried tomatoes
1 tablespoon nutritional yeast

To Assemble

12 ounces small heirloom tomatoes, thinly sliced
3 Campari or small Roma tomatoes, thinly sliced
2 tablespoons pine nuts
Cornmeal, for dusting
Sea salt and ground black pepper

Make the dough: In a large bowl, whisk together the flours and salt. Blend in the olive oil, then gradually add water, using up to ½ cup, until you can form the dough into a ball. Loosely wrap the dough in plastic wrap and press it into a disk. Refrigerate for 20 minutes.

Make the pesto: In a food processor, combine all the pesto ingredients and process to a smooth paste.

Assemble the tart: Preheat the oven to 425°F.

While still wrapped loosely in plastic wrap, gently roll the dough into an even circle. Brush with some of the pesto. Then, place a layer of the tomato slices on the dough, overlapping them slightly and leaving a ½-inch edge clear for the crust. Make two to three layers of tomato slices, drizzling a little pesto between each layer and saving the most colorful tomatoes for the top layer. Using a spoon, place dollops of pesto across the top of the tart in any spots where

(continued)

the tomatoes have left pockets. Drizzle the pesto oil over the top, then sprinkle evenly with the pine nuts. Gently fold the edges of the dough over the filling, leaving the center exposed.

Dust a pizza stone or cookie sheet with cornmeal. Gently move the tart to the pizza stone or cookie sheet. Sprinkle two pinches of salt and pepper over the top of your tart.

Bake for 20 to 30 minutes or until the crust is a light golden brown.

PINE NUTS AND SUN-DRIED TOMATOES

Pine nuts can be expensive, mostly due to the fact that they come in packages that contain way more than you actually need. If you can find bulk pine nuts, you can get about a handful for less than $5, which is even more than you'll need for the above recipe. The same goes for sun-dried tomatoes. Pre-packaged sun-dried tomatoes are often more expensive than if you just grab a few from the salad bar at your local grocery store.

Lasagna Bolognese

You may think you know lasagna, with its thick ricotta layer and sweet tomato sauce, but this recipe will surprise you. It combines "meaty" vegan Bolognese sauce and creamy vegan béchamel sauce with several layers of lasagna noodles for a dish that's a bit more highbrow than what you get in the frozen food aisle. It's downright beautiful if you ask me.

MAKES 6 TO 8 SERVINGS   **$2.05 PER SERVING**

Bolognese Sauce

2 tablespoons olive oil

1 red onion, diced

1 stalk celery, diced

1 carrot, diced

1 (8-ounce) package tempeh, crumbled

1 teaspoon fennel seeds

¼ teaspoon crushed black peppercorns

2 pinches of red pepper flakes

1 teaspoon Italian seasoning

¼ teaspoon celery seed

½ teaspoon smoked paprika

Dash of vegan liquid smoke

1 clove garlic, minced

1 tablespoon soy sauce or Bragg's Liquid Aminos

1 (24-ounce) jar marinara sauce or DIY Marinara Sauce (page 226)

2 tablespoons red wine

Lasagna

1 (12-ounce) package lasagna noodles (not oven-ready)

1 tablespoon olive oil (optional)

1 large tomato, sliced

1 recipe Vegan Béchamel Sauce (page 180)

Make the Bolognese sauce: In your deepest cast-iron skillet or saucepan, heat the olive oil over medium heat. Toss in the onion, celery, and carrot and cook, stirring occasionally.

Once the onion and celery are tender, toss in the tempeh crumbles, fennel seeds, black pepper, red pepper flakes, Italian seasoning, celery seeds, paprika, vegan liquid smoke, and garlic. Continue to cook, stirring occasionally and using a spoon to break the tempeh into smaller pieces as it cooks, for 5 minutes. Add the soy sauce, pasta sauce, and red wine, then reduce the heat to maintain a simmer. Simmer, stirring occasionally, until ready to use.

Make the lasagna: Preheat the oven to 350°F.

Bring a large pot of salted water to a boil. Cook the lasagna noodles following the

(continued)

directions on the package until al dente. We recommend adding a tablespoon of olive oil to the pasta water to keep noodles from sticking together while they boil. Drain the noodles and let cool.

Coat the bottom of a baking dish with a thin layer of Bolognese sauce. Try not to get any vegetables or tempeh in this layer. Place a single layer of lasagna noodles across the bottom. Then ladle another thin layer of Bolognese sauce on top of the noodles. Place 2 slices of tomatoes on any spots where the sauce is thin or there are no vegetables or tempeh. Drizzle some béchamel sauce over the top, then repeat the process 8 more times. If you have any broken noodles, use them to patch up any holes or breaks between noodles. Keep the layers of Bolognese sauce thin so that you have enough to make the whole lasagna. Also, it looks really cool to have thin layers of sauce, tempeh, and tomatoes with a little béchamel sauce between the noodles.

Bake the lasagna for 30 to 40 minutes. You'll know it's done when the exposed noodles are slightly crispy and the béchamel sauce has turned a very light golden brown.

Remove the lasagna from the oven and let cool for 10 minutes before serving.

You can use your leftover red wine to make:

Yankee Pot Roast Dinner on page 144

Ratatouille Rice Bake on page 153

Tuesday Night Dinner on page 203

Tofu Spring Rolls with Agave Chili Sauce

There are as many versions of spring rolls as there are regions in Asia. This is what's called a "fresh" spring roll because it's not fried, but in Vietnam I guess it's called a summer roll. Whatever you call it, it's a light dinner that works perfectly as a simple summer meal.

MAKES 8 TO 10 ROLLS   **$1.19 PER SERVING**

Rolls

2 ounces rice vermicelli (also called thin rice sticks)

¼ cup sesame oil

1 (16-ounce) package extra-firm tofu, drained and cut into 8 to 10 thin pieces

2 teaspoons soy sauce or Bragg's Liquid Aminos

8 to 10 (8½-inch) rice paper spring roll wrappers

1 head Bibb lettuce

2 large carrots, grated

⅓ cup fresh basil leaves

⅓ cup fresh mint leaves

½ cup fresh cilantro

Agave Chili Dipping Sauce

¼ cup agave nectar

¼ cup soy sauce or Bragg's Liquid Aminos

¼ cup boiling water

1 tablespoon rice vinegar

2 cloves garlic, minced

2 to 3 pinches of red pepper flakes

Prepare the rice vermicelli either by following the directions on the package, or by soaking the noodles in a large bowl of hot water for 20 minutes or until pliable. While the noodles soak, bring a large pot of water to a boil. Drain the noodles, then carefully toss them in the boiling water. Boil for 1 minute, then drain. Rinse the noodles under cold water and transfer them to a bowl. They will start to stick together as they cool; don't worry, you're not doing anything wrong.

Meanwhile, heat the sesame oil over medium heat in your favorite skillet. Once the oil is hot, add the tofu and brown the pieces on both sides. We like it best when the edges are crispy on both sides. Be careful not to break the tofu; the rolls will look better and be firmer if the tofu is in one piece. Place the cooked tofu on a paper towel–lined plate to drain and cool.

Once the tofu is cool enough to handle, drizzle the soy sauce over the top to add flavor.

To assemble the spring rolls, fill a shallow dish with warm water and place a spring roll wrapper in it until it is pliable. This should

(continued)

take about 30 seconds—do not oversoak. Remove from the water and pat dry with a tea towel. As soon as the wrapper is dry, build a spring roll: Place the wrapper on a cutting board, then fold one leaf of lettuce in half and place it in the center of the wrapper. Add a pinch of the rice vermicelli, and then a pinch of carrots. Then, layer one or two basil leaves and a few mint leaves on top. Place a tofu slice on top of that and carefully arrange the cilantro leaves over the tofu so that all the lacy edges are visible. It'll look beautiful once you wrap it all up. Fold the sides of the wrapper up, then roll the spring roll tightly into a cigar shape, compressing the filling as you roll to get the tightest roll.

Repeat the above process for each spring roll.

Place the spring rolls together on a plate big enough for them all to fit without crowding; they might stick together a little. Refrigerate until ready to serve.

Make the agave chili dipping sauce: While the rolls are chilling, in a small bowl, whisk together all the dipping sauce ingredients until blended.

Serve the spring rolls cold with the sauce on the side.

You can use your leftover agave nectar to make:

Green Tea and Pear Smoothie on
    page 30
Virgin Crêpes Suzette on page 39
PB&J Granola Bars on page 28
Thai Vegan Chicken Slaw on page 69
Avocado and Grapefruit Salad with
    Cilantro Dressing on page 81
Strawberry Salad on page 300

Chickpea à la King Skillet

While writing this book, I spent a few days at the New York Public Library reading vintage ladies' magazines from the 1920s through the 1960s. I was researching the evolution of certain dishes, as well as seeking out hidden recipe gems or tips that could help us save money and time. One recipe that stood out year after year was chicken à la king. This recipe was originally served in fancy restaurants in upscale resorts and hotels in the 1920s, but had become a midweek dinner staple by the 1950s. And it makes sense why. This one-pot wonder isn't just economical; it's the kind of dish that even the pickiest eater will love. Our take on this classic recipe preserves all the flavor of the original, but leaves the birds out of it.

MAKES 4 TO 6 SERVINGS   **$1.32 PER SERVING**

1 tablespoon olive oil

1 cup white mushrooms

1 red onion, diced

2 cloves garlic, minced

4 cups vegetable broth or vegan chicken broth (we recommend Better Than Bouillon)

⅓ cup frozen green beans

2 pinches of celery seed

1 teaspoon poultry seasoning

¼ teaspoon garlic powder

½ teaspoon Italian seasoning

1 (15-ounce) can garbanzo beans, drained and rinsed, or 1½ cups cooked dry garbanzo beans

1½ cups uncooked curly or spiral pasta

¼ cup chopped fresh parsley

½ red bell pepper

½ cup frozen peas

¼ cup nutritional yeast

Salt and ground black pepper

Crusty bread, for serving

In a cast-iron skillet, heat the olive oil over medium heat. Add the mushrooms, onion, and garlic and cook, stirring occasionally with a wooden spoon to make sure everything cooks evenly, until the onions are tender.

Add the broth, green beans, celery seed, poultry seasoning, garlic powder, Italian seasoning, garbanzo beans, and pasta. Continue to mix the ingredients while cooking. Once the pasta is al dente (taste a piece to check), add the parsley, red bell pepper, and peas. Mix in the nutritional yeast 1 tablespoon at a time to avoid clumps. Continue to stir the ingredients while cooking until the pasta is the desired tenderness. Right before you serve, give the sauce a taste test and add any needed salt and pepper.

Serve hot with a crusty slice of bread to mop up any extra sauce.

(continued)

> **You can use the other half of your red bell pepper to make:**
>
> Sesame Peanut Noodles on page 101
>
> Thai Vegan Chicken Slaw on page 69
>
> Greek Garbanzo Bean Salad Pitas on
>   page 109
>
> Groove Is in the Artichoke Heart Salad
>   on page 72
>
> Tom Kha Gai—Spicy Coconut Soup on
>   page 89

Blackstrap Vegan Bangers and Mash with Onion Gravy

This quintessential British pub dish may not be much to look at, but with its stick-to-your-ribs combination of homemade vegan sausages and mashed potatoes and gravy, it's what the British call "top nosh!" If you can't find affordable vital wheat gluten in your area, aren't the DIY type, or just want to save some time, you can always use premade vegan sausages in this recipe. We recommend using either Tofurky Beer Brats or Field Roast Sausages.

MAKES 4 TO 6 SERVINGS　　　　　　　　　　　　　**$2.42 PER SERVING**

Blackstrap Vegan Sausages

1 (6-ounce) can tomato paste

1 cup vegan beef broth or vegetable broth

2 tablespoons olive oil

3 tablespoons soy sauce or Bragg's Liquid Aminos

¼ teaspoon vegan liquid smoke

2 cloves garlic, minced

1 tablespoon blackstrap molasses

½ cup nutritional yeast

2 teaspoons bread crumbs

1 teaspoon smoked paprika

2 cups vital wheat gluten

½ teaspoon onion powder

1 teaspoon rubbed sage

Onion Gravy

3 tablespoons olive oil

2 red onions, diced

2 tablespoons whole wheat flour

½ teaspoon ground black pepper

2 cups vegan beef broth or vegetable broth (we recommend Better Than Bouillon)

2 teaspoons vegan Worcestershire sauce

1 tablespoon soy sauce or Bragg's Liquid Aminos

Mash

1 pound Yukon Gold potatoes, baked

2 tablespoons vegan margarine

2 tablespoons nutritional yeast

½ cup soy milk

1 teaspoon Dijon mustard

1 to 2 tablespoons olive oil, for frying the sausages

Make the blackstrap vegan sausages: Preheat the oven to 400°F. Cut 6 to 10 pieces of parchment paper and 12 to 20 pieces of string to wrap the sausages. The size will depend on how large and thick you want your sausages to be.

In a small bowl, whisk together the tomato paste, broth, olive oil, soy sauce, vegan liquid smoke, garlic, and molasses.

In a large bowl, mix together the nutritional yeast, bread crumbs, paprika, vital wheat gluten, onion powder, and sage. Add

(continued)

the tomato paste mixture to the bread crumb mixture, kneading and folding by hand until completely combined into a dough.

Place 3 to 4 tablespoons of dough on a sheet of parchment paper and roll it like a cigar, tying the ends with string. Repeat until you have used all of the dough. Place the wrapped sausages on a cookie sheet and bake for 15 minutes.

Meanwhile, make the gravy: In a saucepan, heat the olive oil over medium heat. Toss in the onions and stir until coated with hot oil. Cook until the onions are tender and translucent. Stir in the flour and pepper, then add the broth, vegan Worcestershire sauce, and soy sauce. Bring the mixture to a simmer, then reduce the heat to low and cover to keep warm until ready to serve.

Make the mash: Mash the baked potatoes with their skins in a large bowl, then mix in the margarine, nutritional yeast, soy milk, and Dijon mustard with a large spoon.

When the sausages are finished baking, carefully unwrap them. In a cast-iron skillet or frying pan, heat 1 to 2 tablespoons olive oil over medium heat. Add the sausages and brown them until they become firm and have a lightly crispy skin on the outside. For best results, roll the sausages in the hot oil with a spatula.

Serve the sausages warm, plated with the mash on the bottom and an overflowing ladle of warm gravy over the top.

(Don't forget a pint of your favorite ale to wash it all down!)

You can use the rest of your jar of blackstrap molasses to make:

Simple Korean Kimchi BBQ Burgers on
  page 187
Jerk "Chicken" Pasta Salad on page 98
Molasses Crinkle Cookies on page 280

Rosemary Chicklins and Dumplins Stew

Chicken and dumplings is a famous Southern dish. Maybe it's because it's so fun to say "dumplins" like a Sugarbaker in shoulder pads on Designing Women. But before the Great Depression, this dish was actually made famous by French-Canadian trappers, who were thought to have created this rustic version of coq au vin in the heart of the Great White North. During the Great Depression, it became all the rage in the United States because it was the perfect way to use leftovers from other meals. These days, it's just beloved for being gosh darn delicious.

MAKES 4 TO 6 SERVINGS   **$1.99 PER SERVING**

Chicklins Stew

2 tablespoons olive oil

1 cup vegan chicken, defrosted and diced (we recommend Beyond Meat Chicken-Free Strips or Gardein Chick'n Scallopini)

½ cup whole wheat flour

5 cups vegan chicken broth or vegetable broth

1 cup nutritional yeast

2 tablespoons soy sauce or Bragg's Liquid Aminos

1 teaspoon dried thyme

1½ teaspoons rubbed sage

2 teaspoons dried rosemary, crushed

1 teaspoon onion powder

1 clove garlic, minced

¼ teaspoon crushed black peppercorn, plus more to sprinkle over the top

2 tablespoons chopped fresh parsley

¼ teaspoon celery seed

2 bay leaves

2 carrots, chopped

3 stalks celery, chopped

½ cup frozen peas

Dumplins

2 cups all-purpose flour

2 teaspoons baking powder

½ teaspoon sea salt

2 tablespoons vegan margarine

¾ cup soy milk

1 teaspoon dried rosemary, crushed

Make the chicklins stew: In your favorite Dutch oven or stew pot, heat the olive oil over medium heat. Toss in the vegan chicken and cook until it is browned and has crispy edges. Transfer it to a plate lined with a paper towel to soak up any extra oil, leaving the oil in the pan.

Using a wooden spoon, stir the flour into the hot oil left in the pan. Add the vegan chicken broth and whisk in the nutritional

(continued)

yeast. Using a large wooden spoon, stir in the soy sauce, thyme, sage, rosemary, onion powder, garlic, peppercorns, parsley, celery seed, bay leaves, carrots, celery, and peas. Reduce the heat to low, cover, and let simmer for 15 minutes.

Meanwhile, make the dumplins: In a large bowl, combine all the dumplins ingredients and use an electric handheld mixer to mix the ingredients until they form a firm batter. If you like a large dumpling, roll a portion of the dough into a ball about the size of your palm—but if you want to get more servings out of one recipe, use a soup spoon to form smaller dumplings instead.

Raise the heat under the pot of stew to bring it to a boil. Drop the raw dumplings into the hot stew one at a time and stir them in with a wooden spoon. Make sure the dumplings get completely covered so they cook evenly. Let the dumplings simmer in the stew for 10 to 15 minutes.

Single out the largest dumpling for sacrifice, remove it from the stew, and break it open. If it's firm on the inside, you're ready to eat! Mix in the cooked vegan chicken before serving with a few pinches of pepper over the top.

> *You can use your leftover parsley to make:*
>
> Pan-Fried Artichoke Hearts and Sauce
>   on page 227
> French Potato Salad on page 88
> Irish Stout Stew on page 157
> Fire-Roasted Baba Ghanoush on page 293

Cajun Nachos

One day, people will look back and wonder why we weren't all eating Cajun nachos every Wednesday night while we watched Sons of Anarchy *with our loved ones. We can't change the past; all we can do is make things right now.*

MAKES 6 TO 8 SERVINGS   **$2.71 PER SERVING**

Spicy Aioli

⅔ cup vegan mayonnaise (we recommend Vegenaise or Just Mayo)

1 tablespoon hot sauce

1 teaspoon garlic powder

2 teaspoons lemon juice

½ teaspoon ground cumin

¼ teaspoon paprika

Nachos

Cornmeal, for dusting

1 (13-ounce) bag tortilla chips

1 to 1½ cups shredded vegan cheddar cheese (we recommend Daiya)

1 (15-ounce) can red beans, drained and rinsed, or 1½ cups cooked dry red beans

1 tablespoon olive oil

2 cups vegan chicken, diced (we recommend Beyond Meat Chicken-Free Strips or Gardein Chick'n Scallopini)

1 tablespoon Tony Chachere's Original Creole Seasoning

1 red onion, diced

1 green bell pepper, diced

2 stalks celery, diced

4 or 5 cherry tomatoes, quartered

1 jalapeño, sliced

1 tablespoon capers

6 green olives, pitted and sliced

6 black olives, pitted and sliced

Make the spicy aioli: In a bowl, whisk together all the aioli ingredients until blended. Set aside until ready to serve.

Make the nachos: Preheat the oven to 400°F.

Dust a pizza stone or a baking pan with a handful of cornmeal. Spread the tortilla chips out in an even layer and cover them with half the vegan cheese, a layer of beans, and a layer of the remaining vegan cheese. Bake the chips for 10 minutes or until the vegan cheese has melted.

While the chips are baking, in a large skillet, heat the olive oil over medium heat. Add the vegan chicken, Creole seasoning, and onion and cook until the onion is tender and the vegan chicken is a golden brown. Remove from the heat and set aside.

(continued)

Serve the chips warm, topped with a layer of the vegan chicken and onions, then the bell pepper, celery, tomatoes, jalapeños, capers, and olives, and with the aioli drizzled over the top.

You can use the rest of your jar of capers to make:

Angel Hair Pasta with Garlic and Rosemary Mushrooms on page 202

Pan-Seared Tofu with Arugula, Capers, and Tomatoes on page 210

Baked Strapatsada—Greek Baked "Egg" Cups on page 53

Green Gunpowder Gumbo Skillet

There are probably as many versions of "true" Southern gumbo as there are pots to simmer them in. Which is probably why there are a lot of contradicting rules for what makes a "real" gumbo. Some say it's about the perfect roux; others say it's authentic only if you use seafood; some will tell you never to mix seafood and meat; and some say it's not a gumbo unless it has at least three kinds of animals in it. As vegans, we've decided that our love of animals was going to inspire new traditions; this recipe is one of them.

MAKES 4 TO 6 SERVINGS   **$1.96 PER SERVING**

- ¼ cup olive oil
- 1 (16-ounce) package extra-firm tofu, cut into bite-size squares
- 2 cloves garlic, minced
- 1 red onion, diced
- ¼ cup all-purpose flour
- 4 cups vegan beef broth or vegetable broth (we recommend Better Than Bouillon)
- 1 (12-ounce) can beer (we recommend using an IPA)
- 2 to 3 teaspoons Tony Chachere's Original Creole Seasoning (depending on how much heat you like)
- ¼ to 1 teaspoon hot sauce (depending on how much heat you like)
- 1 teaspoon soy sauce or Bragg's Liquid Aminos
- 1 teaspoon onion powder

- 1 teaspoon garlic powder
- ¼ teaspoon celery seed
- ½ teaspoon dried thyme
- Pinch of red pepper flakes
- 3 Roma or Campari tomatoes, quartered
- ⅓ cup frozen okra
- ½ cup celery, chopped
- ½ green bell pepper, diced
- 1 (14-ounce) can artichoke hearts, drained and quartered
- ⅔ cup chopped kale leaves
- 1 (15-ounce) can black-eyed peas, drained and rinsed, or 1½ cups cooked dry black-eyed peas
- 2 cups brown rice, cooked

In a Dutch oven or a large stew pot with a lid, heat the oil over medium heat. Toss in the tofu, garlic, and onion. Cook for 1 minute, then flip with a spatula. Let the tofu cook for another minute, then flip again. Continue to cook and flip until the tofu is golden brown on all sides. Using a slotted spoon or spatula transfer the tofu and onions to a plate lined with a paper towel to drain off any extra oil, leaving as much oil in the pot as possible.

Whisk the flour into the hot oil remaining in the pot to create a very light roux.

(continued)

Continue to whisk your roux for about 10 to 15 minutes so that it can very lightly brown. Gradually add the broth and beer a little at time, whisking to break up clumps. Whisk in the Creole seasoning and hot sauce, starting with a small amount, then whisk in the soy sauce, onion powder, garlic powder, celery seed, thyme, and red pepper flakes. Give it a taste and add more Creole seasoning and hot sauce until you've reached your desired level of heat.

Using a large wooden spoon, stir in the tomatoes, okra, celery, bell pepper, artichoke hearts, kale, and black-eyed peas. Cover the pot and reduce the heat to maintain a simmer. Let the gumbo simmer for 10 minutes. Once the vegetables are tender mix in your tofu and you're ready to eat!

Serve hot, with a scoop of brown rice on top.

You can use the rest of your bottle of Bragg's Liquid Aminos to make:

Blackstrap Vegan Bangers and Mash with Onion Gravy on page 125

Wild Mushroom Risotto on page 135

Sloppy Joel Pie on page 171

Chili-Stuffed Sweet Potatoes on page 167

Apple-Sage Tempeh Sausage over Savory Polenta

Our friend Stephanie once made a bold statement: "I will never like tempeh. It's the worst."
Challenge accepted!

This comment sparked a month of tempeh-focused experiments that resulted in some amazing new ways to enjoy this vegan staple. The polenta part of this recipe is a little labor intensive, but the tempeh sausage is so easy and delicious, you'll forgive it anything. Or you can just use premade polenta to make this a quick and easy weekday dinner. It's more expensive but if your time equals money, you might not mind.

MAKES 4 SERVINGS $2.40 PER SERVING

- 1 (8-ounce) package tempeh, broken in bite-size pieces
- 1 cup vegetable broth (we recommend Better Than Bouillon)
- 1 tablespoon soy sauce or Bragg's Liquid Aminos
- 1 tablespoon rubbed sage
- 1 teaspoon fennel seed
- Pinch of celery seed
- ¼ teaspoon crushed black peppercorns
- 1½ teaspoons onion powder
- 1 teaspoon garlic powder

- 1 teaspoon applesauce
- ½ teaspoon smoked paprika
- Dash of vegan liquid smoke
- 4 tablespoons olive oil
- ¼ teaspoon salt
- 1 cup cornmeal
- 3 tablespoons nutritional yeast
- 1 red onion, chopped
- 1 large green apple, cored and diced
- 1 cup chopped kale leaves

In a large bowl, toss together the tempeh, broth, soy sauce, sage, fennel seed, celery seed, peppercorns, 1 teaspoon of the onion powder, the garlic powder, applesauce, paprika, and vegan liquid smoke. Cover and let marinate while you prepare the polenta.

In a Dutch oven or other large pot, bring 4 cups water to a boil with 2 tablespoons of the olive oil and the salt. Whisking continuously, gradually pour the cornmeal into the boiling water, breaking up any clumps that form. Whisk in the nutritional yeast and remaining ½ teaspoon onion powder. Then, stir the polenta with a wooden spoon every 8 to 10 minutes while it thickens. Be sure to scrape the sides and bottom of the pot while you stir to prevent any sticking. This should take about 40 to 45 minutes

(continued)

total. I apologize for how long it takes; there are some things even I can't hack. Polenta is a needy dish.

Once the polenta is soft but firm, cover and remove from the heat.

Heat the remaining 2 tablespoons olive oil in your deepest skillet over medium heat. Once the oil is hot, toss in the tempeh mixture, the red onion, and the apples. Mix with a spatula until the tempeh has slightly crispy edges. Then toss in the kale and let cook for about 5 minutes, flipping occasionally with a spatula. Once the kale has wilted, you're done!

Serve the tempeh sausage over the polenta. Make sure to include some of the thin "sauce" on the bottom of the skillet—it'll really make a difference.

TEMPEH

One of our highlights of 2013 was visiting the Tofurky headquarters outside of Portland, Oregon. We played bocce ball with Tofurky founder Seth Tibbott and the Herbivore Clothing Company's Michelle Schwegmann on the roof of their new environmentally friendly building, and got to sample some of their new products. One of the best parts was seeing where they make and store their tempeh—using the same techniques that have been used in Indonesia for generations. We have a few great tempeh recipes in this book. Try the Steamed Sesame Seitan Dim Sum on page 141, Tater Tot Pie on page 150, Turkish Pizza—Lahmacun on page 163, or Lasagna Sandwiches featuring Italian Tempeh Sausage on page 107.

Wild Mushroom Risotto

When you're married to someone who hates mushrooms, it's hard not to long for dishes that feature them so beautifully like this one does. Absence does make the heart grow fonder.

MAKES 4 TO 6 SERVINGS   **$1.53 PER SERVING**

¼ cup olive oil

1 cup sliced wild mushrooms or white mushroom mix

1 red onion, diced

1 clove garlic, minced

1½ cups Arborio rice, uncooked

1 cup white wine

4½ cups vegetable broth (we recommend Better Than Bouillon)

¼ cup cooked cannellini beans, crushed

2 tablespoons soy milk

1 teaspoon crushed black peppercorns

1 tablespoon Italian seasoning

1 tablespoon soy sauce or Bragg's Liquid Aminos

1 tablespoon nutritional yeast

⅔ cup baby spinach leaves

In a Dutch oven or your deepest saucepan, heat the olive oil over medium heat. Add the mushrooms, onion, and garlic and cook until the mushrooms and onion are tender. Remove half of the mushroom mix and set aside.

Mix the rice into the mushroom mix remaining in the pan. Stir in the wine until it has been completely absorbed by the rice. Stir in the broth 1 cup at a time, wait until each addition is absorbed before adding the next. Stir the rice and mushroom mixture continuously to make sure it cooks evenly.

Mix in the crushed beans, soy milk, peppercorns, Italian seasoning, soy sauce, nutritional yeast, and the reserved mushroom mixture. Then stir in the spinach leaves. Cook, stirring continuously, for another 5 minutes. Once the spinach is wilted, you're ready to eat.

(continued)

Make Arancini (Fried Risotto Balls) Using Your Leftover Risotto

In 2012, we visited Rome in the middle of a freak snowstorm. With all the major sites like the Coliseum, the Forum, and the Pantheon closed, we found ourselves with a lot of time to wander beautiful, icy cobblestone streets and enjoy all the vegan fare in one of the most famous food meccas on the planet. In a trip full of vegan gnocchi, Roman artichokes, and marinara pizza, the risotto balls at the vegetarian restaurant Il Margutta still stand out. We came home and started making these immediately.

You'll need at least 1½ cups of leftover risotto that's been in the fridge overnight to get started. You'll also need ¾ cup bread crumbs, 1 tablespoon all-purpose flour, 3 tablespoons nutritional yeast, and enough olive oil to fill a saucepan halfway.

In a saucepan, heat the olive oil over high heat.

In a shallow bowl, whisk together the bread crumbs, flour, and 2 tablespoons of the nutritional yeast until completely blended.

Once the oil is hot, remove the risotto from the fridge and use a large spoon to mix in the remaining 1 tablespoon nutritional yeast. Form the risotto into small balls using your hands. Very gently roll the risotto balls in the bread crumb mixture until completely coated. Using a slotted spoon, carefully lower the breaded risotto balls into the hot oil. There might be some oil spatter, so you might want to wear oven mitts or gloves to protect your hands. Fry the risotto balls until golden brown and warmed through.

Once the risotto balls are the desired golden brown, use a slotted spoon to remove them from the hot oil and transfer them to a paper towel–lined plate to soak up any extra oil.

Enjoy warm; but wait 3 to 5 minutes until cool enough to handle.

Buon appetito!

Bubbie's Polish Potato Pierogies

Every country has a favorite dumpling. It would appear that enjoying little pockets full of your favorite vegetables is a fundamental part of the human condition. Pierogies are the Polish form of the popular and affordable little treats you can find all over Eastern Europe. For centuries they were considered peasant food, but these days you can find them in pubs, at lunch counters, and on the menus at restaurants around the world. Traditional Polish potato pierogies often include a little cheese, so feel free to add a few pinches of your favorite vegan cheese to the filling if you have some leftover from another recipe.

MAKES OVER A DOZEN PIEROGIES   **$0.64 PER SERVING**

Filling

3 to 4 Yukon Gold potatoes, baked

1 tablespoon nutritional yeast

1 tablespoon vegan margarine

1 clove garlic, minced

2 green onions, diced

¼ teaspoon sea salt

½ teaspoon crushed black peppercorns

Dough

2 cups all-purpose flour, plus more for dusting

1 teaspoon sea salt

2 tablespoons olive oil

½ cup plus 2 tablespoons warm water

To Assemble

4 tablespoons olive oil

1 red onion, diced

Make the filling: Preheat the oven to 400°F. Bake the potatoes until tender, then transfer to a rack to cool until they can be safely handled. Halve the potatoes and scrape the flesh into a large bowl, then mash the potatoes and mix in nutritional yeast, vegan margarine, garlic, green onions, salt, and pepper.

Make the dough: In another large bowl, combine the flour, salt, olive oil, and warm water using an electric handheld mixer fitted with a bread hook attachment, or knead the mixture with your hands. For the best

results, add the water ¼ cup at a time and stop once the dough is firm.

Transfer the dough to a floured surface and knead for no more than 3 minutes. Then, roll out the dough using a floured rolling pin. Use a biscuit cutter or the top of a pint glass to cut at least a dozen circles from the dough. Take any dough scraps and knead them together, then roll out the dough and cut as many extra circles as you can.

Using a large spoon, drop a small amount of the potato filling into the center of each

(continued)

circle. Gently fold the circle over to enclose the filling and seal the edges of the dough using wet fingertips, a fork, or a dumpling press.

Assemble the pierogies: In your largest cast-iron skillet or frying pan, heat 2 tablespoons of the olive oil over medium heat. Once the oil is hot, toss the onions in and cook until tender, then remove from the heat and set aside.

Fry the pierogies in the hot oil a few at a time, using a spatula to flip them so they brown evenly. Move the cooked pierogies to a paper towel–lined plate to soak up any extra oil. Add a little bit more oil to the pan if you need to keep the pierogies from sticking.

Serve the pierogies warm, with some onions sprinkled over the top.

You can use your leftover nutritional yeast to make:

Vegan Bacon and "Egg" Enchiladas on page 55

Smoky Butternut Squash Scramble on page 57

Kale Caesar Salad on page 78

Chef's Pasta Salad on page 97

Vegan Bacon, White Bean, and Spinach Risotto on page 155

Yankee Doodle Macaroni on page 191

Swiss Chard Rolls with Domestic Goddess Sauce

These beautiful rolls are as easy to make as they are good for you. We first made them during a Brooklyn heat wave that would make a lesser city melt. We survived with some help from chilled dinners like this one and lots and lots of lemonade.

MAKES 12 ROLLS **$1.09 PER SERVING**

Domestic Goddess Sauce

1 cup tahini

Juice of 1 lemon

2 cloves garlic, minced

1 tablespoon sesame seeds

2 tablespoons chopped fresh parsley

Rolls

1 cup cooked bulgur

1½ cups cooked or canned lentils

4 cherry tomatoes, diced

¼ cup chopped fresh parsley

2 tablespoons soy sauce or Bragg's Liquid Aminos

1 teaspoon ground black pepper

2 tablespoons chopped fresh mint

Zest of 1 lemon

1 small red onion, diced

12 large Swiss chard leaves

Make the domestic goddess sauce: In a food processor, combine the tahini, lemon juice, garlic, and sesame seeds and process until creamy. Then add the parsley and process again for just a few seconds—the parsley will liquefy if blended for too long. Pour the dressing into an airtight container and refrigerate while you prepare the rolls.

Make the rolls: In a large bowl, gently combine the bulgur, lentils, tomatoes, parsley, soy sauce, pepper, mint, lemon zest, and onion, being careful not to crush the tomatoes. Cover and refrigerate for 10 minutes.

Meanwhile, bring a pot of water to a boil. One at a time, dip the Swiss chard leaves into the boiling water while carefully holding the stem. Count to 15, then remove the leaves. Without burning your fingers, lay the leaves flat on a clean dishtowel to soak up any extra water. Be careful not to tear the leaves while flattening them out on the towel.

Once all the leaves are prepared, it's time to roll. One at a time, place the leaves flat on a cutting board with the flat, not spiny, side down. Place 2 to 3 tablespoons of filling

(continued)

in the center of the largest end of each leaf. Fold the side of the leaf over the filling, then roll the largest end forward, rolling up the filling and tucking in any odd corners or edges to make a small, fat cigar about the size of your hand.

Serve with the domestic goddess dressing on the side for dipping.

SWISS CHARD

I know kale gets all the attention, but Swiss chard is a great source of vitamins A and C, and just as much a "superfood" as its curly-leaved cousin. You'll probably end up with a few Swiss chard leaves that have tears, or are too small to make a roll with. You can chop those up and use them in the Sriracha and Sweet Onion Stew on page 104 or the Caldo Verde—Portuguese Soup on page 93.

Steamed Sesame Seitan Dim Sum

In New York's Chinatown, there are a few places where you can find extraordinary vegan dim sum dumplings. You can also find vegan dim sum houses in D.C., San Francisco, and Portland. But if you're not lucky enough to live in one of these vegan food meccas, don't fret—you can make your own using this recipe.

MAKES 10 TO 12 DUMPLINGS   **$0.69 PER SERVING**

Filling

1 tablespoon sesame oil

2 tablespoons soy sauce or Bragg's Liquid Aminos

1 tablespoon rice vinegar

½ teaspoon ginger paste

1 clove garlic, minced

1 teaspoon sesame seeds

2 tablespoons chopped fresh cilantro

1 cup crumbled tempeh or seitan (we recommend Upton's Naturals)

½ head green cabbage, shredded

Dough

1 envelope active dry yeast

⅓ cup warm water

1 cup all-purpose flour

2 tablespoons sugar

2 teaspoons sesame oil

1 teaspoon baking powder

Before starting, cut out 10 to 12 small circles of waxed paper, about the diameter of a coffee mug, to place the dumplings on.

Make the filling: In a large bowl, whisk together the sesame oil, soy sauce, vinegar, ginger paste, garlic, and sesame seeds. Use a spoon to mix in the cilantro, tempeh, and cabbage. Cover with plastic wrap and refrigerate while you prepare the dough.

Make the dough: Dissolve the yeast in the warm water. In a large bowl, use an electric handheld mixer with bread hooks to blend together the remaining dough ingredients, then knead by hand until smooth. Pour in the yeast and water mixture, then knead for 2 minutes until the dough is springy.

Divide the dough into 12 equal portions and form them into flat disks a little larger than the size of your palm.

Add a few pinches of filling to the center of each dumpling. Fill all the dumplings before you begin folding them to make sure you use up all the filling.

(continued)

Fold the sides of each dumpling up to cover the filling like a taco. Gently press the edges together to seal them. Then, fold the two ends of the taco up to create a small round purse. Gently press together all the seams at the top, then twist to seal. You can either break off the little tag of dough you're holding on to, or leave it on.

Place the finished dumplings on the waxed paper circles and cover them with a tea towel. Let rise for 1 hour.

Set up a steamer while the dumplings rise. For the best results, I recommend using a bamboo steamer, but I know many of you have steamer attachments on stew pots, rice cookers, and slow cookers. Whatever you're using, set up the steamer using the directions that came with it.

Steam the dumplings for 5 minutes.

Serve hot or cold; I prefer hot.

The American Frugal Housewife—
Lydia Maria Child

"There is no subject so much connected with individual happiness and national prosperity as the education of daughters."—The American Frugal Housewife, *page 91*

During the time of the American Revolution, only an estimated 50 percent of the female population of New England could read and write. But, only a little over a generation later, that number had almost doubled. By 1840, New England boasted a nearly 100 percent literacy rate for the women who lived there. With this boom in female readers came a need for books that were aimed at women, which led to an unprecedented number of women becoming famous literary figures. One of these was Lydia Maria Child.

Lydia first gained notoriety at the young age of twenty-two, when she wrote a controversial romance novel about a love affair between a sadly stereotypical Native American warrior and a female American colonist. I've only read a few pages, but I'd call it a cross between a Harlequin romance (with less bodice ripping) and *The Last of the Mohicans*. It was also more popular than you'd probably guess an interracial love story would've been in the early 1800s.

In 1829, Lydia fell in love with an abolitionist activist named David Child. He was by most accounts charming and handsome, an articulate debater, a gifted writer—and always broke. I think he had "scoundrel" written all over him—but we shouldn't judge. John Quincy Adams seemed to like him a lot, and Lydia loved him madly despite it all. During a time in history when women weren't even allowed to own property or vote, Lydia became the primary breadwinner in the marriage. The money she had earned with her first novel went toward her husband's debts, so she needed to write more books—and soon.

This time, she wrote about what she knew. Lydia's oftentimes bitterly honest cookbook *The American Frugal Housewife* lacked the rose-colored romanticism of the book that had made her famous, but it was a book that would go on to be even more popular. She was a young wife trying to make a home on a smaller budget than she would've liked, and this required her to reevaluate how meal planning, shopping, and budgeting were typically done in her time. In her book, she stressed the importance of reducing waste and enjoying your meals, while not-so-subtly including messages on the importance of educating your daughters. Lydia pointed out that young women needed to be able to read, write, and do arithmetic so they could grow up to balance their own household budgets and make smart choices about the family finances. She was one of the first writers (male or female) to acknowledge that women played a vital role in managing the finances of the home, and she openly discouraged young women from placing too much importance on getting a man to marry them—or "the game," as she called it.

America was going through a recession when *The American Frugal Housewife* was published, and it resonated with the women who related to Lydia's honest and thrifty approach to housework, as well as her insights into the institution of marriage. When I read it nearly two hundred years later, it helped inspire this book and the new approach we took toward our own kitchen and household budget.

Yankee Pot Roast Dinner

When we started *The Betty Crocker Project* in 2009, we wanted to show people how to use the amazing new vegan products coming out on the market. Making our own seitan, something we'd been doing for years, for that project made no sense whatsoever, so instead we embraced companies like Gardein, Tofurky, Match Meats, Field Roast, and May-Wah like the good friends they are. But this new book has brought us back to our roots. We can still use those wunderkind products in moderation, but if we wanted to get the most for our money, we needed to (and wanted to) start making our own mock meat again.

Not unlike pot roast dinners made in meat-eating homes, if you cut this vegan roast right, you can enjoy several meals out of this one recipe. It does take a while to make, so we suggest making it on Sunday night and then slicing the leftovers up into sandwiches for the next few days.

MAKES 6 TO 8 SERVINGS　　　　　　　　　　　　　　**$1.14 PER SERVING**

. . . .

Vegetable Dinner

3 cups vegan beef broth or vegetable broth

½ pound new potatoes, quartered

⅔ cup baby carrots

4 cloves garlic, minced

2 teaspoons crushed dried rosemary

¼ cup chopped fresh parsley

1 tablespoon red wine

Vegan Pot Roast

2 cups vital wheat gluten

⅓ cup nutritional yeast

1 teaspoon onion powder

1 teaspoon garlic powder

½ teaspoon smoked paprika

1 teaspoon celery seed

1 teaspoon crushed rosemary

¼ teaspoon ground cumin

¼ teaspoon dried thyme

¼ teaspoon crushed black peppercorn

¼ teaspoon rubbed sage

1 tablespoon soy sauce or Bragg's Liquid Aminos

1 tablespoon vegan Worcestershire sauce

2 cups vegan beef broth or vegetable broth (we recommend Better Than Bouillon)

. . . .

Make the vegetables: In a Dutch oven or a large soup pot with a lid, combine all the vegetable dinner ingredients and bring to a boil over medium heat.

Make the vegan pot roast: In a large bowl, whisk together the vital wheat gluten, nutritional yeast, onion powder, garlic powder, paprika, celery seed, rosemary, cumin, thyme, pepper, and sage.

In a separate bowl, whisk together the soy sauce, vegan Worcestershire sauce, and broth. Pour the wet ingredients into the bowl with the dry ingredients and knead with your hands into a firm dough. Form the dough into a round, flat loaf, folding it over a few times to make sure you get a nice springy texture. You should be able to gently poke your dough and have the depression slowly disappear.

Transfer the roast to the pot with the vegetable mixture, carefully setting it on top of the vegetables so it is slightly covered with the boiling broth. Cover and let simmer for 15 to 20 minutes.

Preheat the oven to 400°F.

After the roast has boiled for about 15 minutes, pour a ladleful of the broth into a casserole dish, then very carefully move the roast to the casserole dish using oven mitts and a spatula. Transfer the casserole dish to the oven. Monitor the roast, basting it a few times with the broth while it's baking. Remove the roast from the oven once it develops a crispy golden-brown crust, 15 to 20 minutes.

Serve the roast with the vegetables and a few ladles of broth over the top.

VITAL WHEAT GLUTEN FLOUR

Vegetarian Buddhist monks have been making meat substitutes out of wheat gluten flour since the third century. Since then, these mock meats have been embraced by people around the world as a delicious way to replace animals in a cruelty-free diet. Vital wheat gluten can usually be found in any health food store. Depending on where you live, a good-size bag can be pretty cheap ($4) or not so much ($20). Either way, you can easily make more than a few meals from one bag. Other recipes in this book that use vital wheat gluten flour are the Vegan Gyros on page 219, Budapest Burgers on page 230, Beet "Boudin" Balls with Garlic Aioli on page 206, and Blackstrap Vegan Bangers and Mash with Onion Gravy on page 125. Check out the section on Vital Wheat Gluten on page 8 for information on how to store this ingredient.

Mexican Stuffed Zucchini

People told us we would have a hard time finding vegan food in Mexico when we visited in 2013. However, maybe it was because we stayed in the tourist mecca of Tulum, or maybe it was just Dan's Spanish-speaking abilities, but we never really had a problem. We even had soy milk for our coffee every morning. This is one of the dishes we enjoyed there. It's a stunning dinner that doesn't take long to prepare, making it all the more appealing.

MAKES 4 SERVINGS   **$2.25 PER SERVING**

Olive oil cooking spray

2 large zucchinis, halved lengthwise

2 teaspoons olive oil

1 (15-ounce) can black beans, drained and rinsed, or 1½ cups cooked dry black beans

½ cup frozen corn

2 Roma or Campari tomatoes, diced

2 cloves garlic, minced

1 to 2 teaspoons chili powder (depending on how much heat you like)

1 teaspoon onion powder

2 teaspoons ground cumin

1 teaspoon dried oregano

1½ teaspoons smoked paprika

¼ teaspoon cayenne pepper (optional)

Sea salt and crushed black peppercorns

½ to ¾ cup shredded vegan cheddar cheese or vegan pepper Jack cheese (depending on the size of your zucchini and how cheesy you like your dinner; we recommend Daiya)

½ cup chopped fresh cilantro

1 lime, cut into wedges

Preheat the oven to 375°F. Spray a heavy coating of cooking spray over a lasagna dish.

Bring 3 cups water to a boil in a large Dutch oven or stew pot.

Scoop out the insides of the zucchini to make a bowl or boat. Toss the zucchini "boats" in the boiling water and cook for no more than 2 minutes. Drain and place in the lasagna dish.

In a large bowl, mix the olive oil, beans, corn, tomatoes, garlic, 1 teaspoon chili powder, onion powder, cumin, oregano, paprika, and cayenne. Give your mixture a taste test and add any additional chili powder and needed salt and pepper. Using a large spoon, fill the zucchini boats with the bean mixture. Vegetables come in all different sizes, so you might have to overstuff the zucchini a bit. Sprinkle a little of the vegan cheese over the top.

Bake, uncovered, for 10 to 15 minutes or until the vegan cheese has melted.

Serve hot, garnished with cilantro and a wedge of lime to squeeze over the top.

CILANTRO

When people need to cut corners with their grocery budgets, they often start with the extras. Fresh herbs are replaced with dried ones or "flavor packets." Sadly, cilantro can be seen as a needless expense—and you can still make a delicious dinner without it. But in some meals cilantro plays a role we overlook: It's the only green thing on your plate. I find this a lot with Mexican-themed recipes in particular. Here are some other recipes you can use to keep any leftover cilantro from going to waste: Tofu Spring Rolls with Agave Chili Sauce (page 121), Steamed Sesame Seitan Dim Sum (page 141), Samosa Pizza (page 161), Pan-Seared Corn and Quinoa Salad (page 76), or Tom Kha Gai—Spicy Coconut Soup (page 89). Also, check out page 14 for tips on how to store your fresh cilantro so it lasts longer.

Chimichurri Rice Casserole

* Fast * Date Night * Family Style *

Chimichurri is an Argentinean sauce for beef or steak that's a lot like pesto, with pureed leafy greens, lemon, and garlic. We first started putting it on veggie burgers or Gardein Beefless Tips. Then, we started to pour it over our vegetables and rice as well, and then one day we had this casserole.

MAKES 4 TO 6 SERVINGS   **$2.21 PER SERVING**

Vegan Beef

2 teaspoons olive oil

2 cups vegan beef seitan, defrosted (we recommend Gardein Beefless Tips)

½ cup green beans

½ teaspoon soy sauce or Bragg's Liquid Aminos

1 teaspoon smoked paprika

1 red bell pepper, diced

2 cups brown rice, cooked

Chimichurri Sauce

Zest and juice of 1 lemon

1 cup fresh parsley leaves

3 cloves garlic

½ cup plus 2 teaspoons olive oil

⅓ cup white wine

½ teaspoon garlic powder

Make the vegan beef: Preheat the oven to 375°F.

In a cast-iron skillet, heat the olive oil over medium heat. Once the oil is hot, toss in the vegan beef and green beans, then mix until all the ingredients are coated. Stir in the soy sauce and paprika while your vegan beef cooks.

Meanwhile, make the chimichurri sauce: In a food processor, combine the sauce ingredients and process until the sauce is blended and the garlic is pureed.

Once the green beans are tender, transfer the vegan beef and green beans to a large bowl, add the sauce, bell pepper, and rice. Mix with a spoon until all your ingredients are coated in sauce.

Pour the casserole mixture into a large lasagna dish and use a spoon to smooth it into an even layer.

Put the casserole in the oven and bake for 10 minutes.

Serve hot.

BRAGG'S LIQUID AMINOS

Since we've gone vegan, we've come to love a product called Bragg's Liquid Aminos. This affordable, non-GMO, soy-based liquid protein sauce adds a "beefy" flavor with significantly less sodium than regular soy sauce. It's also a good source of amino acids, which are important to supplement in a vegan diet. If you're wondering what you can do with the rest of your bottle of Bragg's Liquid Aminos, we suggest the Blackstrap Vegan Bangers and Mash with Onion Gravy on page 125, Vegan Bacon and "Egg" Enchiladas on page 55, Green Gunpowder Gumbo Skillet on page 131, Beet "Boudin" Balls with Garlic Aioli on page 206, or Sloppy Joel Pie on page 171.

Tater Tot Pie

Since medieval times, cooks all over Europe have used kitchen scraps in savory pies as a way to reduce waste in their kitchens. This recipe is an über-American take on the classic shepherd's pie that I found gracing the pages of many a women's magazine from the 1950s. We've tweaked our recipe to include vegetables, making it more of a potpie filling. The results are delicious.

MAKES 1 PIE   **$2.04 PER SERVING**

- 1 vegan piecrust, store-bought or homemade (see page 262)
- 1 cup vegan beef broth or vegetable broth (we recommend Better Than Bouillon), plus more as needed
- 1 tablespoon whole wheat flour
- 2 tablespoons nutritional yeast
- 2 teaspoons soy sauce or Bragg's Liquid Aminos
- 1 teaspoon onion powder
- 1 teaspoon garlic powder
- ¼ teaspoon celery seed

- ½ teaspoon dried thyme
- Salt and ground black pepper
- 2 teaspoons olive oil
- 1 cup seitan crumbles or crumbled tempeh (we recommend Upton's Naturals Ground Seitan)
- 1 clove garlic, minced
- 1 red onion, diced
- ½ cup frozen peas
- 1½ cups frozen tater tots, defrosted
- ⅓ cup vegan cheddar or pepper Jack cheese (we recommend Daiya)

Preheat the oven to 400°F.

Prick a few holes in the bottom of the piecrust and bake your vegan piecrust following the directions on the package or according to the recipe on page 262, until it turns a very light golden brown. Remove the crust from the oven and set aside; leave the oven on.

While the piecrust is baking, prepare the gravy. In a saucepan, bring the broth to a boil. Whisk in the flour, nutritional yeast, soy sauce, onion powder, garlic powder, celery seed, and thyme. Give the gravy a taste test

and add salt or pepper to taste. Reduce the heat to maintain a simmer, cover, and let simmer, stirring occasionally to keep clumps from forming.

In a cast-iron skillet or your deepest skillet, heat the olive oil over medium heat. Add the seitan, garlic, and onion and cook until the seitan is evenly browned and the onion is tender.

Stir the seitan mixture and any oil left in the pan into the gravy. Using a large spoon, mix in the peas.

Fill the baked piecrust with the seitan mixture using a slotted spoon. Save any extra gravy, but remove from the heat to keep it from reducing too much. If it does, just mix in more vegetable broth, ¼ cup at a time, until you are happy with the consistency.

Arrange the tater tots over the top of the pie, covering the filling completely so there are very few openings. Put the pie back in the oven to bake for another 20 to 30 minutes. Once the tater tots start to become crispy, remove the pie from the oven and top with a thin layer of vegan cheese. Try to fill any open holes between the tater tots with the vegan cheese. Put the pie back in the oven to bake for another 5 to 10 minutes, or until the cheese has melted. Then set your oven to broil. Let your pie broil close to the flames for 10 seconds or until your cheezy tots are crispy.

Let the pie cool on a rack for 5 minutes before serving. While the pie cools, reheat the gravy and serve it on the side.

VEGAN CHEESE

For many, cheese is the deal-breaker when it comes to maintaining a vegan lifestyle. For years, people struggled between what their heart said and what their stomach wanted. Then food science finally caught up with our hearts. These days, there are any number of vegan cheeses on the market that melt on our pizzas or burgers just like the "real" stuff. Some are cashew based, some soy, and some tapioca; it's up to you to find which you prefer. Since streamlining our kitchen on a budget, we decided the key to keeping these wonderful vegan cheeses in our lives was moderation. So we began rationing the amount of cheese we used in order to get more meals from one package. That means you'll have leftover vegan cheese after making this recipe, but you can use it in several other recipes, including the Cajun Nachos on page 129, Quinoa Taco Casserole on page 152, Cincinnati Chili on page 177, Fajita Pizza on page 160, or Mac and Cheez Pie on page 173.

Quinoa Taco Casserole

Quinoa is a protein-packed grain-like seed that you can use to easily replace ground meat in almost any recipe. I know it sounds too good to be true, but I never lie about tacos.

MAKES 4 TO 6 SERVINGS   **$2.39 PER SERVING**

1 teaspoon olive oil

2 cups cooked quinoa

¾ cup taco sauce

½ teaspoon ground cumin

1 cup cooked or 1 (14-ounce) can black beans

1 cup frozen corn

1 jalapeño, seeded and sliced (more or less, depending how hot you like it)

2 cups broken tortilla chips

1½ cups chunky salsa

2 green onions, diced

½ to 1 cup vegan cheddar cheese (depending on how cheezy you like it; we recommend Daiya)

1 large tomato, diced

1 cup shredded romaine lettuce

Preheat the oven to 350°F.

In a cast-iron skillet or frying pan, heat the olive oil over medium heat. In a large bowl, mix together the quinoa, taco sauce, cumin, and black beans. Toss the quinoa mixture into the skillet and cook for 5 minutes, then transfer back to the bowl and use a large spoon to fold in the corn and jalapeño (using as much as you like to reach the desired heat level).

Layer the tortilla chips over the bottom of a casserole dish. Spread an even layer of the quinoa mixture over the chips, then top with the salsa, then the green onions, and then the vegan cheese. Lay the slices of tomato over the top.

Bake for 20 to 30 minutes, or until the vegan cheese has melted. Serve with the shredded lettuce over the top.

> *You can use any leftover quinoa to make:*
>
> Pan-Seared Corn and Quinoa Salad on page 76
> Cowboy Quinoa Chili on page 241
>
> *For tips on how to toast your quinoa, check out page 77.*

Ratatouille Rice Bake

You've probably seen an adorable animated movie called Ratatouille *about a French rat in Paris who dreamed of becoming a chef. He was enamored with the smell of simmering soups and loved roasting vegetables to perfection. He was a rodent after my own heart. And like Julia Child, this cartoon rat introduced a new generation of Americans to the delight that is French cuisine. This recipe is a take on one of the most famous (and already vegetarian) French dishes, with a few tweaks to make it a meal you can share with the whole family.*

MAKES 6 TO 8 SERVINGS   **$1.74 PER SERVING**

½ cup olive oil

⅓ cup red wine

2 tablespoons soy sauce or Bragg's Liquid Aminos

1 clove garlic, minced

1 red onion, diced

1 eggplant, thinly sliced crosswise

1 red bell pepper, thinly sliced

1 yellow bell pepper, thinly sliced

1 zucchini, thinly sliced crosswise

1 cup brown rice, cooked

½ cup chopped fresh parsley

1 tomato, thinly sliced

4 golden beets, cleaned, peeled and thinly sliced

Preheat the oven to 350°F.

In a small bowl, combine the olive oil, wine, and soy sauce, then heat the mixture in a deep skillet over medium heat. Toss in the garlic and onion and cook until the onion is tender, then transfer to a large bowl and set aside. Cook the eggplant in the hot skillet until tender. You may have to do this in batches, depending on how big the eggplant and the skillet are.

Toss the eggplant with the cooked onion, then add the bell peppers and zucchini.

In a large bowl, mix the rice with the parsley using a large spoon. Fill a casserole dish with an even layer of rice, then layer the tomato slices on top. Top with a layer of sliced beets. Using your hands, place the eggplant, peppers, and zucchini over the top in a fanned layer that alternates the vegetables to really show off their color. Be careful in case your eggplant or oil is still hot.

Bake for 30 minutes, or until the vegetables are tender.

(continued)

> *You can use the rest of your bottle of Bragg's Liquid Aminos to make:*
>
> Blackstrap Vegan Bangers and Mash
> with Onion Gravy on page 125
> Wild Mushroom Risotto on page 135
> Sloppy Joel Pie on page 171
> Chili-Stuffed Sweet Potatoes on
> page 167

Vegan Bacon, White Bean, and Spinach Risotto

The mere fact that we have risotto recipes in a book about saving money is going to confuse and upset some people. Arborio rice, the rice most commonly used for risotto, is often the most expensive rice on the shelf. It can cost 50 to 80 cents more per pound than its brown or jasmine peers—when you buy it prepackaged, that is. But in the bulk section, it's often only 15 cents more per pound, and can provide you with a grain-based dish that's both filling and fabulous. It makes a lovely little date-night-at-home meal that we can enjoy with wine; plus, the leftovers reheat well, so I can spend my Saturdays doing more important things than making lunch—like baking cookies.

MAKES 4 TO 6 SERVINGS $1.87 **PER SERVING**

3 tablespoons olive oil

1 red onion, diced

1½ cups Arborio rice

1 cup white wine

4½ cups vegetable broth or vegan chicken broth (we recommend Better Than Bouillon)

1 teaspoon garlic powder

½ teaspoon onion powder

¼ teaspoon vegan liquid smoke

1 clove garlic, minced

Pinch of celery seed

2 teaspoons crushed rosemary

2 tablespoons nutritional yeast

½ cup baby spinach leaves

⅓ cup chopped fresh parsley

1 (15-ounce) can cannellini beans, drained and rinsed, or 1½ cups cooked dry cannellini beans

¼ cup vegan bacon bits

In a Dutch oven or large soup pot with a lid, heat the oil over medium heat. Add the onion and rice and cook until the onion is tender and the rice begins to look translucent on the outside.

Stir in the wine and let it cook, stirring continuously, until it has been absorbed by the rice. Add ½ cup of the broth, the garlic powder, onion powder, and vegan liquid smoke and cook, stirring, until the broth has been absorbed. Stir in 1 cup broth, the garlic, celery seed, and rosemary and continue to stir until the broth has been absorbed.

Keep adding the broth 1 cup at a time, letting each addition be absorbed before adding the next and stirring continuously. When you get to the last cup, stir in the nutritional yeast, spinach, parsley, and beans.

(continued)

Once the rice is tender and the spinach has wilted, you're ready to eat!

Serve hot, with some vegan bacon bits over the top.

VEGAN BACON BITS

Some people are shocked to find out Bac-Os are vegan. In fact, most bacon bits at your local grocery store are just textured vegetable protein (or TVP), salt, and liquid smoke—which makes them great for adding a smoky, savory crunch to green salads, baked potatoes, pasta salads, and grilled vegan cheese sandwiches. If you're looking for other recipes for your leftover bacon bits, check out the Buffalo Cauliflower Calzones with Vegan Bacon Ranch Dipping Sauce on page 165, Brinner Lasagna on page 169, or Chef's Pasta Salad on page 97.

Irish Stout Stew

Few cultures are as famous for overcoming hardship as the Irish. I mean, seriously, that little island has known famine, disease, invasion, occupation, and all kinds of terrible weather. Yet they endure due to their ability to adapt. They adopted caldrons from the Romans to start making stews, potatoes from the South Americans (via the Spanish), and soda bread from the Native Americans. They did more than just embrace these new culinary advantages—they used them to create a rich food culture that can keep you warm through the worst of winters.

While we were writing this book, the United States got hit by something called a polar vortex. Temperatures in places like Florida dropped as low as 4°F, while the Midwest saw numbers in the negative double-digits. In Brooklyn, we tapped into Dan's Irish side and made this stew. We enjoyed it with some hot black tea and several layers of blankets.

MAKES 8 SERVINGS $1.66 PER SERVING

2 cups vegan beef, defrosted (we recommend Gardein Beefless Tips)

2 tablespoons olive oil

¼ cup all-purpose flour

2 large red onions

1 (6-ounce) can tomato paste

1 large carrot, thinly sliced

2 pounds small red potatoes, cubed

5 white mushrooms, sliced

5½ cups vegan beef broth or vegetable broth (we recommend Better Than Bouillon)

1 bottle Irish stout beer

5 cloves garlic, minced

2 tablespoons fresh parsley leaves

1½ teaspoons dried thyme

2 bay leaves

¾ cup frozen peas

½ teaspoon nutritional yeast

Sea salt and crushed black peppercorns

Preheat the oven to 400°F.

In a shallow baking dish, toss the vegan beef with the olive oil. Sprinkle the vegan beef with the flour and toss to get a light coating.

Slice one red onion into thin slices and place them on top of the vegan beef. Bake for 10 minutes.

While the vegan beef is baking, in your largest Dutch oven or stew pot, toss together the tomato paste, carrot, potatoes, mushrooms, broth, beer, garlic, parsley, thyme, bay leaves, peas, and nutritional yeast. Dice the remaining red onion and add it to the stew. Cover the pot and bring the stew to a boil over medium heat. Once it begins

(continued)

to bubble, reduce the heat to maintain a simmer.

Use a spatula to flip and mix the vegan beef and onions. Bake for another 10 minutes, or until the vegan beef has crispy edges. Then toss the vegan beef, onions, and any extra oil from the baking dish into the stew and mix with a large spoon. The flour will thicken the stew and the onions should pretty much melt. Taste test the stew and add any needed salt and pepper.

Serve hot with some bread, and your favorite beers for the real pub experience.

You can use any leftover mushrooms to make:

Savory Crêpes with Easy "Hollandaise" Sauce on page 42

Smoky Butternut Squash Scramble on page 57

Chop Suey Noodles on page 178

Angel Hair Pasta with Garlic and Rosemary Mushrooms on page 202

Pizza Dough

Making your own dough can make pizza night feel like an honest-to-God meal rather than a fallback plan. In my opinion, the hardest part is having the patience to wait for the dough to rise!

MAKES ENOUGH DOUGH FOR 1 13-INCH PIZZA CRUST　　　　　**$0.17 PER SERVING**

1½ cups bread or all-purpose flour

1 tablespoon sugar

1 teaspoon sea salt

Pinch of nutritional yeast

1 package active dry yeast

3 tablespoons olive oil

1 cup warm water

1½ cups whole wheat flour (plus more to flour surfaces)

In a large bowl, whisk together the flour, sugar, salt, nutritional yeast, and active dry yeast. Blend in the olive oil 1 tablespoon at a time. Then, using an electric handheld mixer fitted with a bread hook attachment, mix in the warm water and whole wheat flour a tablespoon at a time. Use a rubber spatula to scrape the sides of the bowl to make sure all the dough gets blended.

Once the dough is thoroughly mixed, knead it for 5 minutes on a lightly floured surface, stopping once the dough is springy. Cover loosely with plastic wrap and let rise at room temperature for 30 minutes.

Preheat the oven to 425°F.

On a floured surface, use a floured rolling pin to roll the dough into a 13-inch round pizza crust.

Now you're ready to build your pizza!

PREMADE CRUSTS

These days, you can find premade, vegan-friendly pizza dough for around 99 cents at Trader Joe's or Whole Foods—so if you're looking to save time as well as money by enjoying pizza for dinner, check out the frozen food aisle at these stores or your local grocery.

Fajita Pizza

In a world divided by religion, gender, and politics, rare is the individual who can't find some love in their heart for pizza. This recipe combines a classic crust-and-tomato-sauce pizza with the toppings of a Mexican fajita. The result is something pretty special. Like world peace, only on a much, much smaller scale.

MAKES 2 13-INCH PIZZAS   **$1.82 PER SERVING**

2 cups of your favorite vegan chicken (we recommend Beyond Meat Chicken-Free Strips)

1 red bell pepper, sliced

1 yellow bell pepper, sliced

1 green bell pepper, sliced

½ red onion, sliced

Juice of 1 lime

2 pizza crusts, store-bought or homemade (see page 159)

Cornmeal, for dusting

⅓ cup pizza sauce

½ cup shredded vegan pepper Jack or cheddar cheese (we recommend Daiya)

Preheat the oven to 425°F.

In a shallow bowl, mix the vegan chicken, bell peppers, and red onion. Squeeze the lime over the fajita mixture and let it marinate for 5 minutes. (If you're using Beyond Meat, let it marinate for 15 minutes, because it's a denser product.)

Roll out the pizza crusts following the directions on page 159, or follow the instructions on the package.

Unless you have two pizza stones or baking pans, you'll have to bake the pizzas one at a time. Dust a pizza stone or baking pan

with cornmeal. Place a pizza crust on the pan, and using a large spoon, spread half of the pizza sauce over the center of the pizza crust, leaving a ½- to 1-inch space uncovered along the edge.

Spread half of the fajita mixture over the sauce, then sprinkle half of the vegan cheese evenly over the top.

Bake for 5 to 8 minutes, or until the crust is a light golden brown.

Repeat to build and bake the second pizza, while serving the first pizza.

Samosa Pizza

Indian cuisine is easy to veganize, and since many of the dishes have similar flavor profiles and affordable ingredients like potatoes, curry powder, and peas, it can be inexpensive to make. One of the most popular items on any Indian menu is samosas. We combined the spicy potato-and-pea samosa filling with a pizza crust to create a dinner inspired by this beloved appetizer.

MAKES 2 13-INCH PIZZAS   **$0.76 PER SERVING**

¼ cup olive oil

1 red onion, diced

1 teaspoon ginger paste

2 cloves garlic, minced

2 teaspoons garam masala or medium-spicy curry powder

¼ teaspoon smoked paprika

½ teaspoon ground turmeric

¼ teaspoon crushed coriander seeds

1 tablespoon soy sauce or Bragg's Liquid Aminos

¼ jalapeño, diced (more or less, depending on how hot you like it)

3 to 4 Yukon Gold potatoes, baked and cubed (2 cups)

1 tablespoon chopped fresh cilantro

1 cup frozen peas

2 pizza crusts, store-bought or homemade (see page 159)

Cornmeal, for dusting

2 pinches of crushed black peppercorns

Preheat the oven to 425°F.

In your deepest skillet or a Dutch oven, whisk together the olive oil, onion, ginger paste, garlic, garam masala, paprika, turmeric, coriander, and soy sauce. Set the skillet over medium heat and cook, stirring occasionally with a large spoon, until the onion is tender, then gently stir in the jalapeño (using as much as you like to achieve the desired heat level) and potatoes. The potatoes will become soft and crumbly, and it's okay if they break up. Stir in the cilantro and peas and remove the skillet from the heat.

Roll out the pizza crusts following the directions on page 159, or follow the instructions on the package.

Unless you have two pizza stones or baking pans, you'll have to bake the pizzas one at a time. Dust a pizza stone or baking pan with cornmeal. Place a pizza crust on the pan, and using a large spoon, spread half of the potato topping over the center of the pizza crust, leaving a ½- to 1-inch space

(continued)

uncovered along the edge. Sprinkle a pinch of black pepper over the top.

Bake for 5 to 8 minutes or until the crust is a light golden brown and the potatoes have crispy edges.

Repeat to build and bake the second pizza, while serving the first pizza.

You can use your leftover ginger paste to make:

Simple Korean Kimchi BBQ Burgers on
    page 187

Steamed Sesame Seitan Dim Sum on
    page 141

Sesame and Soy Marinated Mushroom
    Steaks on page 198

Tom Kha Gai—Spicy Coconut Soup on
    page 89

Turkish Pizza—Lahmacun

We found lahmacun in shops and stands all over Istanbul. Usually made with ground lamb meat, this portable meal is rolled up like a New York slice or folded like a taco and wrapped in paper. We didn't eat it in Istanbul for obvious reasons; but when we got back to our kitchen, we veganized our lahmacun into a pizza so we could get more servings from our seitan.

MAKES 2 13-INCH PIZZAS　　　　　　　　　　　　　**$1.28 PER SERVING**

⅓ cup pizza sauce

¼ teaspoon ground cumin

½ teaspoon smoked paprika

Dash of vegan liquid smoke

1 teaspoon onion powder

¼ teaspoon dried marjoram

¼ teaspoon dried oregano

¼ teaspoon crushed black peppercorns

1 teaspoon soy sauce or Bragg's Liquid Aminos

1 tablespoon olive oil

½ red onion, diced

¼ cup fresh mint leaves, chopped

1 cup tempeh or seitan, crumbled (we recommend Upton's Naturals Seitan)

2 pizza crusts, store-bought or homemade (see page 159)

Cornmeal, for dusting

Preheat the oven to 425°F.

In a large bowl, whisk together the pizza sauce, cumin, paprika, vegan liquid smoke, onion powder, marjoram, oregano, pepper, soy sauce, and olive oil until smooth. Using a large spoon, mix in the onion, mint, and tempeh.

Roll out the pizza crusts following the directions on page 159, or following the instructions on the package.

Unless you have two pizza stones or baking pans, you'll have to bake the pizzas one at a time. Dust a pizza stone or baking pan with cornmeal. Place a pizza crust on the pan, and using a large spoon, spread half of the toppings over the center of the pizza crust, leaving a ½- to 1-inch space uncovered along the edge.

Bake for 5 to 8 minutes or until the crust is a light golden brown.

Repeat to build and bake the second pizza, while serving your first pizza. They're best when served hot!

(continued)

You can use any leftover mint leaves to make:

Swiss Chard Rolls with Domestic Goddess Sauce on page 139

Tofu Spring Rolls with Agave Chili Sauce
on page 121

Lemon-Tahini Fattoush on page 71

Strawberry Salad on page 300

Buffalo Cauliflower Calzones with Vegan Bacon Ranch Dipping Sauce

Buffalo cauliflower "wings" are the superstars on many a vegan restaurant menu, for obvious reasons. They're tasty, inexpensive, easy to make, and just plain amazing. We turned this appetizer headliner into a meal by wrapping it into a calzone. The vegan bacon ranch dressing on the side is for dipping or drizzling and goes great with a celery stick chaser.

MAKES 2 CALZONES   **$1.64 PER SERVING**

Vegan Bacon Ranch Dipping Sauce

- ½ cup vegan mayonnaise (we recommend Vegenaise or Just Mayo)
- ¼ cup coconut milk, from a carton, not a can
- ½ cup vegan sour cream
- 1 teaspoon chopped fresh parsley
- ½ red onion, diced
- 1½ teaspoons soy sauce or Bragg's Liquid Aminos
- 2 cloves garlic, minced
- 1 teaspoon fresh dill or ¼ teaspoon dry dill
- ½ teaspoon onion powder
- Pinch of celery seed
- Pinch of crushed black peppercorns
- Dash of vegan liquid smoke
- 2 tablespoons vegan bacon bits

Calzones

- ¾ cup hot sauce (we recommend Frank's Red Hot)
- ⅓ cup vegan margarine
- 1 teaspoon vegan Worcestershire sauce
- ½ teaspoon celery seed
- 1 clove garlic, minced
- Dash of vegan liquid smoke
- ½ head cauliflower, cut into small florets
- 1 (16-ounce) package extra-firm tofu, drained and crumbled
- 2 pizza crusts, store-bought or homemade (see page 159)
- Cornmeal, for dusting

Make the vegan bacon ranch dipping sauce: In a bowl, mix together all the ranch dressing ingredients except the vegan bacon bits with a whisk or hand mixer. Put in an airtight container and refrigerate.

Make the calzones: Preheat the oven to 425°F.

In your deepest cast-iron skillet, whisk together the hot sauce and margarine over medium heat. Once the margarine has melted, remove the skillet from the heat and

(continued)

whisk in the vegan Worcestershire sauce, celery seed, garlic, and vegan liquid smoke. Using a large spoon, mix in the cauliflower florets and tofu crumbles.

Roll out the pizza crusts following the directions on page 159, or following the instructions on the package.

Dust a pizza stone or baking pan with cornmeal. Place a pizza crust on the pan, and using a large spoon, spread half of the buffalo-cauliflower topping over half of the pizza crust, leaving a ½- to 1-inch space uncovered along the edge. Fold the uncoated side of the dough over the filling, then use your wet fingers to fold, press, and seal the edges.

Repeat the process on the other side of the baking pan to build a second calzone.

Bake for 10 minutes, or until the crust is a light golden brown and the calzone makes a sound like a ripe melon when you lightly thump it.

Using a large spoon, mix the vegan bacon bits into the vegan ranch dressing while the calzones bake.

Serve the calzones hot with a cup of the dipping sauce on the side.

Use the other half of your cauliflower head to make:

Yankee Doodle Macaroni on page 191

Chili-Stuffed Sweet Potatoes

I'm not ashamed to admit this: Once a month, we host a Dungeons & Dragons night at our home. Well, actually, we use the more rules-light GURPS system, but that's not really the point of this story. See, whenever we host game night, we have a few friends over who are what we like to call not-yet-vegans. I mean, they're great guys who can throw some mean dice, but when they come over we're always aware of how aware they are about what we're eating. Cooking vegan food for omnivores can feel a little like cooking for the FBI sometimes, am I right? So many questions. Needless to say, this recipe was welcomed and enjoyed by all the brave heroes of our game, with little to no investigation into what exactly nutritional yeast is or why we'd want a vegan pot roast as compared to a bunch of carrots.*

MAKES 8 TO 10 SERVINGS $1.77 PER SERVING

8 to 10 sweet potatoes

2 teaspoons olive oil

1 red onion, diced

3 cloves garlic, minced

1 (15-ounce) can lentils, drained and rinsed, or 1½ cups cooked dry lentils

1 (15-ounce) can garbanzo beans, drained and rinsed, or 1½ cups cooked dry garbanzo beans

1 (15-ounce) can black beans, drained and rinsed, or 1½ cups cooked dry black beans

1 (28-ounce) can diced tomatoes

2 cups vegetable broth or vegan beef broth

1 tablespoon plus 1 teaspoon chili powder

2 teaspoons dried oregano

2 teaspoons ground cumin

¾ cup frozen corn

2 tablespoons soy sauce or Bragg's Liquid Aminos

1 teaspoon onion powder

1 teaspoon garlic powder

¼ teaspoon crushed black peppercorns

Dash of vegan liquid smoke

Sea salt and ground black pepper

½ cup chopped fresh cilantro

Preheat the oven to 400°F.

Cut a slit in the top of each potato, then put the potatoes on the oven rack and bake for 20 to 25 minutes, or until the centers are tender. Set aside.

In a Dutch oven or your largest soup pot with a lid, heat the olive oil over medium heat. Add the onions and garlic and cook until the onion is tender, then toss in the remaining ingredients except the cilantro, salt, pepper, and sweet potatoes. Bring the mixture to a boil, stirring occasionally. Once the chili begins to bubble, reduce the heat to

(continued)

---

* I'm only 80 percent serious. No one ever says "carrots"…except maybe with their eyes.

maintain a simmer, cover, and let simmer for 15 minutes. Give your chili a taste test and add any needed salt and pepper.

Serve the potatoes hot, with as much chili and cilantro over the top as your heart desires.

You can use your leftover cilantro to make:

Tofu Spring Rolls with Agave Chili Sauce on page 121

Steamed Sesame Seitan Dim Sum on page 141

Samosa Pizza on page 161

Pan-Seared Corn and Quinoa Salad on page 76

Tom Kha Gai—Spicy Coconut Soup on page 89

Check out page 14 for tips on how to store fresh cilantro so it lasts longer.

POTATOES: THE PERFECT BRING-TO-WORK LUNCH

When we moved to Brooklyn and Dan couldn't come home for lunch anymore, we invested in a wonderful stainless-steel lunchware set so he could take leftovers with him to work. Chili-Stuffed Sweet Potatoes (page 167) work great for that. We just moved one potato fully loaded with vegan chili over to one of the containers the night before and refrigerated it overnight; by the time Dan reheated it in the microwave the next day, the potato and chili had fused into an outstanding and delicious mash worthy of my handsome husband. Of course, always remove your leftovers from their stainless-steel containers before putting them in the microwave. That's a disaster waiting to happen.

Brinner Lasagna

The year we fine-tuned and streamlined our kitchen was a serious year in our lives. It was the kind of year during which you realize all that growing up you did in your twenties wasn't nearly enough, and yet you know your thirties are still way more awesome than your twenties ever were. It was also the year we combined all our favorite breakfast foods into a lasagna and enjoyed it for a week with decaf coffee, because we're too old to drink caffeinated beverages after five p.m. these days.

MAKES 6 TO 8 SERVINGS   **$3.18 PER SERVING**

- 1 (9-ounce) package lasagna noodles, cooked (not oven-ready)
- 4 tablespoons olive oil
- 4 vegan sausages, crumbled (we recommend Field Roast Original Sausages, Tofurky Italian Sausages, or Upton's Naturals Italian Seitan)
- 2 (16-ounce) packages extra-firm tofu, drained
- 1 cup nutritional yeast
- 2 teaspoons ground cumin
- 1 teaspoon onion powder
- 1 teaspoon garlic powder
- ⅓ cup vegan bacon bits

- 1 small red onion, diced
- ½ green bell pepper, diced
- ½ teaspoon sea salt
- ½ teaspoon ground black pepper
- Pinch of celery seed
- ½ teaspoon smoked paprika
- 1 large sweet potato, peeled and shredded
- ½ cup shredded vegan cheddar cheese (we recommend Daiya)
- 1 large tomato, sliced
- 2 green onions, diced

Preheat the oven to 400°F.

Bring a large pot of salted water to a boil. Cook the lasagna noodles according to the package instructions, adding a tablespoon of the olive oil to the water to keep the noodles from sticking together. Drain and set aside to cool.

In your always-faithful cast-iron skillet, heat 1 tablespoon of olive oil over medium heat. Toss in the vegan sausage and cook until it has crispy edges and is a light golden brown. Set aside.

In a large bowl, use a fork to mash the tofu into bite-size pieces. Using a large spoon, mix in the nutritional yeast, cumin, onion powder, garlic powder, vegan bacon bits, red onion, bell pepper, salt, black pepper, celery seed, and paprika.

In a separate bowl, mix the sweet potato with the remaining 2 tablespoons olive oil and the vegan cheese.

Build the lasagna: In a shallow casserole dish or lasagna pan, arrange a layer of

(continued)

noodles. Top the noodles with an even layer of the tofu and vegetable mixture, distributing the vegetables evenly. Add another layer of noodles, a layer of tomato slices, and then a layer of crumbled vegan sausage. Place one last layer of lasagna noodles over the vegan sausage and tomatoes, then spread the sweet potato and cheese mixture over the top.

Bake for 30 minutes, or until the vegan cheese has melted and the sweet potatoes are lightly crispy.

Serve hot, with some green onions sprinkled over the top.

You can use any leftover vegan cheddar cheese to make:

Cajun Nachos on page 129

Mac and Cheez Pie on page 173

Chipotle Avocado Sandwiches on page 106

Cincinnati Chili on page 177

Fajita Pizza on page 160

Sloppy Joel Pie

This here's the story of a pie named Sloppy Joel. It was the neatest way ever for a Sloppy Joel to be prepared, served, and enjoyed, yet it never lost that messy-sounding moniker. Some things just stick around forever, like when you spill glitter on a carpet. But our friend Joel still wears the epithet with pride, because how often do you get both a sandwich and a pie named after you?

Combining the signature flavors of a classic American sandwich full of savory and saucy "beef" and tomatoes with the clean-cut convenience of one of Betty Crocker's impossibly easy Bisquick pies in a completely vegan way...well, this pie has it all.

MAKES 1 PIE   **$0.90 PER SERVING**

1 (8-ounce) package tempeh

1 tablespoon vegan Worcestershire sauce

3 tablespoons soy sauce or Bragg's Liquid Aminos

Dash of Tabasco or other hot sauce (optional)

Dash of vegan liquid smoke

¾ teaspoon onion powder

Pinch of celery seed

Olive oil cooking spray

1 to 2 tablespoons olive oil

1 red onion, diced

1 green bell pepper, diced

3 Campari tomatoes, or 6 cherry tomatoes, quartered

1 tablespoon chopped fresh parsley

½ cup vegan Bisquick mix

1 tablespoon ground flaxseed

½ teaspoon Ener-G egg replacer

1 cup soy milk, plus more as needed

1 tablespoon applesauce

Ketchup or A.1. steak sauce for topping

Crumble the tempeh into a large bowl. In a small bowl, whisk together the vegan Worcestershire sauce, soy sauce, Tabasco, vegan liquid smoke, ½ teaspoon of the onion powder, and the celery seed. Pour the sauce over the tempeh and mix together with a large spoon until the tempeh is well coated. Cover and let sit for 10 minutes, tossing the tempeh occasionally to make sure it marinates evenly.

Preheat the oven to 400°F. Spray a pie dish with a heavy coating of olive oil cooking spray.

In your favorite cast-iron skillet, heat the olive oil over medium heat. Toss in the marinated tempeh and cook for 3 minutes, then add the onion, bell pepper, and any leftover marinade from the tempeh. Cook for another 5 minutes, or until the vegetables are tender.

(continued)

Toss in the tomatoes and parsley, then cook for another 3 to 5 minutes, or until the onion is translucent.

In a large bowl, whisk together the Bisquick, remaining 1/4 teaspoon onion powder, the flaxseed, and the egg replacer. Add the soy milk and applesauce and blend with an electric handheld mixer until the batter is smooth; it should look a little runny. If your mixture is too thick, you might need to add more soy milk, 1 teaspoon at a time, until the desired consistency is reached.

Pour the tempeh mixture into the pie dish and spread it into an even layer. Pour the Bisquick batter over the top.

Bake for 30 to 35 minutes, or until a bamboo skewer stuck in the center comes out clean.

Serve warm, with ketchup or A.1. steak sauce.

You can use your leftover vegan Bisquick mix to make:

Mac and Cheez Pie on page 173

BLT Pancake Stacks on page 36

Sweet Potato Pancakes on page 34

Easy Mixed Berry Muffins on page 45

You can use the rest of your bottle of vegan Worcestershire sauce to make:

Beefless Brussels Sprout Shepherd's Pie on page 183

Vegan Gyros on page 219

Roasted Red Flannel Hash on page 38

Yankee Pot Roast Dinner on page 144

Mac and Cheez Pie

If you read our blog, you know this pie recipe has been through some trial and error. Apparently not all Bisquick or premixed biscuit mix is created equal and different types have different thicknesses. For the best results, you want your Bisquick batter to have the consistency of thin cake batter, so add more liquid if your batter is too thick. This recipe was inspired by a circa-1970s Betty Crocker recipe, and is not unlike the Cheezburger Pie we made in our first book, Betty Goes Vegan, or the Sloppy Joel Pie on page 171. You'll need to soak the cashews overnight, so be sure to plan ahead.

MAKES 1 PIE   **$0.78 PER SERVING**

⅓ cup raw cashews

¼ cup nutritional yeast

Dash of vegan liquid smoke

¼ teaspoon ground cumin

1 tablespoon olive oil, plus a little more to brush the pie plate

1 cup elbow macaroni, uncooked

¾ cup shredded vegan cheddar cheese (we recommend Daiya)

1 dash hot sauce

2 cups soy milk

1 teaspoon soy sauce or Bragg's Liquid Aminos

Pinch of crushed black peppercorns

1 cup vegan Bisquick mix

Soak the cashews overnight in enough water to cover them.

The next day, drain the cashews. Transfer them to a food processor with the nutritional yeast, vegan liquid smoke, and cumin. Blend the mixture into a thick, smooth paste.

Preheat the oven to 400°F.

Brush a glass pie dish with an even coating of olive oil. Pour the uncooked macaroni into the dish and smooth it into an even layer. Sprinkle ½ cup of the vegan cheese over the top, followed by little clumps of the cashew blend. Keep the cashew blend clumps no bigger than a teaspoon.

In a large bowl, blend all the remaining ingredients except the vegan cheese with an electric handheld mixer until smooth. Once blended, pour the batter over the vegan cheese and uncooked macaroni. Use a fork or butter knife to gently stir the pie to make sure the batter gets through the layer of vegan cheese and surrounds the macaroni. You can look through the bottom of the glass dish to confirm. Use a rubber spatula to smooth the batter out on top. Sprinkle the remaining 1/4 cup vegan cheese over the top, then bake for 30 to 40 minutes, or until the pie is golden brown and a bamboo skewer

(continued)

inserted into the center of the pie comes out clean. The edges will brown more quickly than the center. Once the edges begin to brown, test the pie with a skewer. Note that the deeper your pie dish is, the longer the pie might take to bake.

CASHEWS

Cashews have become the new darling of the vegan food scene. But sadly—at least where we live—they're really frakking expensive. Most raw cashews cost us about $14 a pound unless we can find them in bulk, and even then it's still as high as $8 a pound (although I once saw $5). So when we invest in some cashews, we want to really get the most bang for our buck. We suggest you make up some Tofu, Green Beans, and Cashews on page 185 with any leftover nuts you might have.

Aloha Dogs

We've had a few friends visit the island paradise of Kauai and return with stories and photos of tropical flowers, jade-colored pools of water, copper-colored feral island chickens, and great big vegan hot dogs from a little food stand in Poipu called Puka Dogs. So when we were choosing where to go for our babymoon, Kauai was the clear winner.

As I type this I am still a little tan from our week on this beautiful island and still very much in love with the time we spent there. Although this recipe isn't exactly like those famous Puka Dogs, we created it to bring a little piece of that nirvana back home with us and to share it with you.

MAKES 4 HOT DOGS   **$2.95 PER SERVING**

Pineapple Salsa

1 (4-ounce) can sliced pineapple, drained (reserve the juice for the hot dogs, below)

1 red bell pepper, diced

½ red onion, diced

1 jalapeño, seeded and diced (more or less, depending on how hot you like it)

⅓ cup chopped fresh cilantro

Juice of 1 lime

¼ teaspoon ground cumin

Hot Dogs

1 tablespoon olive oil

4 favorite vegan sausages (we recommend Tofurky Beer Brats or Field Roast Sausages)

3 tablespoons pineapple juice (from the can of pineapple slices)

Dash of vegan liquid smoke

1 teaspoon ground cumin

4 whole wheat hot dog buns

Make the pineapple salsa: Combine all the salsa ingredients in a small bowl, adding the jalapeño a pinch or two at a time to gauge how hot you want your salsa to be. Toss to combine. Cover and refrigerate.

Make the hot dogs: In a cast-iron skillet or your deepest frying pan, heat the oil over medium heat. Gently place the vegan sausages in the pan and pour the pineapple juice over the top. Add a dash of vegan liquid smoke and sprinkle with cumin. Roll the vegan sausage in the oil a few times to give it a light, even coating.

While the vegan sausages are cooking, toast the hot dog buns.

Once the vegan sausages are tender and have a golden brown crust, you're ready to eat!

Serve the vegan sausages hot in their buns with a few heaping scoops of pineapple salsa on top.

(continued)

Handling Jalapeños

It might sound funny to hear that there are safety precautions you should take when handling jalapeños, because they're so little and cute. But it's all an act. These little buddies pack a punch.

The first thing to do is get some plastic gloves. I know this sounds like I'm overreacting—but anyone who's ever rubbed their eyes an hour after cooking with jalapeños can testify that the pepper's oil stays on your hands even after washing and can make your eyes feel like they're on fire. If you don't have plastic gloves, use a paper towel or sandwich bag to hold your jalapeño. Just be careful—this'll make it harder to see what your knife is doing.

Start by cutting the stem and tip off your jalapeño, and then slice it in half the long way. Using a small knife, cut the seeds and white parts out of the center and throw them away. Now go ahead and dice up your jalapeño into small bits. Store any leftovers in an airtight container.

You can use any leftover jalapeño to make:

Tom Kha Gai—Spicy Coconut Soup on
    page 89

Cajun Nachos on page 129

Quinoa Taco Casserole on page 152

Samosa Pizza on page 161

Cincinnati Chili

Cincinnati chili is a regional dish that consists of a beany, beefy chili seasoned with cinnamon and served over spaghetti. But when you order your chili, you better be clear what way you want it. You can just get the chili bowl, which is (predictably) a bowl of chili. You can get it two-way, which means you want your chili served over spaghetti. Three-way means you want cheese on top of your chili and spaghetti, while four-way means you toss some onions on top of your three-way. The recipe we've made is the Cincinnati chili five-way, veganized: Bean chili over spaghetti with vegan cheese and onions.

MAKES 4 TO 6 LARGE SERVINGS $2.45 PER SERVING

- 1 (16-ounce) package spaghetti
- 1 (15-ounce) can kidney beans, drained and rinsed, or 1½ cups cooked dry kidney beans
- 1 (15-ounce) can lentils, drained and rinsed, or 1½ cups cooked dry lentils
- 1 red onion, diced
- 3 cloves garlic, minced
- 1 (28-ounce) can crushed tomatoes
- 1 tomato, diced
- 1 teaspoon apple cider vinegar
- 1 teaspoon ground cinnamon

- 1 teaspoon ground all-spice
- 1 teaspoon ground cumin
- Dash of vegan liquid smoke
- 2 bay leaves
- 1 tablespoon cocoa powder
- 2 tablespoons chili powder
- ⅔ cup vegetable broth
- ½ teaspoon cayenne pepper
- 2 cups shredded vegan cheddar cheese (we recommend Daiya)
- Green onions, diced

Bring a large pot of salted water to a boil and prepare the pasta following the directions on the package.

While the pasta is cooking, toss all the remaining ingredients except the vegan cheese and green onions in a large soup pot or Dutch oven. Cover the pot and heat over medium heat until the chili begins to bubble.

Then reduce the heat to a simmer and stir occasionally with a spoon.

Let the chili simmer for 5 to 15 minutes. You'll know it's ready when the beans are tender.

Drain the spaghetti. Serve the chili hot, over the spaghetti, with some vegan cheese and green onions sprinkled on top.

Chop Suey Noodles

Chop suey is not a traditional Chinese dish. In fact, if you were to ask for it in China, you'd get more than a few dirty looks. This dish was actually credited to the then Chinese ambassador to the United States, Li Hung Chang, in 1896.

When Li Hung Chang arrived in New York, the newspapers followed his every move with admiration and curiosity. The president at the time was the uncharismatic Grover Cleveland, so having such an exotic visitor come to the United States wearing brightly colored silk garments and refusing to eat any of our food, was humbling and gave the press something to talk about.

It's rumored that Chang left behind this recipe, but I'd bet money the truth is that someone took note of what he was eating and made chop suey as a hybrid of whatever Americanized Asian food Chang could find during his stay. Over a hundred years later, this dish has lost a lot of its fame, but for generations it was an economical dinner full of vegetables that was notoriously popular with children (if the ladies' magazines from 1920 through the 1960s are to be believed).

MAKES 4 TO 6 SERVINGS $1.58 PER SERVING

½ to 1 cup vegetable broth or vegan chicken broth (we recommend Better Than Bouillon)

2 tablespoons soy sauce or Bragg's Liquid Aminos

1 teaspoon agave nectar

1 teaspoon Sriracha or Thai chili sauce

1 teaspoon cornstarch

1 cup tofu or vegan chicken (we recommend Beyond Meat Chicken-Free Strips or Gardein Chick'n Scallopini)

1 (13-ounce) package chow mein or udon noodles

1 to 3 tablespoons sesame oil

3 cloves garlic, minced

1 red onion, diced

4 stalks celery, chopped

4 mushrooms, sliced

½ cup snap pea pods

½ cup mung bean sprouts (optional)

1 (5-ounce) can sliced water chestnuts, drained

1 green onion, diced

In a large bowl, whisk together ½ cup of the broth, the soy sauce, agave nectar, Sriracha, and cornstarch. Add the tofu to the marinade and let it sit for 15 minutes. (If you're using Beyond Meat, add the additional ½ cup broth.)

While the tofu marinates, prepare the noodles following the directions on the package.

In a wok or your deepest cast-iron skillet, heat 1 to 3 tablespoons of sesame oil over high heat. How much oil you need depends on how big your wok or skillet is.

Once the oil is hot, carefully toss the tofu in and cook, flipping the tofu occasionally to make sure it cooks evenly. Once the tofu has crispy edges, remove from the heat and set aside, leaving the oil in the pan.

Toss the garlic, onion, celery, mushrooms, snap peas, bean sprouts, and water chestnuts into the hot pan and cook until they become tender.

Add the noodles and tofu to the vegetables. Pour any extra marinade/sauce over the top and continue to cook while mixing and flipping occasionally to make sure it cooks evenly.

Serve hot, with a pinch of green onions over the top.

You can use the rest of your bottle of agave nectar to make:

Virgin Crêpes Suzette on page 39

Avocado and Grapefruit Salad with Cilantro Dressing on page 81

Tofu, Green Beans, and Cashews on page 185

Strawberry Salad on page 300

Spinach and Tempeh Pastitsio

Pastitsio is often called "Greek lasagna," but it is really more of a baked ziti. It's often made with a goat- or lamb-based tomato sauce over tube pasta, and then topped with a goat's-milk-based béchamel sauce and dry cheese. Honestly, we've never had the "meaty" version of this recipe, and we're both fine with that. Our recipe uses crumbled tempeh and a vegan cream sauce to replace all the meat, but retains just the right amount of Oompaa!

MAKES 6 TO 8 SERVINGS   **$1.89 PER SERVING**

Pasta and Tempeh Red Sauce

1 (1-pound) box ziti pasta

1 tablespoon olive oil

1 red onion, diced

2 cloves garlic, minced

1 (8-ounce) package tempeh, crumbled

2 teaspoons dried oregano

¼ teaspoon ground cinnamon

¼ teaspoon smoked paprika

1 teaspoon sesame seeds

1 teaspoon crushed black peppercorns

1 tablespoon soy sauce or Bragg's Liquid Aminos

1 (14-ounce) can roasted tomatoes

⅓ cup red wine

1 red bell pepper, diced

¼ cup raw spinach leaves

Vegan Béchamel Sauce

2 tablespoons vegan margarine

¼ cup nutritional yeast, plus more to sprinkle over the top

3 tablespoons whole wheat flour

1 tablespoon white wine

1 tablespoon soy sauce or Bragg's Liquid Aminos

1 teaspoon onion powder

2 teaspoons garlic powder

¼ teaspoon ground nutmeg

2 teaspoons vegan Parmesan cheese

1½ cups soy milk

2 teaspoons lemon juice

Preheat the oven to 375°F.

Make the pasta and tempeh red sauce: Bring a large pot of salted water to a boil and prepare the ziti following the instructions on the package. Drain and set aside.

Meanwhile, in a saucepan, heat the oil over medium heat. Add the onion, garlic, tempeh, oregano, cinnamon, paprika, sesame seeds, peppercorns, and soy sauce and cook, stirring occasionally, until the onion is tender. Mix in the tomatoes, wine, and bell pepper and reduce the heat to maintain a simmer while you make the béchamel.

Make the béchamel sauce: In a separate saucepan, melt the vegan margarine over medium heat. Once it begins to bubble, whisk in the nutritional yeast and flour. Whisk in the white wine, soy sauce, onion powder, garlic powder, nutmeg, vegan Parmesan, soy milk, and lemon juice until the sauce becomes thick and creamy.

Pour the cooked pasta into a casserole dish and use a spatula to arrange it into a tight, uniform layer. Spread the spinach leaves over the pasta, then pour the tempeh red sauce over it. Use a ladle to pour the vegan béchamel over the red sauce; you may need to smooth it into an even layer with a rubber spatula. Sprinkle

nutritional yeast over the top and bake for 20 to 25 minutes.

Once the top of the casserole is a light golden brown, you're ready to eat!

WHITE WINE

Cooking with wine can be one of the healthiest ways to add flavor to your recipes without adding salt. White wine in particular is great at adding that unique fermented flavor you often find in cream sauces that have Parmesan in them. If you're not much of a drinker, you can always substitute vegetable broth for wine. If you're wondering what you can do with your leftover white wine, try making the Wild Mushroom Risotto on page 135, Sesame and Soy Marinated Mushroom Steaks on page 198, Cauliflower Fettuccine Alfredo on page 238, or Pan-Seared Tofu with Arugula, Capers, and Tomatoes on page 210.

Sweet Potato and Black Bean Tacos

Back in 2011, there was a celebrity gossip piece titled "Fergie Isn't Pregnant—She Just Really Likes Tacos."[†] This might be the only thing I have in common with the buxom Black Eyed Peas singer. Tacos are amazing.

MAKES 8 TO 10 TACOS   **$0.73 PER SERVING**

2 sweet potatoes, cubed

1 tablespoon olive oil

2 (15-ounce) cans black beans, drained and rinsed, or 1½ cups cooked dry black beans

1 red onion, diced

½ teaspoon dried oregano

2 teaspoons ground cumin

1 clove garlic, minced

1 tablespoon hot sauce

2 tablespoons soy sauce or Bragg's Liquid Aminos

Juice of 1 lime

¼ cup chopped fresh cilantro

1 or 2 radishes, sliced

8 to 10 (8-inch) flour tortillas

2 limes, cut into wedges

Preheat the oven to 400°F.

In a baking dish, toss the sweet potatoes with the olive oil. Bake for 5 minutes. Using a spatula, flip the potatoes and put them back in the oven to bake until tender.

While the potatoes bake, in a large bowl, mix together the black beans, red onion, oregano, cumin, garlic, hot sauce, soy sauce, and lime juice with a wooden spoon.

Use a spoon to gently mix the baked sweet potatoes in with the black bean mixture. Stir in the cilantro and radishes just before serving.

Warm the tortillas following the directions on the package.

Serve the sweet potato and black bean mixture warm, with lightly toasted tortillas and lime wedges for squeezing over the top.

Store any leftovers separately from the tortillas so the tortillas don't get soggy from the sweet potatoes and black beans.

[†] Yes, I still remember it, because it made me like her. Any time anyone ever makes a comment on my baby weight gain, I always want to quote this article, but know I'm the only one who would get the joke.

> **You can use any leftover tortillas to make:**
>
> Vegan Bacon and "Egg" Enchiladas on page 55
>
> Roasted Pear, Walnut, and Brussels Sprout Taco on page 197

Beefless Brussels Sprout Shepherd's Pie

"The way to a man's heart is paved in pie."
I'm not sure who said that, but I think they knew Dan.

MAKES 1 PIE   **$1.40 PER SERVING**

1 vegan piecrust, store-bought or homemade (see page 262)

Filling

1 tablespoon olive oil

1 (9-ounce) package Gardein Beefless Tips or your favorite beef seitan

6 Brussels sprouts, trimmed and quartered

1 (15-ounce) can lentils, drained and rinsed, or 1½ cups cooked dry lentils

3 to 4 mushrooms, sliced

⅓ cup white wine

2 tablespoons soy sauce or Bragg's Liquid Aminos

1 tablespoon vegan Worcestershire sauce

1 teaspoon dried thyme

1 clove garlic, minced

2 tablespoons chopped fresh parsley

Pinch of celery seed

1½ teaspoons crushed dried rosemary

½ cup frozen peas

Topping

4 large Yukon Gold potatoes, baked

1 tablespoon plus 1 teaspoon vegan margarine

2 tablespoons nutritional yeast

1 recipe Onion Gravy (page 125)

Preheat the oven to 425°F.

Prepare the piecrust following the directions on the package, or following the directions on page 262. Poke a few holes in the bottom of the raw piecrust and bake it for 1 to 2 minutes or until the crust begins to brown. Set aside, leaving the oven on.

Make the filling: In a large saucepan, heat the oil over medium heat. Add the vegan beef tips and cook until they have lightly crispy edges. Add the remaining filling ingredients and cook, stirring with a wooden spoon. Once the mixture begins to bubble, reduce the heat to maintain a simmer. Let simmer for 2 to 3 minutes.

Fill the piecrust with the filling and set aside.

Make the topping: In a large bowl, mash together the potatoes, vegan margarine, and nutritional yeast until completely blended. Then spoon the potato topping on top of the filling in the pie crust into a smooth, sloping mound that covers all the filling, sealing it in.

(continued)

Bake the pie for 30 to 40 minutes, or until the potato topping is golden and crispy.

Meanwhile, reheat the onion gravy, if necessary.

Serve the pie hot, with lots of gravy.

You can use any leftover mushrooms to make:

Savory Crêpes with Easy "Hollandaise" Sauce on page 42

Smoky Butternut Squash Scramble on page 57

Sriracha and Sweet Onion Stew on page 104

Angel Hair Pasta with Garlic and Rosemary Mushrooms on page 202

Sloppy Joel Pie, page 171

Aloha Dogs, page 175

Cincinnati Chili, page 177

Chop Suey Noodles, page 178

Sweet Potato and Black Bean Tacos, page 182

Tofu, Green Beans, and Cashews, page 185

Betty's Wartime Walnut Burger, page 189

Simple Korean Kimchi BBQ Burgers, page 187

Tofu Vindaloo, page 195

Roasted Pear, Walnut, and Brussels Sprouts Tacos, page 197

Sesame and Soy Marinated Mushroom Steaks, page 198

Vegan BLT Mac and Cheez, page 193

Cruelty-Free Crawfish Broil, page 286

Pasta with Asparagus and Green Onion Pesto, page 200

Angel Hair Pasta with Garlic and Rosemary Mushrooms, page 202

Tuesday Night Dinner, page 203

Pumpkin Curry Soup, page 216

Savory Pumpkin Biscuits, page 218

Pomegranate and Brown Rice Cabbage Rolls, page 224

Pasta with DIY Marinara, page 226

Hungarian Goulash Stew, page 229

Simple Spanish Rice Bake, page 232

Pasta Primavera, page 239

Cowboy Quinoa Chili, page 241

Savannah Pecan Pie, page 266

Chai Spice Cheescake, page 272

Pink Lemonade Cupcakes, page 254

Molasses Crinkle Cookies, page 280

Butternut Squash and
Beer Poutine Party, page 288

Mezze Platter, page 292

Strawberry Salad, page 300

Tofu, Green Beans, and Cashews

It's always tough when you finally figure out how to make one of your favorite dishes from a restaurant at home, only to realize you've been paying way too much for it. Although this recipe includes those pricey cashews, it's still way cheaper to make at home. Plus, now you can skip the tip and not be a total jerk.

MAKES 4 TO 6 SERVINGS   **$1.53 PER SERVING**

- 1 pound green beans
- 1 (16-ounce) package extra-firm tofu, drained
- 3 tablespoons sesame oil
- 2 tablespoons agave nectar
- 2 tablespoons soy sauce or Bragg's Liquid Aminos
- ½ teaspoon ground mustard seed
- ½ cup roasted red peppers in oil
- ½ cup raw cashews
- ¼ cup teriyaki sauce

Bring 3 cups water to a rolling boil in a Dutch oven or large pot with a lid. Toss in the greens beans and cover. Cook for 3 to 5 minutes or until the green beans are tender, then drain and set aside.

While the green beans are cooking, slice the tofu into 10 to 12 thin slices or squares. In a bowl, whisk together 2 tablespoons of the sesame oil, the agave nectar, soy sauce, and mustard seed.

Heat your wok or largest skillet over high heat. Once the wok is hot, carefully toss in the tofu and remaining 1 tablespoon sesame oil. Flip the tofu occasionally until it turns a light golden brown with crispy edges.

Add the cooked green beans, red peppers, cashews, and teriyaki sauce and toss with the cooked tofu until everything is lightly coated in the sauce. Then toss your vegetables, cashews, and tofu with the sesame oil and soy sauce mixture until they're evenly coated.

Cook for another 5 to 8 minutes, or until the sauce has reduced to a desired thickness. Serve warm.

You can use any leftover cashews to make:

Mac and Cheez Pie on page 173
Vegan Cheese Party Pizza on page 278

Pan-Seared Black Tea and Pepper Tofu

For most vegans, marinated tofu is nothing new. But I think tofu marinated in black tea, lemon, and black pepper will surprise you. The tea adds a unique flavor that really complements the lemon, and adds a certain something special to an ingredient we've all come to take for granted.

MAKES 4 OR 5 SERVINGS   **$1.01 PER SERVING**

- 2 cups strong brewed black tea, at room temperature
- 1 tablespoon crushed black peppercorns, plus more to sprinkle over the top
- 2 teaspoons grated lemon zest
- Juice of 1 lemon
- 1 teaspoon soy sauce or Bragg's Liquid Aminos
- 1 (16-ounce) package extra-firm tofu, drained and cut into 10 thin slices
- ¼ cup olive oil
- 1 lemon, cut into wedges

In a shallow dish, whisk together the tea, pepper, lemon zest, lemon juice, and soy sauce.

Pat the tofu pieces dry to remove any extra moisture. Place the tofu in the shallow dish and let marinate for 10 minutes. Flip the tofu and marinate on the second side for 5 minutes.

In your favorite cast-iron skillet, heat the oil over medium heat. Very carefully place 3 or 4 tofu slices in the hot oil and pour a few spoonfuls of the tea marinade over each. Cook for 1 to 2 minutes, then flip with a spatula. Once the tofu has crispy edges and is a light golden brown on both sides, remove from the skillet and transfer to a plate. Repeat until you have cooked all the tofu slices.

Serve hot, with a few pinches of black pepper and a lemon wedge for squeezing over the top.

MAKE A SANDWICH WITH IT

The sketch comedy show *Portlandia* has a great skit about how if you're struggling as an artist, *just stick a bird on it!* And people will love whatever it is you made. This show helps alleviate the homesickness I get from time to time for the Pacific Northwest. The same approach can be taken with leftovers. *No,* don't put an actual bird on or in anything. But most leftovers are delicious made into a sandwich on a toasted baguette or bagel.

Leftover Pan-Seared Black Tea and Pepper Tofu in particular is wonderful on a toasted everything bagel with a slice of tomato, some lettuce, and some vegan mayo. Serve it with an iced tea and a cup of soup and you've made a lunch anyone would be jealous of...vegan or not.

Simple Korean Kimchi BBQ Burgers

Years ago, I had a vegan Korean BBQ burrito in Los Angeles. The burrito had jackfruit to replace the steak, and I still think about it when I'm figuring out what to have for lunch. Jackfruit is pretty pricey and hard to come by in Brooklyn, but whenever I get nostalgic for that burrito, I make these spectacular burgers. They combine the signature sweet Korean BBQ sauce with a "beefy" veggie burger and spicy kimchi (a sort of hot Korean sauerkraut usually made with napa cabbage, radishes, and green onions) to create a dinner just as good as those burritos. Plus, you'll hopefully have some leftover kimchi as a side for lunch the next day.

MAKES 4 BURGERS   **$2.68 PER SERVING**

Burger

2 cups Lightlife Gimme Lean Burger or Match Vegan Meats Burger

1 green onion, diced

1 tablespoon blackstrap molasses

½ teaspoon ginger paste

1 tablespoon soy sauce or Bragg's Liquid Aminos

Dash of vegan liquid smoke

½ teaspoon onion powder

1 clove garlic, minced

BBQ Sauce

1 (6-ounce) can tomato paste

2 tablespoons soy sauce or Bragg's Liquid Aminos

Dash of vegan liquid smoke

1 tablespoon Sriracha or Thai chili sauce

¼ cup applesauce

2 teaspoons agave nectar

2 teaspoons sesame seeds

¼ teaspoon ginger paste

1 clove garlic, minced

To Assemble

2 tablespoons sesame oil

4 whole wheat hamburger buns

1 cup vegan kimchi (read labels to make sure yours is vegan; some contain fish sauce)

Make the burger: In a large bowl, use your hands to mix together the vegan beef, green onion, molasses, ginger paste, soy sauce, vegan liquid smoke, onion powder, and garlic until blended. The molasses is really sticky, so this is kind of messy and weird, but it's totally worth it. Promise.

Form the mixture into 4 patties about the size of your hand. Place them on a plate, cover with plastic wrap, and refrigerate for 5 minutes.

(continued)

Meanwhile, make the BBQ sauce: In a small bowl, whisk together all the BBQ sauce ingredients. Set aside.

In a cast-iron skillet or frying pan, heat 1 tablespoon of the sesame oil over medium heat. Working in batches, fry the burgers until lightly crispy around the edges, then reduce the heat to low and brush the burgers with BBQ sauce. Flip and coat the burgers a few times to get a nice saucy patty, but watch out for the hot oil. Repeat with the remaining burgers, adding the remaining oil after the first batch.

Toast the burger buns while the burger patties are cooking.

Serve each burger in a toasted bun with lots of kimchi on top.

You can use the rest of your bottle of sesame oil to make:

Sesame and Soy Marinated Mushroom Steaks on page 198

Sesame Peanut Noodles on page 101

Betty's Wartime Walnut Burger

In 1943, Betty Crocker produced one of the first cookbook leaflets to help women feed their families using only rations. It was titled Your Share, *and it was designed to guide homemakers through the process of "making do" with a lot less. It contained recipes for meat substitutes made from cornflakes, oats, and even potatoes. The only one that sounded slightly good to us had the unfortunate name "The Nut Burger." We've tweaked the recipe quite a bit: We added more flavor, replaced the eggs with a bean puree and flaxseeds, and borrowed techniques from other recipes to improve the texture. In the end, we've come up with a nice recipe that tastes amazing and feels damn patriotic. I think we'd make Betty proud.*

MAKES 4 TO 6 SMALL BURGERS   **$1.99 PER SERVING**

1½ cups raw walnuts

1 (15-ounce) can cannellini beans, drained and rinsed, or 1½ cups cooked dry cannellini beans

3 tablespoons garbanzo bean flour

1 tablespoon applesauce

1 tablespoon ground flaxseed

2 teaspoons onion powder

1 teaspoon dried thyme

1 clove garlic, minced

3 tablespoons nutritional yeast

⅓ cup vegan beef broth or vegetable broth (we recommend Better Than Bouillon)

½ teaspoon vegan Worcestershire sauce

2 pinches crushed black peppercorns

3 tablespoons quick-cooking rolled oats

½ red onion, diced

¼ cup chopped fresh parsley

2 tablespoons olive oil

4 to 6 hamburger buns

Your favorite hamburger fixings

In a food processor, combine the walnuts, beans, garbanzo bean flour, applesauce, and flaxseed and process into a puree.

In a large bowl, whisk together the onion powder, thyme, garlic, nutritional yeast, vegan broth, vegan Worcestershire sauce, and pepper. Use a spoon to mix in the walnut puree, then mix in the oats, onion, and parsley. Cover and let sit for 5 minutes.

Using your hands, form the mixture into 4 to 6 patties. They'll cook better if you don't make them too thick.

In your favorite cast-iron skillet or favorite frying pan, heat 1 tablespoon of the olive oil over medium heat. Working in batches, carefully move the patties to the skillet. Brown on the first side for 1 minute, then carefully flip with a spatula and gently press the

(continued)

patties down. Once the patties are browned on both sides, transfer to a plate. Repeat with the remaining patties, adding the remaining olive oil to the pan after the first batch.

Toast the hamburger buns while the patties are cooking.

Place one patty on each bun and top your burger with mustard, BBQ sauce, pickles, or whatever your favorite hamburger fixings are. I recommend trying it with some A.1. steak sauce. Yep, it's vegan!

You can use the rest of your jar of applesauce to make:

Apple-Sage Tempeh Sausage over Savory Polenta on page 133

Sloppy Joel Pie on page 171

Simple Korean Kimchi BBQ Burgers on page 187

S'mores Cookie Bars on page 260

Yankee Doodle Macaroni

I admit we took a lot of liberties when updating this wartime classic. It needed more flavor than what was available to our grandmothers—and a lot less salt. I'm one of those folks who believe salt should be used to bring out flavor, not be a flavor, but there's a "salt to taste" option in the recipe for those who feel otherwise. We also took out the evaporated milk and bacon fat because that's how we roll in 2014.

MAKES 6 TO 8 SERVINGS   **$0.83 PER SERVING**

Olive oil cooking spray

½ pound carrots, thinly sliced

½ pound cauliflower (about ½ head), cut into small florets

1 teaspoon sea salt, plus more as needed

1½ teaspoons ground black pepper, plus more as needed

1 (1-pound) package medium-size tube or shell pasta (we recommend elbow macaroni)

¼ cup olive oil

1 red onion, diced

2 cloves garlic, minced

3 tablespoons all-purpose flour

2 cups almond or soy milk

5 tablespoons nutritional yeast

1¼ teaspoons garlic powder

1 teaspoon onion powder

Pinch of celery seed

2 dashes of vegan liquid smoke

2 tablespoons soy sauce or Bragg's Liquid Aminos

¼ teaspoon ground turmeric

¼ teaspoon smoked paprika, plus more to sprinkle over the top

Preheat the oven to 400°F. Spray a shallow baking dish with a heavy coating of olive oil cooking spray. Spread the carrots and cauliflower in an even layer in the dish and spray them with a coating of the cooking spray. Sprinkle the salt and pepper over the vegetables. Roast the vegetables until they become tender, tossing them with a wooden spoon every 8 to 10 minutes to make sure they cook evenly. It took about 20 minutes for our vegetables to roast, but yours might take

more or less time depending on how small you cut them.

While the vegetables are roasting, bring a large pot of salted water to a boil and prepare the pasta following the instructions on the package. Drain the pasta and set aside in the colander.

In the pasta pot, heat the olive oil over medium heat. Add the onion and garlic and cook until the onion is tender. Stir in the flour using a wooden spoon. The vegetables

(continued)

in the oven should be tender by now; toss them in the pot with the onion and add the almond milk and 3 tablespoons of the nutritional yeast. Bring to a boil, stirring, then reduce the heat to maintain a simmer.

Use an immersion blender, food processor, or blender to puree the sauce. If you're using a food processor or blender, you may have to do this in batches—be careful, as the sauce will be hot. Once the sauce is smooth, whisk in the remaining 2 tablespoons nutritional yeast, the garlic powder, onion powder, celery seed, vegan liquid smoke, soy sauce, turmeric, and paprika. Remove from the heat

and give it a taste test, adding salt and pepper as needed. Gradually mix in the cooked pasta using a wooden spoon until it's completely coated in the sauce.

Serve hot, with some smoked paprika sprinkled over the top for a bit of color.

You can use the other half of your head of cauliflower to make:

Buffalo Cauliflower Calzones with
Vegan Bacon Ranch Dipping Sauce on
page 165

Vegan BLT Mac and Cheez

If vegan mac and cheese with smoky tempeh bacon, leeks, and tomatoes sounds like your thing . . . this recipe is for you!

MAKES 4 TO 6 LARGE SERVINGS   **$2.06 PER SERVING**

1 (1-pound) package elbow macaroni or small tube or shell pasta

Cheez Sauce

½ cup vegan margarine

½ cup whole wheat flour

3½ cups boiling water

2 tablespoons soy sauce or Bragg's Liquid Aminos

1 clove garlic, minced

1 teaspoon onion powder

1 teaspoon Dijon mustard

¼ teaspoon ground turmeric

¼ teaspoon rubbed sage

1½ cups nutritional yeast

A few dashes of vegan liquid smoke

Salt and crushed black peppercorns

To Assemble

1 tablespoon olive oil

1 (8-ounce) package tempeh bacon (we recommend Lightlife Smart Bacon or Upton's Naturals Bacon), cut into bite-size pieces

1 large leek, cleaned and cut into half-moons

¼ teaspoon smoked paprika

4 to 6 Roma or Campari tomatoes, quartered or sliced

Bring a large pot of salted water to a boil and prepare the pasta following the instructions on the package. Drain and set aside.

While the pasta is cooking, make the cheez sauce: In a saucepan, melt the vegan margarine over medium heat. Once the margarine begins to bubble, whisk in the flour until the mixture forms a saturated paste, then whisk in the boiling water, soy sauce, garlic, onion powder, mustard, turmeric, and sage. Continue whisking until all the ingredients are completely blended, then reduce the heat to maintain a simmer.

Gradually whisk in the nutritional yeast until it has been completely incorporated and the sauce is creamy. Give the sauce a taste test, then mix in small amounts of the vegan liquid smoke, salt, and pepper until you like the flavor. Cover the sauce and remove it from the heat.

Assemble the mac and cheez: In a cast-iron skillet, heat the olive oil over medium

(continued)

heat. Toss in the tempeh bacon, sliced leeks, and paprika and cook for about 1 minute, then flip with a spatula to make sure the tempeh bacon and leeks brown evenly.

Once the pasta is cooked, the sauce is prepared, and the tempeh bacon is lightly crispy, gently mix them all together in a large bowl. Fold in the tomatoes until all the ingredients are completely mixed. Serve warm.

You can use any leftover nutritional yeast to make:

Vegan Gyros on page 219

Rustic Pesto and Heirloom Tomato Tart on page 117

Roasted Pear, Walnut, and Brussels Sprout Tacos on page 197

Blackstrap Vegan Bangers and Mash with Onion Gravy on page 125

Rosemary Chicklins and Dumplins Stew on page 127

Caldo Verde—Portuguese Soup on page 93

Tofu Vindaloo

We live in Brooklyn: home of more quality ethnic cuisines than any one person could ever eat in a lifetime. Most cuisines offer several options for vegans, ranging from traditional bean burritos and avocado sushi to Senegalese tofu dishes. We have quite a few good Indian restaurants that deliver— so when we made the choice to stop ordering takeout, Indian food was one of the first things we started to miss. This recipe is actually left over from when we lived in Virginia and good Indian food was something we had to make for ourselves. We haven't been to India yet, so I can't say this is an authentic vindaloo recipe. But I can promise it's good by Brooklyn standards. Plus, it has peas, and I love peas.

I recommend a nice root beer to go with it, too. It seems like an odd combo, but I really like it.

MAKES 2 TO 4 SERVINGS   **$2.25 PER SERVING**

Olive oil cooking spray

1 (16-ounce) package extra-firm tofu, drained and cut into cubes

Sauce

¼ cup olive oil, plus more as needed

1 tablespoon ginger paste

¼ cup tomato paste

4 cloves garlic, minced

1½ teaspoons ground cardamom

1 teaspoon ground coriander

2 teaspoons ground cumin

¼ teaspoon ground turmeric

¼ teaspoon onion powder

½ teaspoon ground mustard seed

1 to 2 teaspoons cayenne pepper (more or less, depending on how hot you like it)

1½ teaspoons ground cinnamon

½ teaspoon smoked paprika

½ large sweet onion, chopped

½ cup frozen peas

½ cup cooked cut green beans

3 Campari tomatoes, quartered

2 cups brown rice, cooked

Spray a cast-iron skillet with a heavy coating of olive oil cooking spray and set it over medium heat. Carefully place your tofu pieces in the skillet so they don't overlap or touch too much. Brown the tofu for 3 to 5 minutes or until the edges are a very light golden brown, then flip with a metal spatula and brown the other side. If any edges stick, use the metal spatula to scrape them off—they'll make crunchy, yummy bits that will be delicious in your curry.

(continued)

Meanwhile, make the sauce: Whisk together the olive oil, ginger paste, tomato paste, garlic, cardamom, coriander, cumin, turmeric, onion powder, mustard seed, cayenne, cinnamon, and paprika until creamy.

After you've flipped the tofu once, pour the sauce over the tofu in the hot skillet and reduce the heat to low. Toss in the onion and use a spatula to mix all the ingredients together. Simmer until the onion is tender, stirring occasionally. If the sauce reduces while it simmers, you can add a little bit of water and more oil, 1 teaspoon at a time, until you are happy with the consistency. Once the onions are tender, mix in the peas, green beans, and tomatoes and cook for 5 minutes.

Serve hot over rice.

CARDAMOM

You might already have some neglected cardamom hanging out on your spice rack. There are a lot of different kinds, but the most common is ground green cardamom. It's a multitalented spice that goes with everything from turmeric to vanilla. If you're looking for other recipes in which to use cardamom, we recommend you check out the Spiced Pear Cupcakes with Maple Frosting on page 256, Mezze Platter on page 294, or White Wedding Cupcakes on page 310.

Roasted Pear, Walnut, and Brussels Sprout Tacos

This recipe admittedly sounds weird, but sometimes it's the weirdest songs that need to be sung. That's a saying right? It's a great dinner recipe that's sweet and nutty, like the lead in a romantic comedy. Make this taco your new dream date.

MAKES 4 TO 6 TACOS   **$1.17 PER SERVING**

- 2 tablespoons olive oil
- 1 tablespoon soy sauce or Bragg's Liquid Aminos
- 3 tablespoons nutritional yeast
- 2 teaspoons whole wheat flour
- ¼ teaspoon ground black pepper
- Pinch of cayenne pepper
- Pinch of ground cumin

- 2 ripe Bartlett pears, cored and thinly sliced (keep as much pear juice as you can)
- ½ pound Brussels sprouts, trimmed and halved or quartered if large
- ½ cup raw walnut halves
- 4 to 6 (8-inch) flour tortillas
- ¼ cup chopped fresh cilantro leaves
- Sriracha or Thai chili sauce, for drizzling

Preheat the oven to 400°F.

In a large bowl, whisk together the olive oil, soy sauce, nutritional yeast, flour, black pepper, cayenne, cumin, and any pear juice left from cutting up the pears. Add the Brussels sprouts, walnuts, and pear slices and gently toss with a large spoon until lightly coated, without breaking up the pears.

Pour the mixture into a shallow baking dish and use a spatula to spread it out into a thick, even layer.

Bake for 10 minutes. Remove from the oven, flip with a spatula, and bake for another 5 to 10 minutes, or until the Brussels sprouts are tender.

While the filling is baking, warm the tortillas.

Serve the tacos warm, with a few pinches of fresh cilantro and a drizzle of hot sauce over the top.

WALNUTS

We all know walnuts are good for us. In fact, walnuts are one of the healthiest nuts you can add to your vegan diet—they're a great source of omega-3 fatty acids, which can improve your cholesterol. By adding a few walnuts to your salads, breads, cookies, and pastas, you can get all the omega-3s you need without having to eat meat. We recommend you try Betty's Wartime Walnut Burger on page 189, the Kale Caesar Salad on page 78, the Cookie Pizza on page 276, or the Carrot Cake Cookies on page 282.

Sesame and Soy Marinated Mushroom Steaks

We're taking back the portobello mushroom cap "steak": the most stereotypical of all vegan dinners. This recipe will show you how to make this senior citizen of a vegan dish into something so special and delicious that even your not-yet-vegan friends will be impressed.

MAKES 2 TO 4 SERVINGS   **$1.18 PER SERVING**

- ⅓ cup soy sauce or Bragg's Liquid Aminos
- 2 tablespoons white wine
- 2 teaspoons ginger paste
- 3 tablespoons sesame oil
- 3 tablespoons raw sesame seeds
- 2 tablespoons chopped fresh parsley
- 2 green onions, diced
- 1 clove garlic, minced
- 2 to 4 portobello mushroom caps, cleaned
- Olive oil cooking spray
- 4 lime wedges

In a food processor, combine the soy sauce, white wine, ginger paste, sesame oil, sesame seeds, parsley, green onions, and garlic and process until smooth. Place the mushrooms gill-side up in a shallow dish and pour the soy and sesame marinade over the top. Move the mushrooms around a little so they are covered in the marinade, but do not flip them. Set aside to marinate for 1 hour.

Spray your favorite cast-iron skillet with a heavy coating of olive oil cooking spray and set it over medium heat. We recommend using a cast-iron grill pan to get clean sear lines; this will also keep the mushrooms from absorbing too much oil while cooking. Carefully place the mushrooms gill-side up in the skillet and brown them for 5 minutes. Then very carefully flip them with a spatula and brown the second side for 3 minutes. Flip them again and cook for another 2 to 3 minutes. If you're using

a grill pan, rotate the mushrooms 90 degrees before placing the mushroom caps back on the grill, to get nice crisscrossed grill marks.

Use a fork to gently poke the center of the mushroom to see if it's tender. Once it is, you're good to go. Remove from the heat and place on a dish. Don't leave the mushrooms in the pan; they'll burn or get oily.

Serve hot with lime wedges.

> *You can use any leftover ginger paste to make:*
>
> Simple Korean Kimchi BBQ Burgers on page 187
>
> Jerk "Chicken" Pasta Salad on page 98
>
> Thai Vegan Chicken Slaw on page 69
>
> Tom Kha Gai—Spicy Coconut Soup on page 89

Meatless Mondays

These days, when we think of Meatless Mondays, we think of Paul McCartney and Gwyneth Paltrow talking about the health benefits and environmental impact of eating less meat. But there was a time when going meatless wasn't just a choice—it was our patriotic duty.

In 1917, Woodrow Wilson and the United States Food Administration (USFA) first launched Meatless Mondays as a way to help the World War I war effort and send food to parts of France and Belgium where people were starving due to shipping disruptions. With the slogan "Food Will Win This War!" they were hoping to inspire the home front to reduce the amount of meat in their meals so resources like gasoline, water, and labor used to produce meat and dairy products could be used to the benefit of the war effort instead. USFA printed thousands of recipe books and promotional materials to get the population on board—with, sadly, only mild success.

Voluntary rationing just didn't work during World War I. So when, on the morning of the attack on Pearl Harbor, people flooded their grocers to buy up staples, Washington realized they needed a national institutionalized rationing system. Meat wasn't the only item to be rationed—sugar, gasoline, and even panty hose would be itemized and dispersed to the public in limited quantities. The water and fuel used to produce these items was a drain on an economy that now had to build airplanes and tanks to fight the fascists. Homemakers had no choice but to embrace these new limitations, and cookbooks that illustrated creative ways to make more from less were bestsellers.

These books included some of the very first recipes for veggie burgers, lentil meatloafs, and garbanzo bean cutlets. They proudly sung the virtues of "mock meats" while acknowledging that their audience was learning a whole new way of looking at their kitchens. Honestly, a lot of these recipes sound pretty terrible, and most require an egg or cheese to bind them. There's one in particular that claims you can make a "steak" using just cornflakes, an egg, and some ketchup.

Betty Crocker had already established "herself" as being a reliable source for homemaking tips, having held our hands through the Great Depression. As World War II began, Betty's radio shows became more patriotic and embraced this new rationing system as not just a duty, but as a fun challenge. Her book/leaflet *Your Share*, published in 1943, contains numerous recipes for vegetable-focused casseroles and vegetarian meals featuring homemade mock meats. They still relied heavily on dairy products and eggs, but what else can you expect from a book that outlines seven food groups...the seventh being butter. Not kidding.

These days, Meatless Mondays is an international public health awareness program that strives to educate the public on the links between factory farming, meat production, and climate change, as well as the numerous health benefits that come from adopting a meat-free diet. Everyone from Al Gore to numerous celebrity chefs have endorsed this program as a positive force for good and a huge step in the right direction in fighting obesity, heart disease, and apocalyptic environmental destruction.

Pasta with Asparagus and Green Onion Pesto

Oh, glorious springtime, when the trees in Brooklyn fill with blooming bubblegum-colored flowers and brilliant-red tulips line the streets of Manhattan. It's also when the produce section gets a face-lift. Little water-filled tubs of asparagus and piles of locally grown leafy greens are just some of our many springtime perks. I mean, when was the last time you were like, "Man, I wish I'd eaten fewer green vegetables today"? Never. No one does that. Even the quarter-pounder-with-bacon-and-fries types know in their hearts that they aren't being kept alive by the strawberry milkshake they get on the side. This recipe does a great job of combining asparagus, zinc-packed pumpkin seeds, superfood spinach, and green onions into a creamy pesto sauce that is a bit spicy but mostly dreamy!

MAKES 4 TO 6 SERVINGS $1.09 PER SERVING

. . . .

1 (16-ounce) package small to medium shaped pasta

8 to 10 asparagus spears, cut diagonally into 2 to 3 pieces about 3 inches long

1 (14-ounce) can garbanzo beans, drained and rinsed, or 1½ cups cooked dry garbanzo beans

Pesto

1½ cups baby spinach leaves

2 to 3 green onions

¼ cup fresh basil leaves

1 teaspoon grated lemon zest

Juice of 1 lemon

2 tablespoons olive oil

2 tablespoons white wine

1 tablespoon soy sauce or Bragg's Liquid Aminos

2 tablespoons nutritional yeast

1 teaspoon red pepper flakes

Pinch of celery seed

1 teaspoon crushed black peppercorns

1 clove garlic, minced

2 tablespoons hulled pumpkin seeds

. . . .

Bring a large pot of salted water to a boil and prepare the pasta following the instructions on the package. When the pasta shows the first signs of becoming tender, toss the asparagus and garbanzo beans in with the pasta to cook. Drain and return to the pot.

Make the pesto: In a food processor, combine the pesto ingredients, except the garlic and pumpkin seeds, and process into a thin sauce.

Using a large spoon, mix the pesto, garlic, and pumpkin seeds into the pot with the warm pasta, beans, and asparagus.

Serve hot, with some of the leftover white wine alongside.

PUMPKIN SEEDS

Pumpkin seeds are one of the less famous superfoods. This one little seed is full of protein, iron, zinc, and potassium, and can be pretty affordable if you buy them in bulk. You can toss them in smoothies, salads, and soups; grind them up and use them to thicken creamy sauces; or bake them into bread. If you're looking for other recipes in which to use your leftover pumpkin seeds, check out the Roasted Beet and Lentil Salad on page 73 or the Pan-Seared Corn and Quinoa Salad on page 76. Just make sure you buy your pumpkin seeds hulled (with the thick, white outer shell removed) so you can do more with them.

Angel Hair Pasta with Garlic and Rosemary Mushrooms

There was a trend in the 1930s and '40s of writing recipes that involved a simple and straightforward base recipe, then offered three or four different ways to personalize it. Cakes could be cupcakes with different frosting combos. A giant ham could be basted and baked a few different ways, with rings of pineapple across the top or rows of cloves stuck into it like a pincushion. This recipe is a tribute to those clever multitasking recipes. This simple pasta dish with garlic and rosemary sautéed mushrooms is lovely on its own, but you can also add any seasonal vegetable of your choice to the mushroom sauté and have a different dish every three months. Just adjust the olive oil so that all your vegetables get coated. It's like five-plus recipes in one.

MAKES 4 TO 6 SERVINGS   **$1.23 PER SERVING**

. . . .

1 (1-pound) package angel hair pasta

2 tablespoons olive oil

¾ cup white wine

2 tablespoons vegan Parmesan cheese or nutritional yeast, plus more to sprinkle over the top

3 cloves garlic, minced

6 or 7 white or baby portobello mushrooms, sliced

1 tablespoon crushed dried rosemary

1 tablespoon drained capers

1½ teaspoons crushed black peppercorns

Sea salt and ground black pepper

Red pepper flakes, for sprinkling

. . . .

Bring a large pot of salted water to a boil and prepare the pasta following the directions on the package.

While the pasta cooks, in your deepest skillet or saucepan, heat the oil over medium heat. Toss in the white wine, vegan Parmesan, garlic, mushrooms, rosemary, capers, and crushed pepper. Cook until the mushrooms are tender.

Drain the pasta and add it to the skillet a little bit at a time, ensuring that all the pasta gets completely coated in hot oil before adding more.

Reduce the heat to low and cook the pasta and mushrooms, tossing occasionally, for 3 minutes. Give the pasta a taste test and add salt and ground pepper as needed.

Serve hot, with some vegan Parmesan and red pepper flakes sprinkled over the top.

You can use any leftover mushrooms to make:

Smoky Butternut Squash Scramble on page 57

Chickpea à la King Skillet on page 123

Tuesday Night Dinner on page 203

Irish Stout Stew on page 157

Primavera Pizza on page 240

Tuesday Night Dinner

Every year, I help my friend Michelle Schwegmann from the Herbivore Clothing Company sell T-shirts at the N.Y. Vegetarian Festival, and every year, I get to meet some pretty awesome folks. In 2013, Michelle introduced me to Dan and Nicole, the adorable couple who run Upton's Naturals. We hadn't used many Upton's products in the past because they were hard to find in our area, but that's changed recently—and boy, are we glad it has. Every time I get a chance to try some Upton's, I half faint from joy. You remember those old Bugs Bunny cartoons when he falls in love and little hearts float up from his chest and his eyes get all swirly? That's Upton's and me. It's firm, flavorful, and versatile enough to work perfectly in a ton of different recipes, including this one. But honestly, this recipe can showcase any vegan Italian sausage, and is easy and fast enough that you can make it, eat it, and have your dishes done in time to watch Supernatural in your pj's.

MAKES 2 TO 4 SERVINGS   **$2.86 PER SERVING**

- 1 (1-pound) package whole wheat penne
- 1 tablespoon olive oil
- 1 cup diced defrosted vegan Italian sausage (we recommend Upton's Italian Seitan, Tofurky Italian Sausage, or Field Roast Italian Sausage)
- 5 Campari or Roma tomatoes, halved
- 5 white mushrooms or baby bella mushrooms, halved
- 1 cup chopped raw spinach leaves
- 2 cloves garlic, minced
- ½ cup red wine
- 1 teaspoon garlic powder
- ¼ teaspoon onion powder
- ¼ cup fresh basil leaves
- 2 teaspoons dried oregano
- 1 teaspoon Italian seasoning
- ¼ teaspoon red pepper flakes
- Vegan Parmesan cheese or nutritional yeast, for topping

Bring a large pot of salted water to a boil and prepare the pasta following the instructions on the package.

While the pasta is cooking, in your deepest saucepan, skillet, or Dutch oven, heat the olive oil over medium heat. Toss in the vegan Italian sausage and cook, flipping occasionally, until the sausage begins to brown. Add all the remaining ingredients except the vegan Parmesan and cook, mixing gently without squishing the tomatoes.

Drain the pasta. Once the spinach and basil begin to wilt, toss in ⅓ cup of the pasta, mix it in, then add another ⅓ cup pasta. Continue adding and mixing the pasta until you've added it all.

(continued)

You'll know dinner is ready when the tomatoes are tender, the greens are wilted, and the pasta is coated.

Serve hot, with some vegan Parmesan sprinkled on top.

You can use any leftover fresh basil leaves to make:

Ribollita Soup on page 103

Tuscan Eggplant and White Bean Sandwiches on page 110

Rustic Pesto and Heirloom Tomato Tart on page 117

Spinach and Broccoli Stuffed Shells on page 205

DIY Marinara Sauce on page 226

Fresh Herb and Heirloom Tomato Salad on page 304

Spinach and Broccoli Stuffed Shells

These stuffed shells are a great dinner choice when you're craving ravioli but don't feel like the hassle. They capture the spirit of stuffed pasta, without the headache of tracking down vegan ones or rolling out pasta dough. They're easy, tasty, and fancy enough that you can feel like a proper adult serving them at a dinner party. This recipe is potluck-tested and approved.

MAKES 4 TO 6 SERVINGS   **$1.68 PER SERVING**

18 large pasta shells, uncooked

2 cups raw spinach, chopped very small

2 cups raw broccoli florets, chopped very small

½ cup cooked or canned cannellini beans

¼ cup fresh basil leaves

¼ cup nutritional yeast

½ cup white wine

1 clove garlic, minced

1 (24-ounce) jar of your favorite marinara sauce or 3 cups DIY Marinara Sauce on page 226

1 tomato, diced

1 teaspoon dried oregano

¼ teaspoon garlic powder

½ cup shredded vegan mozzarella (we recommend Daiya)

Preheat the oven to 350°F.

Bring a large pot of salted water to a boil and prepare the pasta shells following the directions on the package. Drain and set aside.

In a large bowl, toss together the spinach, broccoli, beans, and basil.

In a small bowl, whisk together the nutritional yeast, wine, and garlic, then add the mixture to the bowl with the vegetables and toss to combine. Set the vegetable filling aside.

In a medium bowl, mix the marinara sauce with the diced tomato, oregano, and garlic powder.

Spread 1 cup of the marinara mixture in a 2-quart glass baking dish. Fill each cooked shell with 2 tablespoons of the vegetable filling and place them side by side in the dish. Pour the remaining marinara mixture over the shells and sprinkle the vegan mozzarella evenly over the top.

Bake the shells for 20 to 30 minutes, until the vegan cheese has melted.

> *You can use any leftover vegan mozzarella to make:*
>
> Lasagna Sandwiches featuring Italian Tempeh Sausage on page 107
>
> Hermes' Pizza on page 221
>
> Pocket Calzones on page 228
>
> Vegan Cheese Party Pizza on page 278

Beet "Boudin" Balls with Garlic Aioli

These beet-based vegan sausage balls combine everything we love about Cajun cooking, without any of the secrecy surrounding the ingredients used to make those meat-based sausages. While the mystery might be gone, we don't think you'll miss it, because honestly, these little guys are damn good.

MAKES 4 TO 6 SERVINGS   **$1.56 PER SERVING**

Beet "Boudin" Balls

2 small or medium beets, roasted

1 (14-ounce) can garbanzo beans, drained and rinsed, or 3 cups cooked dry garbanzo beans

1 cup brown rice, cooked

2 tablespoons ground flaxseed

1 tablespoon tomato paste

1 tablespoon smoked paprika

2 tablespoons soy sauce or Bragg's Liquid Aminos

1 teaspoon vegan Worcestershire sauce

1 to 2 teaspoons hot sauce (more or less, depending on how hot you like it)

Dash of vegan liquid smoke

½ red onion, minced

3 cloves garlic, minced

4 tablespoons olive oil, you may need more for frying

½ cup vegan beef broth or vegetable broth (we recommend Better Than Bouillon)

¼ cup vital wheat gluten

¾ cup bread crumbs

1½ teaspoons garlic powder

¼ teaspoon crushed black peppercorns

Pinch of cayenne pepper

Garlic Aioli

1 cup vegan mayonnaise (we recommend Vegenaise or Just Mayo)

2 cloves garlic, minced

2 tablespoons lemon juice

1 teaspoon Dijon mustard

1 teaspoon garlic powder

1 green onion, diced

1 tablespoon chopped fresh parsley

Pinch of celery seed

Pinch of ground black pepper

Preheat the oven to 350 degrees.

Make the beet "boudin" balls: In a food processor, puree the roasted beets and garbanzo beans and transfer to a large bowl. Use a large spoon to stir in the brown rice, flaxseed, tomato paste, paprika, soy sauce, vegan Worcestershire sauce, hot sauce to taste, and vegan liquid smoke. Stir in the red onion and garlic, then mix in 2 tablespoons of the olive oil and the broth. Once everything is blended, use your hands to mix in the vital wheat gluten, sprinkling it in a little bit at a time, then mixing it in with your hands before adding a little more. You'll eventually have a loose, wet dough. We recommend wearing plastic gloves or sandwich bags on your hands to prevent any staining.

Pour the bread crumbs into a shallow bowl and use a whisk to mix in the garlic powder, black pepper, and cayenne.

Use your hands to form the dough into firm balls smaller than your palm. Roll the balls in the bread crumbs until completely coated.

Place your balls on a foil lined cookie sheet. Once your balls are all formed, put them in the oven to bake for 20 minutes.

In a cast-iron skillet or frying pan, heat the remaining 2 tablespoons olive oil over medium heat. Working in batches, very carefully fry the breaded "boudin" balls in the skillet. Use a spatula to roll the balls in the hot oil so they brown evenly. Add more oil a tablespoon at a time when needed.

Once the "boudin" balls are brown and crispy, transfer them to a paper towel–lined plate to soak up any extra oil.

Make the garlic aioli: When the last "boudin" balls make it into the skillet, toss all the aioli ingredients in a bowl and blend with an electric handheld mixer until smooth.

Serve the beet "boudin" balls hot with some garlic aioli drizzled over the top or in a bowl on the side for dipping.

BEETS

Beets are so good for us. They're full of potassium, fiber, iron, beta-carotene, and folic acid. Yeah, they'll turn your teeth and hands pink, but who doesn't like a little blush? If you're wondering what to do with the rest of your bunch of beets, we recommend you bake them into some chips using the Sweet Beet Mix recipe on page 113, or make the Roasted Beet and Lentil Salad on page 73. If you happened to buy your beets with the greens intact, don't throw those out! You can use them as a substitute for almost any kind of leafy green in pestos, salads, pilafs, and quiches.

Chipotle Chicken Chilaquiles

Chilaquiles is a classic Mexican dish created to use up leftover tortillas, chilies, shredded chicken, and cheese. Ours obviously uses vegan chicken and cheese, but the spirit of this almost effortless dish remains the same.

MAKES 4 TO 6 SERVINGS $1.85 PER SERVING

1 (28-ounce) can whole tomatoes

2 chipotle chilies in adobo sauce

1½ tablespoons olive oil

1 red onion, diced

3 cloves garlic, minced

1½ cups vegan chicken broth or vegetable broth (we recommend Better Than Bouillon)

½ cup frozen corn

1 teaspoon ground cumin

1 cup chopped defrosted vegan chicken (we recommend Beyond Meat Chicken-Free Strips or Gardein Chick'n Scallopini)

Sea salt and crushed black peppercorns to taste

2 cups tortilla chips

⅓ cup shredded vegan cheddar or pepper Jack cheese (we recommend Daiya)

¼ cup vegan sour cream

⅓ cup fresh cilantro leaves

In a food processor, blend the tomatoes and chipotles in adobo until smooth. Add 1 to 2 peppers depending on how hot you like it.

In your deepest cast-iron skillet, heat the olive oil over medium heat. Add the onion and garlic and cook until the onion starts to become tender. Pour in the pureed tomato mixture and reduce the heat to maintain a simmer. Stir the sauce continuously until it begins to thicken. Stir in the vegan broth, corn, cumin, and vegan chicken and simmer for 3 minutes. (If you're using Beyond Meat, just toss it in, but if you're using Gardein, fry it up in a little olive oil first to give it a crispy skin and keep it from getting soggy.)

Remove the sauce from the heat, give it a taste test, then add salt and pepper as needed. Keep in mind that the tortilla chips have salt on them, so when you add them to your sauce, they'll make it saltier.

Gently stir the tortilla chips into the sauce, ensuring that they are well coated. Top with the vegan cheese and sour cream, then sprinkle with cilantro.

Serve immediately so the chips don't get too soft.

VEGAN SOUR CREAM

Good news: Not only do we live in a world with a few different vegan sour cream brands on the market, but you can usually find one in any grocery store for about the same price as dairy-based sour cream. If you're wondering what to do with the rest of your vegan sour cream, we recommend blending 1 tablespoon at a time into mashed potatoes to make them creamy. You can also serve it with a pot of Green Shchi—Russian Cabbage Soup (page 92), or with a batch of Bubbie's Polish Potato Pierogies (page 137). You can also use it to make the Vegan Bacon Ranch Dipping Sauce that goes with the Buffalo Cauliflower Calzones on page 165.

Pan-Seared Tofu with Arugula, Capers, and Tomatoes

While some nights of experimental cooking were more successful than others, this recipe stood out as a perfect date-night dinner. It's quick enough to make while talking about the highlights of your day, and easy enough that you can actually listen to what the other person is saying while you make it.

MAKES 4 SERVINGS   **$2.00 PER SERVING**

. . . .

¾ cup white wine

½ teaspoon onion powder

2 tablespoons olive oil

1 (16-ounce) package extra-firm tofu, drained and cut into 10 to 12 thin slices

1 cup cherry tomatoes, halved

¼ teaspoon red pepper flakes

2 cups arugula leaves

¼ cup vegan margarine

Juice of 1 lemon

1 tablespoon plus 2 teaspoons drained capers

2 cloves garlic, minced

Sea salt and crushed black peppercorns

. . . .

In your largest cast-iron skillet, heat the white wine, onion powder, and olive oil over medium heat. When the wine begins to bubble, carefully add the tofu slices, tomatoes, and red pepper flakes. Cook for 2 minutes before flipping the tofu so it browns on the other side.

Arrange ½ cup of the arugula on each plate like a little nest. Once the tofu and tomatoes have a nice sear on both sides, place an equal amount in the arugula nest on each plate.

In the hot skillet, melt the margarine. Whisk in the lemon juice, capers, and garlic. Give the sauce a quick taste test, then add salt or pepper as needed. Drizzle the lemon and caper sauce over the tofu right before serving.

CHAPTER 6

NO MORE LEFTOVERS!

You don't save money on food you throw out. According to the EPA, the average American household throws away 25 percent of the food they prepare. On a global scale, between 1.3 and 1.6 billion tons of food are estimated to be wasted each year. Most of this food ends up in landfills that are one of the leading sources of methane—a greenhouse gas. So long story short: Eat your leftovers and save the world (and your money). This chapter will show you how to reinvent leftovers you can enjoy all week.

> Slow-Cooker Tempeh Jambalaya 213

> Leftover Recipe: The Big
Easy Tacos with Garlic Aioli 214

> Leftover Recipe: Corn Beignets 215

> Pumpkin Curry Soup 216

> Leftover Recipe: Pumpkin and
Spinach Orzo 217

> Leftover Recipe: Savory Pumpkin
Biscuits 218

> Vegan Gyros 219

> Leftover Recipe: Hermes' Pizza 221

> Leftover Recipe: Hestia's Biscuits . . . 222

> Pomegranate and Brown
Rice Salad 223

> Leftover Recipe: Pomegranate and
Brown Rice Cabbage Rolls 224

> Leftover Recipe: Turkish Stuffed
Peppers 225

> Pasta with DIY Marinara. 226

> Leftover Recipe: Pan-Fried Artichoke
Hearts and Sauce 227

> Leftover Recipe: Pocket Calzones . . . 228

> Hungarian Goulash Stew 229

> Leftover Recipe: Budapest
Burgers 230

> Leftover Recipe: Mayday
Noodles. 231

> Simple Spanish Rice Bake. 232

> Leftover Recipe: Vegan Pollo
Gumbo. 233

> Leftover Recipe: Spanish
Rice Quiche 234

> Aloo Saag 235

> Leftover Recipe: Curry Spinach
and Potato Biscuits. 236

> Leftover Recipe: Indian
Takeout Pizza 237

> Cauliflower Fettuccine Alfredo 238

> Leftover Recipe: Pasta Primavera . . . 239

> Leftover Recipe: Primavera
Pizza 240

> Cowboy Quinoa Chili. 241

> Leftover Recipe: Roasted Red
Pepper Tamale Pie 242

> Leftover Recipe: Cahoots Quiche. . . . 243

> Leftover Recipe: Not-cho
Everyday Chili Dogs. 244

Slow-Cooker Tempeh Jambalaya

This is a Creole jambalaya with some Spanish paella influences. It's pretty spicy, so you may want to adjust the ingredients a bit if you're not a fan of heat.

MAKES 6 TO 8 SERVINGS   **$1.03 PER SERVING**

2 tablespoons olive oil

1 (8-ounce) package tempeh, crumbled

1 red onion, diced

3 cloves garlic, minced

1 (15-ounce) can kidney beans, drained and rinsed, or 1½ cups cooked dry kidney beans

1 green bell pepper, diced

4 stalks celery, diced

1 (28-ounce) can diced tomatoes

2 teaspoons soy sauce or Bragg's Liquid Aminos

1 teaspoon Italian seasoning

½ teaspoon smoked paprika

½ teaspoon fennel seed

1 tablespoon Tony Chachere's Original Creole Seasoning

1 teaspoon dried thyme

1¼ teaspoons dried oregano

1 to 2 teaspoons hot sauce (more or less depending on how hot you like it)

Dash of vegan liquid smoke

2½ cups vegan chicken broth or vegetable broth (more, if your rice is stubborn)

2 cups brown rice, uncooked

¼ cup of your favorite beer

Sea salt and crushed black peppercorns to taste

Fresh parsley, for sprinkling

In a cast iron skillet, heat your oil over a medium heat. Once your oil is hot, toss your crumbled tempeh, onion, and 1 clove of garlic in and brown while flipping with a spatula so your ingredients cook evenly.

Toss all the ingredients except the tempeh mix and parsley in your slow cooker and set it to low. Cook for 1 hour or until the rice is tender. If, after an hour, the rice isn't tender but the broth has been completely absorbed, add more broth, 2 tablespoons at a time, until the rice is tender.

Once your rice is tender, mix in your tempeh mix and give your jambalaya a taste test and add any needed salt and pepper.

Serve hot with a few pinches of parsley sprinkled over the top.

Leftover Recipe: The Big Easy Tacos with Garlic Aioli

MAKES 4 TO 6 SERVINGS   **$0.71 PER SERVING**

1 tablespoon olive oil

1½ cups leftover Slow-Cooker Tempeh Jambalaya (page 213)

2 tablespoons frozen corn

4 to 6 hard taco shells

1 avocado, halved, pitted, and sliced

¼ cup fresh cilantro leaves, chopped

1 recipe Garlic Aioli (page 206)

1 lemon, cut into wedges

To reheat the jambalaya, heat the olive oil in a cast-iron skillet over medium heat. Toss in the jambalaya and the corn. Use a spatula to flip the jambalaya a few times to make sure it reheats evenly.

Heat the taco shells following the instructions on the package.

Once the jambalaya is hot, you're ready to eat! Fill the taco shells with a scoop of jambalaya, avocado slices, and cilantro leaves. Drizzle aioli and squeeze a lime wedge over the top and BAM-O, or something like that.

Leftover Recipe: Corn Beignets

MAKES 6 TO 8 SERVINGS   **$0.81 PER SERVING**

Vegetable oil, for frying

1 cup soy milk

1 tablespoon applesauce

2 teaspoons egg replacer powder (we recommend Ener-G or Beyond Eggs)

2 ears raw corn

1 cup leftover Slow-Cooker Tempeh Jambalaya (page 213)

1½ cups all-purpose flour

2 green onions, diced

2 tablespoons minced fresh parsley

1 recipe Garlic Aioli (page 206)

1 to 2 lemons, cut into wedges

Fill a soup pot or Dutch oven halfway with oil and heat the oil over high heat. If you have a deep fryer thermometer, check your oil. Once it's around 350 degrees you're ready to deep fry your beignets.

In a small bowl, whisk together the soy milk, applesauce, and egg replacer.

One at a time, cut the kernels off the cob. Hold the cob narrow side up. Using a sharp knife, start at the narrow end and cut down, slicing all the kernels off the cob. Continue doing this till you've cut all the kernels off both cobs.

In a large bowl, mix together the jambalaya, corn kernels, flour, green onions, and parsley with a large spoon until blended. Then mix in the applesauce mixture.

Using a large spoon, scoop out about 2 tablespoons of the batter and drop it into the hot oil. Drop in a few fritters at a time and use a slotted spoon to keep the fritters from touching in the pot as they fry. Once the fritters rise to the top and are a golden brown, use the slotted spoon to remove them from the oil and transfer them to a paper towel–lined plate to soak up any extra oil. Repeat until you've used all the batter.

Serve the fritters in a basket with a bowl of aioli alongside for dipping and lemon wedges to squeeze over the top.

Pumpkin Curry Soup

You never regret the soups you make—only the Pumpkin Curry Soup you don't.

MAKES 8 TO 10 SERVINGS   **$0.89 PER SERVING**

¼ cup olive oil

2 red onions, diced

4 cloves garlic, minced

6 cups vegan chicken broth or vegetable broth (we recommend Better Than Bouillon)

1 cup coconut milk, from a carton, not a can

2 (15-ounce) cans pumpkin puree

3 tablespoons soy sauce or Bragg's Liquid Aminos

2 tablespoons curry powder

1 teaspoon crushed black peppercorns, plus a little more to sprinkle over the top

2 teaspoons ground cumin

½ teaspoon ground turmeric

1 teaspoon smoked paprika

Bread, for serving

In your largest Dutch oven or stew pot, heat the olive oil over medium heat. Add the onions and cook until they are tender, then add the remaining ingredients and reduce the heat to maintain a simmer.

Cook the soup, stirring occasionally, until it begins to bubble, then remove it from the heat and use an immersion blender or food processor to puree the soup until creamy and smooth.

Serve hot, with bread and extra crushed pepper over the top.

Leftover Recipe: Pumpkin and Spinach Orzo

MAKES 6 TO 8 SERVINGS **$0.37 PER SERVING**

3 cups leftover Pumpkin Curry Soup (page 216)

1⅓ cups orzo, uncooked

2 tablespoons nutritional yeast

¼ cup coconut milk, from a carton, not a can

1 teaspoon rubbed sage

1 teaspoon soy sauce or Bragg's Liquid Aminos

¼ cup chopped fresh parsley

1 cup baby spinach leaves

Crushed black peppercorns or red pepper flakes, for sprinkling

In your largest Dutch oven or stew pot, use a large spoon to mix all the ingredients except spinach and pepper. Bring to a boil over medium heat, stirring, then reduce the heat to maintain a simmer. Simmer until the orzo is tender, then stir in the spinach.

Serve hot, with pinches of crushed pepper over the top.

Leftover Recipe: Savory Pumpkin Biscuits

MAKES 8 TO 10 SERVINGS $0.15 PER SERVING

2¼ cups all-purpose flour, plus more for dusting

1 tablespoon baking powder

½ teaspoon garlic powder

¼ teaspoon sea salt

½ cup vegan margarine, cold, plus more for serving

1 cup leftover Pumpkin Curry Soup (page 216)

Preheat the oven to 400°F. Line a cookie sheet with parchment paper.

In a large bowl, whisk together the flour, baking powder, garlic powder, and salt. Then, using a pastry blender, mix in the cold vegan margarine until the dough resembles pea-size pebbles. Mix in the soup using an electric handheld mixer fitted with a bread hook attachment.

Once the dough is mixed, use floured hands to move the dough to a floured surface and carefully knead it into a large mound. Don't handle the dough too much; it will melt the margarine and the biscuits won't be as flaky.

Using a floured rolling pin, roll the dough out until it is a little less than 1 inch thick. Use a biscuit cutter or the top of a pint glass to cut out 10 to 12 biscuits. Place the cut biscuits on the lined cookie sheet.

Bake for 15 to 20 minutes, or until golden brown.

Serve warm with margarine.

Vegan Gyros

Many years from now, wouldn't you be willing to trade all your sandwiches for one chance, just one chance, to come back here and make these vegan gyros? Some might think going vegan will take away our delicious food. But this recipe will make it so that while we may give up our meat, they'll never take... OUR GYROS!

MAKES 6 TO 8 GYROS   **$2.21 PER SERVING**

Gyro Meat

8 cups vegan beef broth or vegetable broth (we recommend Better Than Bouillon)

3 cups vital wheat gluten

2 tablespoons garbanzo bean flour

2 tablespoons nutritional yeast

1½ teaspoons dried marjoram

1 teaspoon rubbed sage

2 pinches of celery seed

1 teaspoon dried thyme

½ teaspoon dill seed

½ teaspoon crushed black peppercorns

½ teaspoon smoked paprika

1 teaspoon garlic powder

3 tablespoons soy sauce or Bragg's Liquid Aminos

3 dashes of vegan liquid smoke

1 teaspoon vegan Worcestershire sauce

¼ cup olive oil

Tzatziki Sauce

½ cucumber, chopped

½ (16-ounce) package silken tofu, drained

2 tablespoons soy sauce or Bragg's Liquid Aminos

2 tablespoons fresh dill

1 teaspoon fresh mint, chopped

Grated zest and juice of 1 lemon

2 cloves garlic, minced

To Assemble

6 to 8 Greek-style pocketless pita breads

1 to 2 small tomatoes, sliced

1 cucumber, sliced

Make the gyro meat: Bring 6 cups of the vegan beef broth to a boil in your largest Dutch oven.

In a large bowl, whisk together the vital wheat gluten, garbanzo bean flour, nutritional yeast, marjoram, sage, celery seed, thyme, dill seed, pepper, paprika, and garlic powder.

In a separate bowl, whisk together the remaining 2 cups vegan beef broth, 2 tablespoons of the soy sauce, 2 dashes of the vegan liquid smoke, and the vegan

(continued)

Worcestershire sauce. Pour the wet ingredients into the dry ingredients and mix with your hands. Knead the dough a few times to get a light springy dough.

Form the dough into a loaf shape, then roll it tightly in cheesecloth or a clean kitchen towel that you hate, because it'll never be the same again.

Very carefully place the roast in the boiling vegan beef broth, reduce the heat to maintain a simmer, and simmer for 30 minutes.

Preheat the oven to 400°F.

In a small bowl, whisk together the olive oil, remaining 1 tablespoon soy sauce, and remaining dash of vegan liquid smoke.

Transfer the roast to an oven-safe dish and carefully unwrap it. Brush it with the olive oil mixture, then bake for 20 minutes. Every 8 to 10 minutes, check the roast and brush it with more olive oil.

Once the roast is dark golden brown, remove it from the oven and let cool for 5 minutes.

Meanwhile, make the tzatziki sauce: In a food processor, combine all the tzatziki ingredients and blend until smooth and creamy.

Assemble the gyros: Warm the pita bread before serving. Using a serrated knife, thinly slice 4 to 6 pieces of gyro meat per sandwich. Make the sandwiches with slices of gyro meat, tomato, and cucumber, then drizzle the tzatziki over the top. Fold the pita bread like a taco, and enjoy!

Kalí̱ sas óre̱xi̱!

Leftover Recipe: Hermes' Pizza

MAKES 1 PIZZA   **$0.76 PER SERVING**

1 pizza crust, store-bought or homemade (see page 159)

Cornmeal, for dusting

2 Roma or Campari tomatoes, sliced

⅓ cup thinly sliced leftover Vegan Gyro Meat (page 219)

⅓ cup baby spinach leaves

¾ cup shredded vegan mozzarella (we recommend Daiya)

2 tablespoons diced red onion

¼ cup pitted kalamata olives

1 or 2 pepperoncinis, sliced

Oregano, red pepper flakes, and vegan Parmesan cheese, for sprinkling

Preheat the oven to 425°F.

Roll out the pizza crust following the directions on page 159, or follow the instructions on the package.

Dust a pizza stone or baking pan with cornmeal. Carefully move the pizza crust to the stone or baking pan. Reshape it into a circle if necessary.

Arrange the tomato slices evenly over the pizza crust, leaving 1 inch exposed along the edge for the crust. Arrange the slices of gyro meat and spinach leaves over the tomato slices. Spread a few pinches of vegan cheese over the pizza. Add the red onions, olives, and pepperoncini slices, then sprinkle the remaining vegan cheese evenly over the top.

Bake for 8 to 10 minutes or until the crust is golden and the vegan cheese has melted.

Serve with oregano, red pepper flakes, and vegan Parmesan cheese sprinkled over the top.

Leftover Recipe: Hestia's Biscuits

MAKES 12 BISCUITS   **$0.49 PER SERVING**

Biscuit Batter

Olive oil cooking spray

1 cup vegan Bisquick mix

1 cup almond milk

2 tablespoons ground flaxseed

2 teaspoons egg replacer powder (we recommend Ener-G or Beyond Eggs)

¼ teaspoon red pepper flakes

¼ teaspoon crushed rosemary

¼ teaspoon dried oregano

¼ teaspoon dried marjoram

¼ teaspoon crushed black peppercorns

¼ teaspoon nutritional yeast

¼ teaspoon garlic powder

Filling

1½ cups diced leftover Vegan Gyro Meat (page 219)

1 red bell pepper, diced

½ red onion, diced

2 tablespoons chopped fresh parsley

2 tablespoons chopped pitted kalamata olives

¼ cup cubed vegan feta cheese (we recommend Vegcuisine Soy Feta)

Make the biscuits: Preheat the oven to 375°F. Spray a 12-cup muffin tin with olive oil cooking spray.

In a large bowl, whisk together all the biscuit ingredients.

Make the filling: In a large bowl, toss all the filling ingredients together with a large spoon.

Place 1 tablespoon of the biscuit batter in each well of the muffin tin. Then place 1 tablespoon of the filling into the center and top with 2 to 3 tablespoons of the batter.

Once all the cups are full, bake the biscuits for 20 to 30 minutes or until a bamboo skewer inserted into the center of a muffin comes out clean. These biscuits stay pretty pale, so don't wait for them to get golden.

Let the muffins cool slightly on a rack, then serve warm. We recommend serving with some fresh tomatoes and pickled peppers or olives on the side. You know, like the Greeks do.

Pomegranate and Brown Rice Salad

You can enjoy this recipe as a warm pilaf or a cold rice salad. It's one of those perfect Sunday night recipes that goes great with some Pan-Seared Black Tea and Pepper Tofu (page 186), can make a great lunch all week, or can have an encore in one of the recipes that follow on pages 224 and 225.

MAKES 6 TO 8 SERVINGS   **$1.32 PER SERVING**

1 cup brown rice, cooked

1 (15-ounce) can lentils, drained and rinsed, or 1½ cups cooked dry lentils

2 cloves garlic, minced

Grated zest and juice of 1 lemon

½ red onion, diced

¼ cup chopped fresh parsley

2 tablespoons fresh mint leaves, chopped

⅓ cup roasted red peppers in oil

½ cup raw walnuts, crushed

2 tablespoons soy sauce or Bragg's Liquid Aminos

Seeds from 1 pomegranate

Pita chips, for serving

In a large bowl, mix all the ingredients with a large spoon. Refrigerate for 20 minutes before enjoying with some rosewater lemonade and some pita chips.

Leftover Recipe: Pomegranate and Brown Rice Cabbage Rolls

MAKES 6 TO 8 SERVINGS   **$0.54 PER SERVING**

- 1 head cabbage, cored and with ugly outer leaves removed
- 1½ cups leftover Pomegranate and Brown Rice Salad (page 223)
- 1 (24-ounce) jar marinara sauce, or 3 cups DIY Marinara Sauce (see page 226)
- ½ teaspoon red pepper flakes

Preheat the oven to 350°F.

Bring a pot of water to a rolling boil, then carefully place the cabbage in the water, with the open (cored) end down. The leaves will slowly become more flexible and loosen themselves from the rest of the head. As this happens, carefully remove the leaves and place them on a plate.

Once the leaves are cool enough to handle, cut away the stiff stem in the center to make rolling easier.

Use a spoon to fill each cabbage leaf with rice salad. Fold the sides of the leaf over the rice, then roll the leaf forward, creating a fat cigar shape. If the leaf splits, just grab another and roll it over the first. You'll have extra leaves, so don't worry. Repeat this process 6 to 8 times until you have a nice little row of cabbage rolls ready for the oven.

Pour half of the marinara sauce into your favorite casserole dish. Place the rolls into the marinara sauce, seam-side down, and pour the remaining sauce over the top, then sprinkle with some red pepper flakes.

Bake for 15 to 20 minutes.

Serve warm, with lots of the sauce from the dish.

Leftover Recipe: Turkish Stuffed Peppers

MAKES 4 SERVINGS

$1.92 PER SERVING

4 large green bell peppers

2 vegan Italian sausages, diced (we recommend Tofurky Italian sausages, Field Roast Italian sausages, or 1 package Upton's Naturals Italian Seitan)

1 cup leftover Pomegranate and Brown Rice Salad (page 223)

1 (24-ounce) jar marinara sauce, or 3 cups DIY Marinara Sauce (see page 226)

Cut off the tops of the peppers (keep the top with the stem) and carefully clean out all the seeds, white ribs, and other stuff. If you've ever cleaned out a pumpkin for a jack-o'-lantern, it's a lot like that.

In a large bowl, mix the vegan sausage and rice salad together with a large spoon. Fill the peppers with the rice mixture.

Pour half the marinara sauce into a casserole dish, then take the filled peppers and stand them in the dish, filled-side up. Using a large spoon, pour a little sauce over each stuffed pepper, then replace the pepper cap.

Bake for 20 minutes, or until the peppers are tender.

Pasta with DIY Marinara

I am a woman with few talents. I'm a decent card player and I can ice skate. I make a pretty good vegan cheesecake, and I know how to make traditional Italian marinara from scratch. It is undeniably faster to use a jar of premade sauce, but there's something downright soulful about making your own marinara for the people you love.

MAKES 4 TO 6 SERVINGS   **$2.34 PER SERVING**

DIY Marinara Sauce

3 tablespoons olive oil

1 red onion, diced

3 cloves garlic, minced

3½ pounds Roma tomatoes, chopped

⅓ cup red wine

⅓ cup water

2 tablespoons soy sauce or Bragg's Liquid Aminos

½ teaspoon celery seed

2½ teaspoons dried oregano

¼ teaspoon dried marjoram

1 teaspoon crushed rosemary

¼ teaspoon crushed black peppercorns, plus more as needed

Sea salt to taste

Pasta

1 (16-ounce) package spaghetti

½ cup whole fresh basil leaves

1 (15-ounce) can artichoke hearts, drained (optional)

Vegan Parmesan cheese, for sprinkling

Make the marinara sauce: In your largest Dutch oven or stew pot, heat the oil over medium heat. Toss in the onion and garlic and use a large spoon to toss them a few times to make sure they get a light coating of hot oil. Once the onion is tender, toss in the chopped tomatoes and stir to combine. Pour the wine and water into the pot while stirring continuously. Reduce the heat to maintain a simmer, cover, and simmer for 4 to 5 minutes. Then stir in the soy sauce, celery seed, oregano, marjoram, rosemary, pepper, and salt to taste. Cover and let simmer, stirring occasionally, for another hour. Use a large spoon to mash any large pieces of tomato that are still hanging around. If you have a lot of larger pieces, use an immersion blender or food processor to puree the sauce. Give the sauce a taste test and add salt and pepper as needed.

Make the pasta: While the sauce is simmering, bring a large pot of water to a boil and prepare the pasta following the instructions on the package.

Right before serving, stir in the basil leaves and artichoke hearts.

Serve the pasta hot, with marinara sauce ladled over the top and sprinkled with vegan Parmesan cheese.

Leftover Recipe: Pan-Fried Artichoke Hearts and Sauce

MAKES 4 TO 6 SERVINGS   **$1.20 PER SERVING**

1 teaspoon onion powder

1 teaspoon garlic powder

1 teaspoon crushed black peppercorns

1½ cups all-purpose flour

¼ cup garbanzo bean flour

2 tablespoons baking powder

¼ cup nutritional yeast

3 tablespoons Dijon mustard

⅓ cup vegan chicken broth or vegetable broth (we recommend Better Than Bouillon)

⅓ cup olive oil

2 (15-ounce) cans quartered artichoke hearts, drained

2 tablespoons chopped fresh parsley leaves

1 cup leftover DIY Marinara Sauce (page 226), chilled

In a deep bowl, mix together the onion powder, garlic powder, pepper, all-purpose flour, garbanzo bean flour, baking powder, and nutritional yeast.

In a separate bowl, whisk together the mustard and vegan chicken broth.

Add 2 tablespoons of the flour mixture to the mustard mixture and stir.

In your deepest cast-iron skillet, heat the oil over medium heat.

Dip the artichoke hearts in the mustard batter, then coat them with the flour mixture.

Carefully drop the battered artichoke hearts into the hot oil and cook until golden brown, using a spatula to flip as needed. Transfer the fried artichoke hearts to a paper towel–lined plate to soak up any extra oil. Repeat until all the artichoke hearts are fried.

Serve hot in a basket with fresh parsley sprinkled over the top and a bowl of cold marinara sauce alongside for dipping.

Leftover Recipe: Pocket Calzones

MAKES 4 SERVINGS   **$1.69 PER SERVING**

1 pizza crust, store-bought or homemade (see page 159)

Cornmeal, for dusting

1 Roma or Campari tomato, sliced

1 cup vegan Italian sausage, crumbled (we recommend Upton's Naturals Italian Seitan or chopped Tofurky Italian Sausages)

1 tablespoon pitted kalamata olives, drained

¼ teaspoon drained capers

½ cup shredded vegan mozzarella cheese (we recommend Daiya)

2 or 3 mushrooms, sliced

1 cup leftover DIY Marinara Sauce (page 226)

Preheat the oven to 425°F.

Roll out the pizza crust following the directions on page 159, or follow the instructions on the package. Cut the dough in half, then roll each half out into a separate small round.

Dust a pizza stone or baking pan with cornmeal.

Place a few tomato slices on one half of each pizza dough round. Then sprinkle half of the vegan sausage over each round. Place the remaining tomato slices over the sausage, then sprinkle equal amounts olives, capers, vegan cheese, and mushrooms over the top. Fold the open side of each pizza round over the top and use wet fingers to seal the edges. Make sure the calzones are completely sealed, then use a spatula to carefully move them to the baking pan.

Bake for 10 minutes, or until the crust is golden brown and makes a thumping noise when you tap it.

Serve hot with some Marinara Sauce on the side for dipping.

Hungarian Goulash Stew

We first fell in love with Hungarian goulash in 2008 after a trip to Budapest. Since then, we've been inspired by this paprika-seasoned and "beefy" peasant stew, using the same flavor profile to spice up Tofurky holiday roasts and baked potatoes. This recipe will always have a place in our hearts, and remind us of those seven rainy days we spent in Hungary that were also some of the best of our lives.

MAKES 6 TO 8 SERVINGS   **$2.85 PER SERVING**

¼ cup olive oil

2 yellow onions, diced

2 cloves garlic, minced

2 cups vegan beef seitan, defrosted (we recommend Gardein Beefless Tips)

¼ cup smoked paprika

2 teaspoons dried marjoram

2 teaspoons caraway seeds

1 teaspoon ground cumin

2 tablespoons soy sauce or Bragg's Liquid Aminos

4 cups vegan beef broth or vegetable broth (we recommend Better Than Bouillon)

1 (28-ounce) can stewed tomatoes

1 large tomato, diced

2 carrots, chopped

1 parsnip, chopped

1 pound small potatoes, quartered

1 green bell pepper, chopped

2 tablespoons chopped fresh parsley

Sea salt and crushed black peppercorns to taste

In a large Dutch oven or stew pot, heat the olive oil over medium heat. Add the onions and garlic. Toss in the vegan beef and mix until completely coated in hot oil. Let the vegan beef and onions cook until the onions are tender and the vegan beef has a light, crispy skin. Move the vegan beef to a bowl and set aside.

Toss all the remaining ingredients in the pot, season with salt and black pepper, mix, cover, and bring to a boil. Reduce the heat to maintain a simmer, stirring a few times while simmering. Once the potatoes and other vegetables are tender, remove the pot from the heat and mix in the vegan beef.

Serve hot with bread and a cold beer alongside.

Leftover Recipe: Budapest Burgers

MAKES 4 SERVINGS   **$1.85 PER SERVING**

½ cup leftover Hungarian Goulash Stew
(page 229)

3 tablespoons nutritional yeast

1 tablespoon soy sauce or Bragg's Liquid
Aminos

½ teaspoon garlic powder

1 cup vital wheat gluten

1 tablespoon olive oil

4 whole wheat hamburger buns, toasted

4 slices vegan provolone slices (optional; we
recommend Daiya)

Mustard, lettuce, pickles, and other toppings

Pour the leftover Hungarian Goulash Stew into a food processor—potatoes, vegan beef, and all—and process for 30 seconds. Then pour the pureed stew into a large bowl and mix in the nutritional yeast, soy sauce, and garlic powder with a spoon.

Add half of the vital wheat gluten to the stew blend and mix it in with your hands. Then mix in the remaining half. Knead the wheat gluten into the stew blend for 1 minute. Use your hands to form the mixture into four patties about the size of your palm.

In a cast-iron skillet, heat the olive oil over medium heat. One at a time, fry up the burgers in the hot oil. Once both sides of each burger are browned, place them on the bottom half of a toasted hamburger bun and top with a slice of vegan provolone.

Set the oven to broil.

Put each burger on an oven-safe plate and broil for no more than 1 minute, until the cheese has melted and has a light golden crispiness to it.

Top the burgers with all your favorite fixings.

Leftover Recipe: Mayday Noodles

MAKES 4 TO 6 SERVINGS $0.14 PER SERVING

. . . .

½ package whole wheat bow-tie pasta

2 cups leftover Hungarian Goulash Stew
(page 229)

2 tablespoons vegan sour cream

2 green onions, diced

. . . .

Bring a large pot of salted water to a boil and prepare the pasta following the instructions on the package.

While the pasta is cooking, reheat the goulash in a saucepan over medium heat. Once it begins to bubble, reduce the heat to maintain a simmer and stir in the vegan sour cream.

Drain the pasta and serve hot with the goulash sauce and a pinch of diced green onions over the top.

Simple Spanish Rice Bake

For nearly a century, (mostly) women have been sending in tips and recipes to women's magazines and ladies' journals just for the honor of being published. Some of these mailed-in recipes introduced us to dishes now considered classics, like German Chocolate Cake, Tater Tot Pies, and Spanish Rice. In reality, Spanish rice is neither a Spanish nor a Mexican dish, but is inspired by both these international cuisines, borrowing flavor profiles and common ingredients found in both. Every so often, someone has a new take on this modern classic, but they all seem to include the same spicy tomato sauce, green bell pepper, and tender rice. We've added black beans and vegan cheese to make it a simple, complete meal that can be enjoyed as a pilaf or later as a gumbo or quiche.

MAKES 6 SERVINGS $1.24 PER SERVING

1 cup brown rice, uncooked

2 cups vegetable broth

1 large red onion, diced

1 green bell pepper, diced

⅔ cup frozen corn

1 (15-ounce) can black beans, drained and rinsed, or 1½ cups cooked dry black beans

1 jalapeño, seeded and diced (more or less, depending on how hot you like it; we added 1 teaspoon)

1 (28-ounce) can diced tomato

1½ teaspoons chili powder

1½ teaspoons ground cumin

1 tablespoon soy sauce or Bragg's Liquid Aminos

2 tablespoons chopped fresh cilantro

1 teaspoon smoked paprika

1½ teaspoons onion powder

½ cup shredded vegan cheddar cheese (we recommend Daiya)

Preheat the oven to 375°F.

In a large casserole dish, mix all the ingredients except the cheese. Sprinkle the cheese over the top.

Bake for 25 to 30 minutes, or until the rice is tender.

Leftover Recipe: Vegan Pollo Gumbo

MAKES 6 SERVINGS   **$1.23 PER SERVING**

- 1 cup vegan chicken, defrosted (we recommend Beyond Meat Chicken-Free Strips—Grilled or Gardein Chick'n Scallopini)
- 1 tablespoon olive oil
- ⅓ cup of your favorite beer
- 1 large red onion, diced
- 1 tablespoon Tony Chachere's Original Creole Seasoning
- 2 stalks celery, diced
- 1 clove garlic, minced
- 3 cups vegan chicken broth or vegetable broth (we recommend Better Than Bouillon)

- ½ teaspoon vegan Worcestershire sauce
- ¼ teaspoon cayenne pepper
- 2 large tomatoes, diced
- ¼ teaspoon celery seed
- 1 teaspoon dried oregano
- 8 Spanish olives, pitted and sliced
- ½ teaspoon hot sauce
- 2 tablespoons chopped fresh parsley
- 1 bay leaf
- ½ cup leftover Simple Spanish Rice Bake (page 232)

Cut the vegan chicken into strips.

In a shallow dish, whisk together the olive oil, beer, red onion, and Creole seasoning. Toss in the vegan chicken and marinate for 1 minute. (If you're using Beyond Meat, we recommend letting it marinate for 10 minutes since it's a denser product.)

While the vegan chicken marinates, throw all the remaining ingredients in a large Dutch oven or large stew pot and bring to a boil over medium heat, stirring occasionally.

When the gumbo begins to bubble, reduce the heat to maintain a simmer.

While the gumbo is simmering, toss the vegan chicken mixture in your deepest cast-iron skillet or frying pan and heat over medium heat. Use a spatula to flip the vegan chicken a few times to make sure it browns evenly. Once the vegan chicken has crispy edges and the onions are tender, toss the contents of the skillet into the gumbo.

Serve the gumbo hot with some cold beer.

Leftover Recipe: Spanish Rice Quiche

MAKES 6 SERVINGS   **$1.88 PER SERVING**

- 1 vegan piecrust, store-bought or homemade (see page 262)
- 1 (16-ounce) package extra-firm tofu, drained
- ¼ cup nutritional yeast
- 1 tablespoon olive oil
- 1 clove garlic, minced
- 1 teaspoon onion powder
- 1 teaspoon garlic powder
- 1 teaspoon ground turmeric
- 1½ teaspoons ground cumin
- 1 teaspoon smoked paprika
- ¼ teaspoon vegan liquid smoke
- 1 tablespoon soy sauce or Bragg's Liquid Aminos
- ¼ cup shredded vegan cheddar cheese (we recommend Daiya)
- 3 or 4 Spanish olives, pitted and sliced
- ½ teaspoon capers, drained
- 1 tablespoon sliced almonds
- ¼ cup leftover Simple Spanish Rice Bake (page 232)
- 1 Roma or Campari tomato, sliced

Preheat the oven to 375°F.

Either prepare the piecrust following the directions on page 262, or completely defrost the premade crust.

In a food processor, combine the tofu, nutritional yeast, olive oil, garlic, onion powder, garlic powder, turmeric, cumin, paprika, vegan liquid smoke, soy sauce, and vegan cheese and process into a smooth paste.

Transfer the tofu mixture to a large bowl and add the olives, capers, almonds, and Spanish rice. Gently stir the mixture with a large spoon to combine. Fill the piecrust with the tofu and rice mixture, using a rubber spatula to get everything out of the bowl and to smooth the top flat. Then gently press the tomato slices into the quiche.

Bake for 20 to 30 minutes, or until the quiche is a light golden brown and the tofu mixture is firm.

Aloo Saag

Coming to terms with eating in more often can be tough when you don't know how to make your take-out favorites. That's why we made it a mission to figure out how to make this spicy Indian meal that combines potatoes and spinach with a curry sauce served over rice. If you've never had it before, that description might not do this delicious dish justice. Just try it—you'll like it.

MAKES 4 TO 6 SERVINGS   **$1.00 PER SERVING**

1 pound potatoes, peeled and cubed

⅓ cup olive oil

1 red onion, diced

2 teaspoons ginger paste

3 cloves garlic, minced

2 cups baby spinach leaves

1½ teaspoons soy sauce or Bragg's Liquid Aminos

2 teaspoons ground cumin

2 teaspoons curry powder

½ teaspoon ground turmeric

2 teaspoons ground coriander

¼ teaspoon cayenne pepper

Pinch of ground cinnamon

5 tablespoons water

½ cup coconut milk, from a carton, not a can

1 tablespoon vegan margarine

2 cups brown rice, cooked

Bring a large pot of water to a boil over high heat. Once it begins to bubble, toss in the cubed potatoes and cook for 5 minutes. You don't want the potatoes to be completely boiled, just partially. Drain and set the potatoes aside.

In your largest cast-iron skillet or frying pan, heat the oil over medium heat. Toss in the onion and ginger paste and sauté for 3 minutes. Add the garlic and spinach and sauté for another 2 minutes.

Mix in the soy sauce, cumin, curry powder, turmeric, coriander, cayenne pepper, and cinnamon. Reduce the heat to maintain a low simmer.

Mix in about 3 tablespoons water to create a light sauce. Add the potatoes and sauté for 3 minutes. Then mix another 2 tablespoons water, the coconut milk, and the vegan margarine. Cook, stirring continuously, for another 5 minutes, then remove the skillet from the heat. The mixture will thicken a bit once you take it off the heat.

Serve hot over brown rice.

Leftover Recipe: Curry Spinach and Potato Biscuits

MAKES A DOZEN BISCUITS   **$0.09 PER SERVING**

Olive oil cooking spray

Biscuit Batter

1 cup vegan Bisquick mix

1 cup almond milk

2 tablespoons ground flaxseed

2 teaspoons egg replacer powder (we recommend Ener-G or Beyond Eggs)

¼ teaspoon nutritional yeast

1 teaspoon curry powder

¼ teaspoon garlic powder

1½ cups leftover Aloo Saag (page 235)

Preheat the oven to 375°F. Spray a 12-cup muffin tin with olive oil cooking spray.

Make the biscuit batter: Using a whisk, mix all the biscuit ingredients in a large bowl until you have a creamy batter.

If you have any big pieces of potato in your leftover aloo saag, use a fork to break them into small pieces.

Place 1 tablespoon of the biscuit batter in each well of the muffin tin. Place 1 tablespoon of the aloo saag into the center of each cup and top with 2 to 3 tablespoons of biscuit batter.

Bake the biscuits for 20 to 30 minutes, or until a bamboo skewer inserted into the center comes out clean. Let cool slightly on a rack, but serve warm.

Leftover Recipe: Indian Takeout Pizza

MAKES 1 PIZZA   **$0.34 PER SERVING**

1 pizza crust, store-bought or homemade (see page 159)

Cornmeal, for dusting

1½ cups leftover Aloo Saag (page 235)

½ red bell pepper, diced

¼ cup fresh cilantro leaves, chopped

Preheat the oven to 425°F.

Roll out the pizza crust following the directions on page 159, or follow the instructions on the package.

Dust a pizza stone or baking pan with cornmeal.

Place the pizza crust on the pizza stone or pan. Use a spoon to spread the aloo saag over the crust, leaving 1 inch exposed along the edge for the crust. Sprinkle the bell pepper evenly over the aloo saag.

Bake for 8 to 10 minutes, or until the crust is golden.

Top with cilantro and serve.

Cauliflower Fettuccine Alfredo

Looking through rationing leaflets and cookbooks from World War II, some recurring themes emerge. One of these is trying to get Americans to fall in love with a vegetable-heavy diet. Page after page features dancing carrots and potatoes with big smiles, singing the praises of the vitamins and minerals they contain. One vegetable you see over and over again is cauliflower. Creamed into soup and sauces, roasted with olive oil, baked au gratin...there is hardly a dish cauliflower can't make. This vegan Alfredo sauce is inspired by a few different cauliflower sauces we found, with the heavy cream and butter replaced with healthier and kinder ingredients. We also added white wine, artichoke hearts, and nutritional yeast to get more of that signature Alfredo flavor.

MAKES 8 TO 10 SERVINGS   **$1.07 PER SERVING**

1 to 2 (16-ounce) packages fettuccine*

1 head cauliflower, cut into florets

2 tablespoons vegan margarine

3 cloves garlic, minced

1 (15-ounce) can artichoke hearts, drained

1½ teaspoons garlic powder

1½ teaspoons sea salt, plus more as needed

1 teaspoon crushed black peppercorns, plus more as needed

1 tablespoon lemon juice

¼ cup white wine

1 cup soy milk

½ cup nutritional yeast

¼ teaspoon ground mustard seeds

Bring a large pot of salted water to a boil and prepare the pasta following the instructions on the package.

Bring a large Dutch oven or stew pot of water to a boil. Add the cauliflower florets and cook until tender, then drain. Pat dry with a paper towel to remove any extra water.

In the same pot, melt the vegan margarine over medium heat. Toss in the garlic and cook for 10 seconds, then add the cauliflower and the artichoke hearts, using a spatula to toss the vegetables so they get a light coating of the melted vegan margarine. Add the garlic powder, salt, pepper, lemon juice, white wine, soy milk, nutritional yeast, and mustard seeds and bring to a boil over medium heat. Once it begins to bubble, reduce the heat to low. Simmer for 5 minutes, then remove from the heat.

Use an immersion blender or food processor to blend the sauce until creamy. Give it a taste test and add salt and pepper as needed.

Serve the sauce hot over the pasta and sprinkled with some crushed pepper.

---

* In my experience, one package of pasta will feed four or five people, so if you're planning on feeding eight to ten people, make two packages. If you're just feeding your family or significant other, make less, then use the leftover sauce in one of the leftover recipes on pages 239 and 240.

Leftover Recipe: Pasta Primavera

MAKES 4 SERVINGS $1.14 PER SERVING

1 (16-ounce) package whole wheat decorative formed pasta (we recommend using medium shells, bow ties, or capunti)

½ batch leftover Cauliflower Alfredo Sauce (page 238)

1 tablespoon white wine (you may need a little more for the sauce)

1 tablespoon olive oil

1 clove garlic, minced

3 small carrots, cut into thin coins

6 to 8 asparagus spears, trimmed and cut into 3-inch pieces

½ red bell pepper, sliced

5 mushrooms, sliced

Crushed black peppercorns, for sprinkling

Bring a large pot of salted water to a boil and prepare the pasta according to the instructions on the package.

Reheat the leftover Alfredo sauce in a large saucepan over low heat until it starts to bubble. If the sauce reduces too much, add a little white wine, 1 tablespoon at a time, to thin it.

In a deep cast-iron skillet or wok, heat the olive oil over medium heat. Add the garlic, then toss in the carrots and cook until tender. Add the remaining vegetables and the white wine. Cook, tossing with a spatula so the vegetables cook evenly, until the vegetables are tender.

Transfer the contents of the skillet into the pan with the Alfredo sauce. Let the vegetables cook in the sauce for another 5 minutes before serving.

Use a ladle to pour the sauce and vegetables over the pasta and sprinkle a few pinches of crushed pepper over the top. You're ready to eat.

Leftover Recipe: Primavera Pizza

MAKES 1 PIZZA $0.62 PER SERVING

1 pizza crust, store-bought or homemade (see page 159)

Cornmeal, for dusting

¼ cup roasted red peppers in oil

3 mushrooms, sliced

5 or 6 asparagus spears

1 tablespoon drained capers

¼ to ⅓ cup leftover Cauliflower Alfredo Sauce (page 238)

½ cup shredded vegan mozzarella (we recommend Daiya)

A few pinches of vegan Parmesan cheese

Crushed black peppercorns, for sprinkling

Preheat the oven to 425°F.

Roll out the pizza crust following the directions on page 159, or follow the instructions on the package.

Dust a pizza stone or baking pan with cornmeal.

Place the pizza crust on the stone or baking pan. Reshape it back into a circle if necessary.

Lay the roasted red peppers over the pizza crust leaving an exposed ½ inch around the edge (they shouldn't overlap), leaving 1 inch uncovered around the edge for the crust. Brush the crust with some of the oil in which the peppers were packed. Then arrange the mushroom slices and asparagus spears over the red peppers. Sprinkle some capers over the top.

Drizzle the leftover Alfredo sauce over the veggies. Sprinkle vegan mozzarella over that, then add a few pinches of vegan Parmesan.

Bake for 5 to 8 minutes, or until the crust is a light golden brown.

Toss a few pinches of crushed pepper over the top before you serve.

Cowboy Quinoa Chili

Quinoa is the perfect ingredient with which to make a vegan chili "con carne." It's full of protein and has a texture similar to ground meat, but without all that pesky fat, cholesterol, and, you know, those poor cows. This is a chili for cow-hugging fellers.

MAKES 4 TO 6 SERVINGS   **$1.48 PER SERVING**

1 cup quinoa, uncooked

2 tablespoons olive oil

1 red onion, chopped

3 cloves garlic, minced

1 (28-ounce) can diced tomatoes

1 (6-ounce) can tomato paste

1 (12-ounce) bottle of your favorite beer

2 tablespoons chili powder

2½ cups vegan beef broth or vegetable broth (we recommend Better Than Bouillon)

½ teaspoon onion powder

2 teaspoons ground cumin

⅓ cup frozen corn

1 jalapeño, seeded and diced (more or less, depending on how hot you like it; we used 1 teaspoon)

1 (15-ounce) can kidney beans, drained and rinsed, or 1½ cups cooked dry kidney beans

Fresh cilantro leaves, for sprinkling

Unless you're using prewashed quinoa, you need to wash your quinoa with warm water to remove this stuff called saponin. Place the quinoa in a large bowl full of water. Let the quinoa soak for about 30 minutes, then swish it around with a whisk so the saponin comes off. Drain the quinoa in a fine-mesh sieve, rinse, and set aside.

Heat your deepest cast-iron skillet over medium heat. Add the wet quinoa to the skillet and use a spatula to spread it out and flip it a few times to toast evenly.

Once the water evaporates, the quinoa starts to "pop" and toast, and a light nutty fragrance fills the air, you're ready. Set the toasted quinoa aside in a large bowl.

In your largest Dutch oven or stew pot, heat the olive oil over medium heat. Toss in the onion and garlic and cook until the onion is tender. Toss in the quinoa and the remaining ingredients except the cilantro, and simmer until the quinoa is soft.

Serve hot, with some fresh cilantro over the top.

Leftover Recipe: Roasted Red Pepper Tamale Pie

MAKES 4 TO 6 SERVINGS   **$0.95 PER SERVING**

3 cups leftover Cowboy Quinoa Chili (page 241)

¼ cup roasted red peppers in oil

2 tablespoons fresh cilantro leaves, chopped

¼ cup shredded vegan cheddar cheese (we recommend Daiya)

1¼ cups cornmeal

½ teaspoon ground cumin

¼ teaspoon crushed black peppercorns

2 tablespoons nutritional yeast

1 cup vegetable broth (we recommend Better Than Bouillon)

¼ cup vegan margarine, melted

2 dashes of Tabasco or hot sauce

1 teaspoon soy sauce or Bragg's Liquid Aminos

Preheat the oven to 400°F.

Ladle the chili into your deepest, largest cast-iron skillet. Use a rubber spatula to spread the chili into an even layer. Lay the roasted red peppers over the top, then sprinkle evenly with the vegan cheese.

In a large bowl, whisk together the cornmeal, cumin, black pepper, and nutritional yeast.

In a separate bowl, whisk together the melted vegan margarine, hot sauce, and soy sauce. Pour the vegan margarine mixture over the cornmeal mixture and whisk together until creamy.

Pour the cornmeal mixture over the chili. Use a rubber spatula to smooth the cornmeal mixture into an even layer.

Bake for 40 minutes or until the cornmeal topping is golden brown and firm.

Let cool for 10 minutes before serving so the topping can get firm and the chili doesn't resemble lava. Serve warm with a few pinches of fresh cilantro over the top.

Leftover Recipe: Cahoots Quiche

MAKES 4 TO 6 SERVINGS   **$1.48 PER SERVING**

- 1 vegan piecrust, store-bought or homemade (see page 262)
- 1 (8-ounce) package extra-firm tofu, drained
- 3 tablespoons shredded vegan cheddar cheese (we recommend Daiya)
- 1 tablespoon soy milk
- 3 tablespoons nutritional yeast
- 1 tablespoon cornstarch
- ½ teaspoon onion powder
- ¼ teaspoon ground turmeric
- 2 teaspoons soy sauce or Bragg's Liquid Aminos
- ¼ teaspoon smoked paprika
- 1 tablespoon olive oil
- ¾ cup leftover Cowboy Quinoa Chili (page 241)
- Salsa, guacamole, and sliced black olives, for serving

Preheat the oven to 425°F.

Prepare your vegan piecrust following the directions on the package or according to the recipe on page 262.

In a food processor, combine the tofu, 2 tablespoons of the vegan cheese, the soy milk, nutritional yeast, cornstarch, onion powder, turmeric, soy sauce, paprika, and olive oil and process into a smooth paste. Transfer the tofu mixture to a large bowl and mix in the chili.

Pour the filling into the crust and use a rubber spatula to press it into an even layer. Make sure there are no cracks, peaks, or spaces between the filling and crust. Sprinkle the remaining 1 tablespoon vegan cheese over the top. Bake for 10 minutes, then reduce the oven temperature to 325°F and bake for another 30 minutes.

Serve warm, with salsa, guacamole, and sliced black olives on top.

Leftover Recipe: Not-cho Everyday Chili Dogs

MAKES 4 SERVINGS   **$1.83 PER SERVING**

- 1 (12-ounce) can of your favorite beer
- 2 tablespoons olive oil
- 4 vegan sausages (we recommend Tofurky Beer Brats or Field Roast Sausages)
- 1 cup leftover Cowboy Quinoa Chili (page 241)

- 4 hot dog buns, toasted
- ½ cup broken tortilla chips
- ¼ cup shredded vegan cheddar cheese (we recommend Daiya)
- ¼ cup fresh cilantro leaves, chopped

In a cast-iron skillet, heat the beer and the olive oil over medium heat. Once the mixture begins to bubble, carefully place the sausages in the skillet. Use a spatula to roll the sausages in the beer while they cook.

Meanwhile, reheat the chili in a saucepan over low heat, stirring continuously.

Once the chili is hot and the sausages are seared, use a fork to place a sausage in each bun. Use a spoon to pile on the chili, then add a few pinches of tortilla chips, vegan cheese, and fresh cilantro. Then you're ready to go!

CHAPTER 7

SPECIAL OCCASIONS

"A party without cake is just a meeting."
—Julia Child

Try as you might to streamline your life into a fine-tuned machine that is the epitome of productivity and thriftiness, you're not a robot (we hope)—sometimes you need sweet treats for dinner parties and cookies for office potlucks. Life is full of special events and occasions that fill your life with joy and memories—but can also cost a lot of money.

In this chapter, we've included baking tips and modernized recipes from the Great Depression and World War II to help you keep your special occasions special, as well as party and potluck tips so you can still entertain. We've even included a DIY wedding section with recipes, ideas, and tips inspired by the impromptu weddings of World War II to help you personalize, enjoy, and afford "The Happiest Day of Your Life."

SWEET TREATS

> Cuba Libre Cake 248

> Salted Caramel Skillet Cake 250

> Orange Spice USO Cake 252

> Pink Lemonade Cupcakes 254

> Spiced Pear Cupcakes with
  Maple Frosting 256

> Snowball Cupcakes 258

> S'mores Cookie Bars 260

> Vegan Piecrust 262

> Olive Oil Piecrust 263

> Peanut Butter Cup Pie 264

> Savannah Pecan Pie 266

> Humble Apple Pie 267

> Mango Coconut Pie 269

> Chai Spice Cheesecake 272

> Monkey Bread 274

> Cookie Pizza 276

> Fresh Fruit Pizza 277

> Vegan Cheese Party Pizza 278

> Molasses Crinkle Cookies 280

> Chocolate Chip and Banana
  Brownie Cookies 281

> Carrot Cake Cookies 282

> Lemon and Lavender Cookies 284

POTLUCKS AND PARTIES

> Cruelty-Free Crawfish Boil 286

> Butternut Squash and Beer Poutine
  Party 288

> Baked Potato Bar 290

> Mezze Platter 292

> Slow-Cooker Taco Party 296

THE DIY WEDDING

> Strawberry Salad 300

> Chilled Cucumber and
  Avocado Soup 301

> Veg Manchurian 302

> Fresh Herb and Heirloom
  Tomato Salad 304

> Honeydew Skewers 305

> Chocolate Strawberry
  Cheesecake Cups 306

> Lavender and Vanilla
  Cupcakes 308

> White Wedding Cupcakes 310

Sweet Treats

A vegan cannot live on kale alone.

Imagine the faces of your child's classmates if, for her birthday, you brought in little cups of kale instead of cookies. It probably wouldn't convince the next generation of eaters that being vegan is totally fun and normal. I mean it might, but it seems unlikely.

We created this section for those times when you need something sweet for an office pot-luck or baby shower, when you want to add a treat to your kid's lunch box to help distract them from the other lunch boxes full of Lunchables and soda, or when you just want to have some fun. Being vegan on a budget can be challenging in a world full of excess and dollar menus. There's no need to give up celebrating the highlights of our lives, or to miss out on an opportunity to show off how fabulous being vegan can be.

These treats are for the special occasions that call for more than kale—the ones that call for frosting.

Cuba Libre Cake

Rum and Coke is supposedly the second most popular alcoholic drink in the world—and not just among sorority girls. Just combine white rum, cola, and a squeeze of lime and you're done. Yet for a simple drink, its origin story is somewhat mysterious.

Many say the first rum and Cokes were enjoyed by the Rough Riders in Cuba during the Spanish-American War—hence "Cuba Libre," which means "Free Cuba" in Spanish. But others point out that cola drinks weren't available in Cuba until a few years after the war ended in 1898. Some argue the drink was invented in the Havana Club in the early 1920s to draw in American tourists. Whatever the truth may be, whoever invented it did the world a great favor, because the distinct combination of sweet cola and rum with a hint of lime is exceptionally refreshing and fun—especially in cake form. It's the perfect birthday cake for a grown-up!

If alcohol isn't your thing, you can always substitute 1 tablespoon of rum extract for the rum in this recipe. The flavor and texture won't be exactly the same, but still close enough.

MAKES 1 CAKE   **$0.60 PER SERVING**

Cake

Baking spray

2 cups all-purpose flour

1¼ teaspoons baking powder

½ teaspoon baking soda

¼ teaspoon sea salt

1 teaspoon cocoa powder

¼ teaspoon ground allspice

1¼ cups granulated sugar

½ cup vegan margarine

Grated zest and juice of 1 lime

1 tablespoon applesauce

1 tablespoon ground flaxseed

1 cup cola soda

¼ cup rum (we recommend using white rum)

1 teaspoon vanilla extract

Cola Frosting

3 cups powdered sugar

⅓ cup vegan margarine

2 to 3 tablespoons cola soda

Grated zest of 1 lime

Make the cake: Preheat the oven to 350°F. Spray a 9 x 13-inch cake pan with baking spray.

In a large bowl, whisk together the flour, baking powder, baking soda, salt, cocoa powder, and allspice.

In your largest bowl, combine the granulated sugar, vegan margarine, lime zest, lime juice, applesauce, and flaxseed and beat with an electric handheld mixer until creamy. Gradually mix in the flour until the batter is fluffy and smooth. Mix in the cola, rum, and vanilla. The batter will start to look broken, but don't worry, it'll all work out.

Pour the batter into the prepared cake pan and smooth it out with a rubber spatula to make it as flat and even as possible.

Bake for 15 to 20 minutes or until a bamboo skewer inserted into the center comes out clean.

Let cool in the pan for 5 minutes, then put a large serving plate over the pan and invert the pan and the plate together, flipping the cake out onto the plate. Tap the edge of the pan with a wooden spoon to make sure the cake comes out cleanly. Let the cake cool to room temperature before frosting.

While the cake is cooling, make the cola frosting: In a large bowl, beat together the powdered sugar and the vegan margarine using an electric handheld mixer on low speed. Blend in 1 tablespoon of cola at a time until the frosting is the consistency and flavor you want.

Fill a cake-decorating gun or pastry bag with the frosting and cover the top of the cake with peaked dollops of frosting the size of a quarter. They should be touching and should cover the entire top of the cake with frosting.

Sprinkle the lime zest over the top to add a little color and flavor before serving.

Salted Caramel Skillet Cake

Skillet cakes became popular during the Great Depression when many homes couldn't afford proper heating, so families would gather in the kitchen around the stove to stay warm. The cast-iron skillet would retain heat long after it'd been removed from the oven to help keep the cake warm until it could be served.

MAKES 1 CAKE   **$0.38 PER SERVING**

Coconut oil, for coating the skillet

2 cups cake flour

1 cup plus 2 tablespoons packed brown sugar

½ cup vegan margarine

2 tablespoons applesauce

2 teaspoons ground flaxseed

2 tablespoons whole wheat flour

1¼ teaspoons baking powder

½ teaspoon baking soda

¼ teaspoon sea salt

1 cup coconut milk, from a carton, not a can

2 tablespoons coarse sea salt, for sprinkling

Preheat the oven to 350°F. Coat a cast-iron skillet with coconut oil.

In a large bowl, blend all the cake ingredients except the coarse sea salt with an electric handheld mixer for 2 to 3 minutes, or until creamy.

Pour the cake batter into the coated skillet, then use a rubber spatula to smooth the cake into an even layer.

Bake for 20 to 30 minutes, or until the cake begins to look dry around the edges and a bamboo skewer inserted into the center comes out clean.

Sprinkle the sea salt evenly over the top and serve warm in the skillet.

COCONUT MILK

These days, it's not hard to find coconut milk in most grocery stores. In fact, you can find it in most dairy cases by the carton, or by the can in the Asian food aisle. If you haven't figured it out yet, be warned: Coconut milk in a carton is not the same as the stuff in a can.

Canned coconut milk has a higher fat content (yes, even the low-fat versions). You've probably noticed that thick white foam at the top of the can when you open it—that's the fat that'll make it thicker when mixed in. While that might seem like a bad thing, it does make canned coconut milk the perfect substitution for heavy cream, and with only half the calories. Coconut milk in the carton is more processed, but it's intended to be a beverage, so it's thinner and (normally) has a lot less fat than its canned brethren.

If you're looking at your carton of coconut milk wondering what to do with it, try baking some Spiced Pear Cupcakes with Maple Frosting (page 256) or Lavender and Vanilla Cupcakes (page 308).

Orange Spice USO Cake

The United Service Organization (USO) was founded by President Franklin D. Roosevelt in 1941 to help keep up the morale of soldiers fighting overseas. While most of us think of the USO as putting on shows featuring Bob Hope cracking jokes and the Andrews Sisters singing in harmony about the Bugle Boy from Company B, this program did so much more than entertain. One program in particular focused primarily on serving punch and inexpensive baked goods to newly enlisted men to thank them for their service. This program was led and staffed almost completely by female volunteers. African-American women volunteering in USO cake events often worked alongside white women planning similar events in their own neighborhoods, and together, they began to lay the groundwork for the desegregation of the USO. That unfortunately wouldn't officially happen until the Korean War, but it was still way ahead of many other U.S. institutions at the time. This recipe is an adaption of one of the most popular cakes served at these USO events, and, later, in the kitchens of returning soldiers, who would forever think of this cake as being a little part of home.

MAKES 1 CAKE $0.26 PER SERVING

Baking spray

1 cup granulated sugar

¼ cup olive oil

2 tablespoons applesauce

1 teaspoon ground cinnamon

Pinch of grated nutmeg

Pinch of ground black pepper

Pinch of ground allspice

½ teaspoon ground cloves

½ teaspoon sea salt

1 cup water

2 cups all-purpose flour

1 teaspoon baking soda

2 teaspoons apple cider vinegar

Grated zest and juice of 1 large orange

⅓ cup powdered sugar, for sprinkling

Preheat the oven to 350°F. Coat a Bundt pan with baking spray.

In a saucepan, combine the granulated sugar, olive oil, applesauce, cinnamon, nutmeg, pepper, allspice, cloves, salt, and water. Bring to a boil over medium heat, whisking continuously. Once the mixture begins to bubble, remove the pan from the heat.

In a large bowl, mix the flour and baking soda together. Once the sugar and spice mixture is ready, whisk it into the flour mixture. Continue to whisk the batter while you add the apple cider vinegar, orange zest, and orange juice.

Pour the cake batter into the prepared pan. Use a rubber spatula to scrape all the batter out of the bowl and to smooth the top of the cake in the pan.

Bake for 30 to 45 minutes or until a bamboo skewer inserted into the center comes out clean. (It will take more or less time depending on the size of your Bundt cake pan.)

Let cool in the pan on a wire rack for 10 minutes. Use a bamboo skewer to poke 10 to 15 holes in the cake to help it cool and release from pan.

Put a large serving plate over the pan and invert the pan and the plate together, flipping the cake out onto the plate. Before lifting the pan off, tap it a few times on the side and the top with a spoon to make sure the cake comes out cleanly.

Serve with the powdered sugar sprinkled over the top.

APPLESAUCE

During World War II, when dairy products and eggs were being rationed, bakers were forced to think creatively. People tried everything from boiled raisins to ground oats to find a way to bind their cakes without dairy or eggs while still retaining moistness. It's a struggle most vegan bakers know all too well. We've found that applesauce works best. It's an affordable ingredient, can be found at any grocery store, and can be easily substituted for eggs in almost any baking recipe. If you're looking for other recipes in which to use applesauce, try baking a Salted Caramel Skillet Cake (page 250), a batch of Cinnamon Roll Pancakes (page 32), or Pumpkin Pie Muffins (page 46).

Pink Lemonade Cupcakes

The first time I made these cupcakes was for my friend Sarah's birthday. They're pink and girlie, with a tart lemon filling, creating the perfect combination that is pink lemonade. I recommend making these into mini cupcakes, because they're even cuter that way.

MAKES 12 CUPCAKES **$0.69 PER SERVING**

Lemonade Filling

¾ cup granulated sugar

3 tablespoons cornstarch

¼ teaspoon sea salt

⅔ cup lemonade

1 tablespoon vegan margarine

Grated zest and juice of 1 lemon

Cupcakes

2¼ cups unbleached flour

1⅓ cups granulated sugar

⅔ cup vegetable shortening

1¼ cups soy milk

¼ teaspoon apple cider vinegar

1 tablespoon plus ¼ teaspoon baking powder

1 teaspoon sea salt

1 teaspoon vanilla extract

1 teaspoon lemon extract

4 tablespoons egg replacer powder (we recommend Ener-G or Beyond Eggs)

Cherry Glaze

¼ cup frozen cherries with juice, defrosted and pureed

½ cup granulated sugar

½ teaspoon agave nectar

½ teaspoon vanilla extract

⅓ cup vegetable shortening

3 to 4 cups powdered sugar

2 tablespoons cornstarch

Sprinkles, for decorating the cupcakes

Make the lemonade filling: In a saucepan, whisk together the granulated sugar, cornstarch, salt, and lemonade. Cook the filling over medium heat, whisking continuously until the filling thickens. Let the filling boil for 1 minute while you whisk, then remove it from the heat. Stir in the vegan margarine and lemon zest. Once the margarine has melted, gradually whisk in the lemon juice and whisk until smooth. Tightly cover the saucepan and refrigerate for 2 hours.

Make the cupcakes: Preheat the oven to 350°F. Line a 12-cup cupcake tin with paper liners.

In a large bowl, combine all the cupcake ingredients and blend with an electric handheld mixer for 3 minutes.

Using a ladle, fill the cupcake cups halfway. Bake for 20 minutes, or until golden on top and a bamboo skewer inserted into the center of a cupcake comes out clean.

Remove the cupcakes from the pan and let cool on a wire rack.

Make the cherry glaze: In a saucepan, whisk together the cherry puree, granulated sugar, agave nectar, and vanilla and bring to a boil over medium heat. Once the glaze begins to bubble, remove it from the heat and set aside. Let cool to room temperature.

In a large bowl, beat together the vegetable shortening, 2 cups of the powdered sugar, and the cornstarch with an electric handheld mixer until completely blended. Gradually add a few tablespoons of the cherry mixture and blend again. Add another few tablespoons and blend again. Repeat until all the cherry mixture has been incorporated. Beat in the remaining powdered sugar 1 cup at a time until you like the consistency.

Once the cupcakes have cooled to room temperature and the filling has chilled for 2 hours, you can fill your cupcakes!

To fill the cupcakes, fit your frosting gun with the longest and thinnest decorating tip. Fill the frosting gun with the lemonade filling. Very gently poke a hole in the top of each cupcake with the frosting gun and fill the center with filling. Stop when you feel the cupcake expand and you see the filling come out of the top. Repeat the process until all the cupcakes have been filled.

Take each filled cupcake and gently dip the top in the cherry glaze. Move the cupcakes back to the cooling rack. Decorate each cupcake with a few pinches of sprinkles.

Once the glaze sets, you're ready to eat!

You can use any leftover egg replacer to make:

Sloppy Joel Pie on page 171

Snowball Cupcakes on page 258

Chai Spice Cheesecake on page 272

Chocolate Strawberry Cheesecake Cups on page 306

Orange Drop Doughnuts on page 49

Corn Beignets on page 215

Spiced Pear Cupcakes with Maple Frosting

This is the perfect cupcake to bring to a "Friends-giving" potluck. You know, the ones where everyone who can't afford to go home for Thanksgiving gets together to eat way more green bean casserole and pumpkin pie than they should and to pretend they don't miss their moms. These cupcakes will help take the edge off all that.

MAKES 24 CUPCAKES　　　　　　　　　　　　　　　　**$0.29 PER SERVING**

Spiced Pear Cupcakes

2 ripe Bartlett pears, peeled, cored, and cut into chunks

1 teaspoon olive oil

½ cup packed brown sugar

¼ cup vegan margarine

2 teaspoons applesauce

½ teaspoon vanilla extract

¼ cup coconut milk, from a carton, not a can

1 cup all-purpose flour

¼ teaspoon egg replacer powder (we recommend Ener-G or Beyond Eggs)

¼ teaspoon sea salt

¾ teaspoon baking powder

¼ teaspoon baking soda

½ teaspoon ground cinnamon

½ teaspoon ground cardamom

¼ teaspoon ground ginger

¼ teaspoon ground nutmeg

Pinch of ground allspice

Maple Frosting

1 cup vegan margarine, at room temperature

3 tablespoons maple syrup

1 teaspoon vanilla extract

2½ to 3 cups powdered sugar

2 tablespoons raw sugar

1 tablespoon ground cinnamon

Make the spiced pear cupcakes: Preheat the oven to 325°F. Line two 12-cup cupcake tins with paper liners.

In your deepest cast-iron skillet, combine the pear chunks, olive oil, and brown sugar and heat over medium heat. Cook for 20 minutes, using a large spoon to mix and mash the pears as they cook into a sauce.

In a large bowl, blend the vegan margarine, applesauce, vanilla, and coconut milk until creamy. Add this mixture to the warm pear sauce and blend.

In a large bowl, whisk together the flour, egg replacer, salt, baking powder, baking soda, cinnamon, cardamom, ginger, nutmeg, and allspice. Add the pear sauce to the flour mixture and use an electric handheld mixer to blend it into a creamy batter.

Use a ladle to fill each cupcake cup three-quarters of the way with the batter. Bake for

15 to 20 minutes, or until a bamboo skewer inserted into the center of a cupcake comes out clean.

Remove the cupcakes from the pan and let cool on a wire rack.

Meanwhile, make the maple frosting: In a large bowl, blend the vegan margarine, maple syrup, vanilla, and 2 cups of the powdered sugar until smooth. Add more powdered sugar, ⅓ cup at a time, until the frosting has a fluffy consistency.

In a small bowl, mix the raw sugar and the cinnamon.

Once the cupcakes are cool, frost them with the maple frosting and top with a few pinches of the cinnamon-sugar mixture.

You can use any leftover cardamom to make:

Tofu Vindaloo on page 195

Mezze Platter on page 292

Chai Spice Cheesecake on page 272

White Wedding Cupcakes on page 310

Snowball Cupcakes

So, you might ask yourself: "Why in the world would I need a recipe for a dozen homemade snowball cupcakes when I'm trying to save money?" Here's my answer—and I'm going to be honest here, because we're friends, right?

Nobody needs baked goods.

But we want them. This recipe is for those folks who see their friends posting birthday party pictures with fancy bakery-made cupcakes that they either can't afford or don't have access to and think: "How can I make something for my significant other/best friend/child/coworker/Secret Santa designee/whoever that is just as fun as that?"

The original Hostess-brand Sno Balls have a marshmallow coating that is both too labor intensive and too expensive for this book, so we went with a coconut frosting instead. But the spirit of the snowball is there to delight the vegan eight-year-old in all of us.

MAKES 12 CUPCAKES   **$0.36 PER SERVING**

Chocolate Cakes

Baking spray

½ cup vegan margarine, at room temperature

2 cups granulated sugar

1 ripe banana

1 tablespoon applesauce

1½ cups coconut milk, from a carton, not a can

1 teaspoon vanilla extract

½ teaspoon egg replacer powder (we recommend Ener-G or Beyond Eggs)

2 cups all-purpose flour

2 teaspoons baking soda

½ teaspoon sea salt

⅓ cup cocoa powder

Coconut Topping

2 cups shredded raw coconut

2 drops red food coloring (optional)

Coconut Frosting

¼ cup coconut oil, at room temperature

2 cups powdered sugar

1 teaspoon cream of tartar

4 to 6 tablespoons coconut milk, from a carton, not a can

1 teaspoon vanilla or coconut extract

Make the chocolate cakes: Preheat the oven to 350°F. Spray a 12-cup cupcake tin with a light coating of baking spray.

In a large bowl, blend the vegan margarine, granulated sugar, banana, applesauce, coconut milk, and vanilla with an electric handheld mixer until creamy.

In your largest bowl, whisk together the egg replacer, flour, baking soda, salt, and cocoa powder. Add the margarine mixture to the flour mixture and blend into a smooth batter.

Use a ladle to fill the cupcake cups three-quarters of the way with batter. Bake for 15 to 20 minutes, or until a bamboo skewer inserted into the center of a cupcake comes out clean. Remove the cupcakes from the pan and let cool on a wire rack.

Make the coconut topping: If you're going to dye the raw coconut, do it while the cupcakes are baking. In a shallow dish, use a spatula to mix the raw coconut with the food coloring until you have baby pink shreds.

Make the coconut frosting: In a large bowl, blend together the frosting ingredients with a whisk, or use an electric handheld mixer for the fluffiest frosting.

Fit a frosting gun or pastry bag with the smallest tip and fill with the frosting.

Once the cupcakes are cool, flip them over so they are bottom-up. Then, pop the frosting gun or piping tip into the bottom of each cupcake and gently fill the center with a little frosting. Using a rubber spatula, spread the remaining frosting over the top of the cupcakes to make little white mounds.

Using your fingers, sprinkle the coconut over the frosted cupcake mounds to create fluffy coconut hills.

You can use any leftover cocoa powder to make:

Cincinnati Chili on page 177
Cuba Libre Cake on page 248
S'mores Cookie Bars on page 260
Chocolate Chip and Banana Brownie
    Cookies on page 281

S'mores Cookie Bars

Growing up, who didn't love marshmallows in their hot cocoa or Rice Krispie treats? Nowadays, there are a few brands on the market that offer completely compassionate, fluffy white marshmallows that you can bring camping for s'mores or roast over sweet potatoes.

This cookie bars recipe is a step up from your classic blondie recipe, combining a vanilla cookie with a crushed graham crackers, marshmallow, and brownie center. We used Sweet & Sara Vegan Marshmallows when we made this, but you can also use Chicago Vegan Foods Dandies to make that gooey center.

The marshmallows will be the most expensive ingredient in this recipe, but that's why we put it in the Special Occasions chapter! Treat yo'self! (Once in a while.)

MAKES 12 COOKIE SQUARES   **$1.06 PER SERVING**

Baking spray

2 cups all-purpose flour

2 teaspoons baking powder

½ teaspoon sea salt

¾ cup vegan margarine, at room temperature

1¾ cups sugar

2 tablespoons applesauce

1 tablespoon ground flaxseed

1¼ teaspoons vanilla extract

⅓ cup cocoa powder

⅓ cup soy milk or almond milk

¼ cup crushed graham crackers

¾ cup vegan marshmallows (we recommend 1 small package of Sweet & Sara Vegan Marshmallows)

¼ cup vegan chocolate chips

Preheat the oven to 350°F. Spray a heavy coating of baking spray over a 9 x 9-inch baking pan.

In one of your largest bowls, whisk together the flour, baking powder, and salt.

In a separate bowl, combine the vegan margarine, sugar, applesauce, flaxseed, and 1 teaspoon of the vanilla using a handheld electric mixer until blended. Gradually blend in the flour mixture to make a smooth vanilla batter.

In a separate bowl, whisk together the cocoa powder, soy milk, and remaining ¼ teaspoon vanilla.

Put one-third of the vanilla batter into a bowl with the cocoa mixture and blend with an electric handheld mixer until a chocolate cookie batter forms.

Using your hands, press half of the remaining vanilla batter into the prepared cake pan. Sprinkle half of the crushed graham crackers in an even layer covering the center of the vanilla batter layer, keeping it away from the edge. Using a rubber tipped spatula, spread the chocolate batter over the vanilla batter layer and graham crackers. Then, arrange the vegan marshmallows in the center of the chocolate batter layer, keeping it away from the edge. Sprinkle the remaining graham crackers over the marshmallows. Using a rubber tipped spatula, spread the remaining vanilla batter over the top. Then sprinkle your chocolate chips over the top. You will probably have some marshmallows that peek out. That's actually a good thing. When you bake your cookie bars the exposed marshmallows will toast.

Bake for 45 minutes to 1 hour, or until a bamboo skewer inserted into the center of the cookie bars comes out clean.

Let your cookie bars cool in the pan on a wire rack for 20 minutes. Once your pan is cool enough to hold with your bare hands, cut your cookie bars into 12 square pieces. Use a fork to lift your bars out of the pan.

Serve warm to get the full "campfire" effect!

GRAHAM CRACKERS

It can be disappointing to learn that many graham crackers have honey in them. Many people aren't aware that commercial honey production can be just as inhumane as most factory farms. Bees in commercial honey farming are often hurt and killed in pretty horrific ways, while the farms themselves are bad for the environment because they can kill off native bee populations with diseases and aggressive genetically manipulated honeybees. Once you find a brand of graham crackers that doesn't contain honey, you'll be pleasantly surprised by how many things you can do with just one package. There's the obvious s'mores and faux-gingerbread houses at Christmas, but you can also make graham cracker crusts for cheesecakes and other pies. We recommend you try the Mango Coconut Pie on page 269 or the Chocolate Strawberry Cheesecake Cups on page 306 if you're looking for ways to use your leftover graham crackers.

Vegan Piecrust

For everything there is a season, and for every pie there is a crust.

MAKES 1 PIECRUST   **$0.25 PER SERVING**

. . . .

2 cups flour, plus more for dusting

1 teaspoon salt

⅔ cup plus 2 tablespoons vegetable shortening

4 to 6 tablespoons cold water

. . . .

In a medium bowl, mix together the flour and salt. Cut in the shortening with a pastry blender or fork, then mix it in until the dough forms little clumps that look like small peas. While mixing the dough, sprinkle in the cold water 1 tablespoon at a time until the dough is moist but not wet.

Using your hands, roll the dough into a ball inside the bowl. On a floured surface, roll out the dough ball with a floured rolling pin.

Gently wrap the flattened dough in plastic wrap and refrigerate for 45 minutes. Once the dough is firm but still pliable, remove it from the fridge. Using wet fingers, press together any cracks, then let the dough warm until it is more pliable, 1 to 2 minutes.

The crust is now ready to be rolled out or pressed into a pan or tart dish. Go forth and make pies, my friend!

Olive Oil Piecrust

I grew up eating olive oil piecrusts. My mom used olive oil for everything: salad dressing, cooking, baking, garlic bread, deep-frying, coating cast-iron pans. When I went away to college and started baking with friends, I was introduced to vegetable shortening and my world got bigger. But I always had a place in my heart for my mom's olive oil crust. Just be sure to put your olive oil in the fridge about twelve hours before you use it, so you get those little solidified blobs that will make your crust flaky.

MAKES 1 PIECRUST   **$0.13 PER SERVING**

. . . .

2 cups all-purpose flour, plus more for dusting

¼ teaspoon sea salt

½ cup olive oil, refrigerated overnight

2 to 3 tablespoons cold water

. . . .

In your largest bowl, whisk together the flour and salt. Gradually mix in the olive oil, 1 tablespoon at a time, until all the olive oil has been incorporated and the dough forms large crumbles. Sprinkle 1 tablespoon of the cold water over the flour mixture and mix with an electric handheld mixer, adding the remaining cold water until the dough is firm.

Using your hands, roll the dough into a ball inside the bowl. Cover the bowl with plastic wrap and refrigerate for 15 to 20 minutes. While the dough is in the refrigerator, place a large piece of waxed paper on the countertop.

Using a rolling pin dusted with flour, roll out the dough on the waxed paper into a 12-inch circle.

Very carefully lift the dough and move it to a 9-inch glass pie dish. Use your wet fingers to seal up any cracks, then press the crust into the dish so it fits snugly. Trim off any extra dough hanging over the dish so that the crust is perfectly round. If you have just a little bit of extra dough left, gently fold it under the edge and press it together to form a nice rim. Use a fork or your fingers to create waves, crimps, or another decorative rim. Prick the sides and bottom of the crust all over with a fork. Bake for 12 minutes, or until very light brown.

Now you're ready to add your filling and finish your pie!

Peanut Butter Cup Pie

You may find yourself living a vegan life. You may find yourself feeling healthier and looking better than most of the people you went to high school with. You may find yourself enjoying tofu and visiting farm animal sanctuaries with a huge smile. You may find yourself in a beautiful life with a beautiful wife. And you may ask yourself, well, how did I get here? Living a cruelty-free lifestyle has so many rewards . . . vegan peanut butter cup pie is only one of them.

MAKES 1 PIE   **$1.88 PER SERVING**

. . . .

1 vegan piecrust, store-bought or homemade (see page 262)

2 cups vegan chocolate chips

2 (8-ounce) packages vegan cream cheese

1½ cups creamy peanut butter (we recommend using the kind of peanut butter with not a lot of oil to get the firmest pie)

1 tablespoon all-purpose flour

1½ cups powdered sugar

1 teaspoon cornstarch

½ teaspoon vanilla extract

3 tablespoons coconut milk, from a carton, not a can

⅓ cup dry-roasted peanuts

. . . .

Prebake the piecrust until golden brown following the directions on the package, or following the recipe on page 262. Let the piecrust cool to room temperature.

While the piecrust is cooling, melt half the chocolate chips following the instructions on the package. Use a ladle to pour the melted chocolate into the piecrust, making sure to evenly coat the sides and bottom of the pie. Refrigerate for 10 minutes, or until the chocolate is solid.

In a large bowl, blend the vegan cream cheese, peanut butter, flour, powdered sugar, cornstarch, vanilla, and coconut milk until creamy.

Remove the piecrust from the refrigerator. Pour the peanut butter filling into the piecrust and use a rubber spatula to scrape down the sides of the bowl and spread the filling evenly.

Melt the remaining vegan chocolate chips following the instructions on the package. Drizzle the melted chocolate over the top of the pie, then sprinkle the peanuts over the chocolate.

Refrigerate the pie for 2 hours before serving.

PEANUT BUTTER

Although people have eaten crushed peanut paste for years in the South Pacific and Asia, it was John Harvey Kellogg—breakfast cereal tycoon, vegetarian advocate, and infamous health-crazed sanitarium founder—who patented it in 1895 as a "nut meal" and its popularity spread in the United States. For generations, kids all over America have enjoyed a vegan lunch of peanut butter and jelly sandwiches without even realizing they're doing something nice for animals. We recommend you check out the Sesame Peanut Noodles on page 101 or the PB&J Granola Bars on page 28 for other recipes with peanut butter.

Savannah Pecan Pie

Dan and I visited Savannah, Georgia, for our first wedding anniversary. It was a great weekend full of mossy trees and tall sweet teas. This recipe is a tribute to that trip, and to the pralines Savannah is so famous for.

MAKES 1 PIE　　　　　　　　　　　　　　　　　　　　**$0.99 PER SERVING**

1 vegan piecrust, store-bought or homemade (see page 262)

1 cup pecan halves

⅓ cup vegan margarine

½ cup granulated sugar

1 cup packed brown sugar

2 tablespoons maple syrup

2 tablespoons applesauce

2 dashes of hot sauce

1 tablespoon plus 2 teaspoons vanilla extract or bourbon

Pinch of sea salt

2 tablespoons powdered sugar

2 tablespoons cornstarch

Prebake the piecrust following the instructions on the package, or following the recipe on page 262.

Grind ½ cup of the pecans in a food processor or blender—be careful not to grind them into a paste.

In a saucepan, melt the margarine over medium heat. Use a whisk to blend in the granulated sugar and brown sugar. Once the sugars are blended and begin to bubble, whisk in the maple syrup, applesauce, hot sauce, vanilla, and salt. Then mix in the ground pecans, powdered sugar, and cornstarch and remove from the heat. Continue to whisk until completely blended. The mixture will be super-sticky, but that's part of what you sign up for when you make pecan pie.

Use a rubber spatula to fill the piecrust with half the filling and smooth out the top. Arrange the remaining ½ cup pecans over the top, then pour the remaining filling over the top and use a spatula to smooth it out. Cover the pie with foil and bake for 5 minutes. Then carefully remove the foil, being careful to avoid steam—it can burn your fingers just as easily as touching a hot pan. Put the pie back in the oven to bake for another 5 to 8 minutes.

Refrigerate the pie for 20 minutes before serving.

Humble Apple Pie

We've talked a lot in this book about the kitchen ingenuity displayed during the Great Depression and World War II when it came to mock meat—but we haven't yet mentioned the famous mock apple pie.

This extremely popular 1930s recipe used buttery Ritz crackers mixed with corn syrup, lemon juice, and vanilla to replace the apples that were too expensive for some at the time. I was intrigued, but knew deep down that it wasn't a recipe that needed veganizing. I mean, I might do so for fun on our blog later, but as far as this book goes, it was a bad fit—a package of Ritz crackers can cost around $4, at least $1 more than the four apples needed for a pie. Plus, cracker pie is just weird.

So I searched out other popular apple pies from the same time period and found this humble apple pie that doesn't require a pie pan because it's wrapped up like a galette. It's a beautiful, rustic dessert that looks really impressive on any table with some after-dinner coffee or tea.

MAKES 1 PIE **$0.43 PER SERVING**

Crust

1 cup all-purpose flour, plus more for dusting

¼ cup whole wheat flour

2 tablespoons granulated sugar

2 pinches of sea salt

¼ teaspoon ground cinnamon

½ cup vegan margarine, cold

3 tablespoons cold water

Filling

½ cup plus 1 tablespoon packed brown sugar

2 tablespoons all-purpose flour

½ teaspoon ground cinnamon

¼ teaspoon ground allspice

¼ teaspoon ground cloves

2 Gala or Pink Lady apples, cored and thinly sliced

2 Granny Smith apples, cored and thinly sliced

2 tablespoons old-fashioned oats

Make the crust: In a medium bowl, whisk together the flours, granulated sugar, salt, and cinnamon. Using a pastry blender, mix in the vegan margarine until the dough starts to form small crumbles the size of peas.

Sprinkle the water over the flour mixture 1 tablespoon at a time while mixing continuously until the dough is moist but firm.

Using your hands, form the dough into a ball inside the bowl. On a floured surface,

(continued)

flatten the dough into a round disk. Wrap the dough in plastic wrap and refrigerate for 35 minutes.

Preheat the oven to 400°F.

With a floured rolling pin, roll the dough into a 12-inch round on a floured surface and place it on a pizza stone or cookie sheet.

Make the filling: In a large bowl, whisk together the brown sugar, flour, cinnamon, allspice, and cloves. Using a large spoon, stir in the apple slices and oats until they are completely coated.

Pile the apple mixture in the center of the rolled-out dough, leaving 2½ inches uncovered along the edge. Fold the uncovered edge of the dough over the apples, leaving the center exposed.

Bake for 30 minutes, or until the crust is golden brown. Cut into wedges and serve warm, with some vegan vanilla ice cream, if you really love yourself.

You can use any leftover old-fashioned oats to make:

Granola Grrrl Bars on page 29
Betty's Wartime Walnut Burger on page 189
Carrot Cake Cookies on page 282
PB&J Granola Bars on page 28

Mango Coconut Pie

This is a tropical-themed dessert that combines all the goodness of sweet golden mangoes with the soft heart of a coconut to make sunshine in a graham cracker crust.

MAKES 1 PIE   **$1.82 PER SERVING**

Graham Cracker Crust

2 cups crushed vegan graham crackers

⅓ cup vegan margarine

2 tablespoons granulated sugar

1 tablespoon packed brown sugar

Filling

1 (14-ounce) can coconut milk

3 tablespoons powdered sugar

½ cup plus 2 tablespoons sweetened shredded coconut

1 ripe banana

2 tablespoons coconut oil

2 tablespoons cornstarch

1 teaspoon vanilla or coconut extract

2 tablespoons all-purpose flour

2 (8-ounce) packages vegan cream cheese

1 teaspoon vegan egg replacer (we recommend Ener-G Egg Replacer or Beyond Eggs)

Topping

2 ripe mangoes, peeled and pitted

Grated zest and juice of 1 lemon

2 tablespoons granulated sugar

¼ cup fruit juice (we recommend using orange and mango cocktail)

1 tablespoon agar-agar powder

Make the graham cracker crust: Preheat the oven to 350°F.

In a food processor, blend all the crust ingredients until crushed and well mixed. Gently press the crust into the bottom and up the sides of a pie dish. Bake for 8 to 10 minutes, or until light golden brown. Let the crust cool while you prepare the filling.

Make the filling: Clean out your food processor, then toss in all the filling ingredients and puree until creamy and smooth.

Use a rubber spatula to scrape all the filling ingredients into the piecrust.

Make the topping: Clean out the food processor and puree the mango flesh until liquefied, then add the lemon zest, lemon juice, and granulated sugar and process to combine.

In a small saucepan, bring the fruit juice to a boil, then whisk in the agar-agar powder. Bring the juice mixture to a boil, whisking continuously, about 10 minutes.

(continued)

Quickly pour the juice mixture into the food processor and blend for a count of 3.

Pour the topping mixture over the filling, using a rubber spatula to spread it into an even layer.

Refrigerate for 20 minutes or until the topping sets and has a loose gel-like texture.

Serve cold.

COCONUT OIL

If you'd told me ten years ago that coconut oil would be praised as a health food, I would have called you a liar to your face. I mean, I would have done it in a nice way, probably using humor to soften the blow. But I would have been wrong to do that, and not just because it would be sort of jerky. Research into Polynesian diets that rely heavily on coconut oil has shown that it can be a great way to diversify your diet and make healthier baked goods. We also use it to "season" our cast iron, since it solidifies at room temperature. But if you have any coconut oil that you're just not sure what to do with, you can always use it to make the Salted Caramel Skillet Cake on page 250 or Snowball Cupcakes on page 258.

Treat Yo'self!

Any lifestyle change can seem like a pretty big sacrifice. So here are a few tips I've picked up over the years that have helped me stick to a smaller budget. I'm not saying you must do all these things at once—but picking one a week or a month might make living on less seem a little more fun.

- *Find a trustworthy friend to trade with.* Maybe you love baked goods but not baking, or you love wearing a different outfit every day but you aren't Sarah Jessica Parker. Find a friend with whom you can trade babysitting for baked goods, or who wears your size and can double your closet. Just remember: If you're borrowing clothes or books, have each party write their names in their things to keep organized.

- *Check out what's free in your hometown.* We're lucky to live in New York City where you can always find a free museum, concert, or event. But I've lived all over the country, and I know that this isn't just a big-city thing. Most college towns have free art shows and plays. Bookstores and libraries usually have speakers and readings. Take advantage of what's free in your area to save money for the things that aren't.

- *Make your own fun.* Home movie nights, board game nights, and book clubs are inexpensive ways to socialize without tipping waitresses and bartenders.

- At least once a month, *treat yourself to a reward* for sticking to your budget. This doesn't mean go get a new car or buy a round of drinks for the house. Just look at what you have saved that month, and then give yourself 10 percent to 15 percent of that as a "tip." Yeah, it's a crappy tip, but if you know that at the end of the month you'll have an extra $20 to do whatever you want with...well, it's a pretty nice feeling. You might even want to hold on to that $20 so the next month you have $40 to spend. It won't get you a new car, but you'll be surprised how quickly you'll be able to afford small splurges like manicures or new video games again. And not to sound like your mother or anything, but I find I value them more now, too.

Chai Spice Cheesecake

This recipe combines everything good in the world. Just remember that this is the Special Occasions section—so share the wealth of this creamy treat with loved ones.

MAKES 1 LARGE CHEESECAKE   **$1.75 PER SERVING**

Crust

Vegetable shortening, for the pan

1 cup all-purpose flour

½ cup vegan margarine

¼ cup sugar

1 tablespoon applesauce

¼ teaspoon ground cinnamon

Filling

1¼ cups almond milk

6 chai tea bags

3 (8-ounce) packages vegan cream cheese

1 cup sugar

3 tablespoons applesauce

1 tablespoon egg replacer (we recommend Ener-G or Beyond Eggs)

½ teaspoon ground cinnamon

¼ teaspoon whole cardamom pods, crushed (optional)

1 teaspoon vanilla extract

1 tablespoon grated orange zest

1 tablespoon all-purpose flour

Pinch of sea salt

Cinnamon-Sugar Topping

3 tablespoons sugar

2 teaspoons ground cinnamon

Make the crust: Preheat the oven to 350°F. Lightly coat a springform pan with vegetable shortening.

In a large bowl, mix all the crust ingredients together using a pastry blender or fork until the mixture is blended and crumbly. Using your hands, press the crust into a springform pan to create a shallow bowl. Bake for 5 to 6 minutes, or until the crust is a very light golden brown. Remove the crust from the oven and set aside; reduce the oven temperature to 300°F.

Make the filling: In a small saucepan, heat the almond milk and chai tea bags over medium heat until it begins to boil, then remove from the heat.

In a large bowl, use an electric handheld mixer to combine the remaining filling ingredients. Once the almond milk mixture is cool enough to handle, use your hands to squeeze the tea bags into the almond milk. Mix the chai-infused almond milk into the filling mixture.

Pour the filling into the crust. Use a spatula to scrape all the filling out of the bowl and smooth it into an even layer.

Make the cinnamon-sugar topping: In a small bowl, mix the sugar and cinnamon together. Sprinkle the cinnamon-sugar topping over the cheesecake in swirls.

Bake the cheesecake for 20 minutes, then reduce the oven temperature to 200°F and bake for another hour. The cheesecake may not look done, but if a small area in the center still seems soft, it will become solid as it cools. Don't test it with a toothpick/bamboo skewer as you would normally with a baked good.

Turn off the oven and leave the cheesecake in the oven for another 30 minutes.

Remove from the oven and let cool in the pan on a wire rack for another 30 minutes.

Without releasing or removing the side of the pan, run a metal spatula or a butter knife carefully along the side of the cheesecake to loosen it. Refrigerate, uncovered, overnight.

Before serving, run a metal spatula or butter knife carefully along the side of the cheesecake in the pan to loosen it again. Unsnap and gently lift off the sides of the springform pan. Serve the cheesecake on the bottom of the springform pan.

You can use any leftover almond milk to make:

Banana Churro Waffles on page 44
Pumpkin Spice Latte on page 64
S'mores Cookie Bars on page 260
Green Tea and Pear Smoothie on page 30

Monkey Bread

Not all special occasions are cake focused. I know that might sound like blasphemy, but it's true. This is a wonderful sweet treat for a bridal shower brunch or Easter Sunday spread. It's easy to make and goes perfectly with a Pumpkin Spice Latte (page 64).

MAKES 8 TO 10 SERVINGS $0.37 PER SERVING

Baking spray

Dough

2½ cups all-purpose flour, plus more for dusting

1 tablespoon granulated sugar

1 teaspoon sea salt

1 package active dry yeast

3 tablespoons olive oil

1 cup warm water

Coating

⅔ cup granulated sugar

2 tablespoons ground cinnamon

½ cup vegan margarine

½ cup packed brown sugar

2 tablespoons soy milk

Preheat the oven to 350°F. Spray a heavy coating of baking spray over a fluted cake pan. Many Bundt cake pans have decorative peaks and ridges that might be problematic, so for the best results use a simple pan.

Make the dough: In a large bowl, whisk together the flour, sugar, salt, and yeast. Blend in the olive oil 1 tablespoon at a time until all the olive oil has been incorporated. Then, using an electric handheld mixer fitted with a bread hook attachment, mix in the warm water. Use a rubber spatula to scrape down the sides of the bowl to make sure all the dough is blended.

Once the dough is thoroughly mixed, knead it for 5 minutes on a lightly floured surface, stopping once it is springy. Cover the dough loosely with plastic wrap and let it rise at room temperature for 30 minutes.

On a floured surface, use a floured rolling pin to roll out the dough so it's about an inch thick. Then, using a pizza cutter or large knife, cut the dough into a grid with squares about 1 inch wide. You'll want about 50 pieces. Place a kitchen towel over the dough and let it rise for another 10 minutes.

Make the coating: Put the granulated sugar and the cinnamon in a large freezer bag, then shake to mix. Toss a few pieces of dough into the bag at a time. Shake to coat, remove from the bag, and place in the cake pan. Repeat until all the dough pieces are coated and the cake pan is filled with dough pieces arranged evenly to make a flat bottom for the cake. Pour any extra cinnamon-sugar over the top of the cake.

In a saucepan, heat the vegan margarine over medium heat. As the margarine begins to melt, whisk in the brown sugar and the soy milk. As the mixture begins to bubble, whisk continuously to avoid clumps. Once both the margarine and brown sugar have melted, remove the pan from the heat. Pour the sauce over the dough pieces, coating all the pieces rather than pouring in a single location.

Bake for 45 minutes, or until the dough is golden brown. Let cool on a wire rack for about 5 minutes, or until you can handle the pan with bare hands.

Place a serving plate on top of the pan and holding the pan and the plate together, flip them so the monkey bread is inverted onto the plate.

Serve with extra napkins—you'll be pulling apart this sticky treat with your fingers and eating with your hands. This could get messy.

Use any leftover brown sugar to make:

Ginger-Plum Oatmeal on page 26

Cinnamon Roll Pancakes on page 32

Virgin Crêpes Suzette on page 39

Cinnamon Peach Skillet Rolls on
     page 47

Cookie Pizza on page 276

Pumpkin Pie Muffins on page 46

Veg Manchurian on page 302

Cookie Pizza

In the summer of 2007, I went to Chicago to help collect signatures for a citywide ban on foie gras. It was an excruciatingly hot summer full of sunburns, Bears fans, and parking lots. It was also the summer I had a vegan cookie pizza for the first time. Someone brought one to a vegan potluck (one of many I attended) along with a little note that said: "Welcome to Chicago—where everything's a pizza!"

MAKES 1 PIZZA   **$0.64 PER SERVING**

1¼ cups all-purpose flour

½ teaspoon baking soda

Pinch of sea salt

¾ cup packed brown sugar

½ cup vegan margarine, at room temperature

1 teaspoon vanilla extract

1 tablespoon applesauce

½ teaspoon egg replacer (we recommend Ener-G or Beyond Eggs)

¼ cup raw walnuts, crushed

1 cup vegan chocolate chips

Preheat the oven to 375°F.

In a large bowl, whisk together the flour, baking soda, and salt.

In a separate bowl, blend together the brown sugar, vegan margarine, vanilla, applesauce, and egg replacer with an electric handheld mixer until creamy. Then, pour the applesauce mixture into the flour mixture and blend until smooth. Use a large spoon to fold in the walnuts and chocolate chips.

Spread the cookie batter over an ungreased cookie sheet or baking pan. (Sorry, you can't use a pizza stone this time.) Use your hands to form the cookie batter into a big, round cookie.

Bake for 10 minutes, or until the cookie pizza is brown and crispy around the edges.

You can use your leftover walnuts to make:

Kale Caesar Salad on page 78

Betty's Wartime Walnut Burger on page 189

Roasted Pear, Walnut, and Brussels Sprout Tacos on page 197

Carrot Cake Cookies on page 282

Fresh Fruit Pizza

This recipe was quite popular in 1950s women's magazines for being a "fruit dessert that kids will love!" We can't vouch for those kiddos—but we like it!

MAKES 1 PIZZA   **$2.36 PER SERVING**

Cookie Crust

1½ cups powdered sugar

1 cup vegan margarine

¼ cup almond milk

¼ teaspoon grated orange zest

1½ teaspoons vanilla extract

2½ cups all-purpose flour

2 tablespoons cornstarch

1 teaspoon baking soda

1 teaspoon cream of tartar

Topping

1 (8-ounce) package vegan cream cheese

Grated zest and juice of 1 lemon

1 tablespoon powdered sugar

Berries and sliced fresh fruit (we used blueberries, strawberries, and raspberries, 1 peach, 1 mango, and 1 kiwifruit)

1 tablespoon fresh mint leaves

Make the cookie crust: In a large bowl, blend the powdered sugar, vegan margarine, almond milk, orange zest, and vanilla with an electric handheld mixer until smooth. Gradually mix in the flour, cornstarch, baking soda, and cream of tartar and blend into a soft dough. The mixture will form small pebbles at first, but as you continue to blend it will become a proper dough. Be patient. Cover the bowl with foil and refrigerate for 1 hour.

Preheat the oven to 375°F.

Use your hands to press the chilled dough into a large round cookie on a cookie sheet or baking pan. You can roll it out, if you like, but for best results, use your hands so you can create a crust around the edge.

Bake for 5 to 7 minutes, or until the cookie is a very light golden brown. Remove from the oven and use a spatula to carefully transfer the cookie to a wire rack or serving dish. Let cool to room temperature.

Make the topping: In a large bowl, blend the cream cheese, lemon zest, lemon juice, and powdered sugar using an electric handheld mixer.

Once the cookie crust has cooled, spread the cream cheese mixture over the cookie crust, leaving 1 inch uncovered along the edge.

Arrange the fresh fruit on top of the cream cheese in either a colorful fan or spiral design. Sprinkle fresh mint over the top right before you serve.

Vegan Cheese Party Pizza

The year 2013 could be called the Renaissance of Vegan Cheese. Visit any vegan's social media page and you'll find at least one photo of a vegan pizza with cheese that really melts and a post singing the praises of cashews. This recipe follows the guidelines of a classic cheese plate: something sweet, something crunchy, and three types of cheese.

Because cashews can be pricey, this recipe includes a small batch of homemade soft cashew cheese to go with the pears, dried apricots, almonds, and grapes to create a lovely, schmancy vegan cheese platter pizza. Serve it at a party as an appetizer or save it for a special night with your significant other.

MAKES 1 PIZZA   **$1.07 PER SERVING**

⅓ cup raw cashews

2 tablespoons plus 1 teaspoon olive oil

Dash of vegan liquid smoke

½ teaspoon soy sauce or Bragg's Liquid Aminos

1 tablespoon nutritional yeast

1½ teaspoons crushed black peppercorns

¼ teaspoon smoked paprika

1 teaspoon sesame seeds

½ teaspoon lemon juice

1 pizza crust, store-bought or homemade (see page 159)

Cornmeal, for dusting

1 teaspoon dried rosemary

¼ cup shredded vegan mozzarella (we recommend Daiya)

3 tablespoons cubed vegan cheese (we recommend Heidi Ho Smoked Gouda or Daiya Jalapeno Havarti)

½ pear, cored and sliced

¼ cup whole dried apricots

3 tablespoons sliced almonds

2 tablespoons pitted kalamata olives or Spanish green olives

Vegan Parmesan cheese, for sprinkling

¼ cup halved red grapes

Soak the cashews overnight in enough water to cover them.

Twenty minutes before serving, drain the cashews and place them in a food processor with a bottom blade. Add 1 tablespoon of the olive oil, the vegan liquid smoke, soy sauce, nutritional yeast, ½ teaspoon of the

black pepper, the paprika, sesame seeds, and lemon juice and process until creamy and smooth. Transfer to an airtight container and refrigerate until ready to use.

Preheat the oven to 400°F.

On a floured surface, roll out the pizza crust until it is very thin, then move it to a pizza stone or baking pan dusted with cornmeal.

In a small bowl, mix together 1 tablespoon of the olive oil and the rosemary. Brush the pizza crust with the olive oil mixture, leaving 1 inch uncovered around the edge.

Sprinkle half the vegan mozzarella over the pizza crust. Remove the cashew mixture from the fridge and use a tablespoon to scoop out one portion at a time. Form the mixture into small patties by hand. Place the cashew patties all over the pizza, leaving a lot of space between each patty. Distribute the vegan cheese cubes, pear slices, dried apricots, almonds, and olives in the spaces between the cashew patties and sprinkle with leftover vegan mozzarella. Drizzle the remaining 1 teaspoon olive oil and sprinkle the vegan Parmesan and black pepper over the top.

Bake for 8 to 10 minutes, or until the crust is a golden brown and the cheese has melted. Before serving, toss the grape halves on top and maybe open a bottle of wine or apple cider.

You can use any leftover cashews to make:

Mac and Cheez Pie on page 173
Tofu, Green Beans, and Cashews on
    page 185

Molasses Crinkle Cookies

During the sugar rationing of World War II, molasses became a very popular way to sweeten baked goods. This cookie also uses brown sugar to create a chewy, spicy treat that will be a hit at any office potluck.

MAKES 18 COOKIES   **$0.25 PER SERVING**

¾ cup vegan shortening

1 cup packed brown sugar

⅓ cup blackstrap molasses

1 tablespoon applesauce

2 cups all-purpose flour

2 teaspoons baking soda

¼ teaspoon ground allspice

1 teaspoon ground cinnamon

1 teaspoon ground ginger

½ teaspoon ground cloves

¼ teaspoon sea salt

⅓ cup raw sugar

Preheat the oven to 325°F. Line a cookie sheet with aluminum foil.

In a large bowl, mix the shortening, brown sugar, molasses, and applesauce with an electric handheld mixer until blended.

In a separate bowl, blend the flour, baking soda, allspice, cinnamon, ginger, cloves, and sea salt. Add the applesauce mixture to the flour mixture and blend until creamy.

Pour the raw sugar into a bowl. Roll 1 tablespoon of the cookie dough into a ball, then gently press the ball into the raw sugar. Place the cookie, sugar-side up, on the lined cookie sheet. Repeat with the remaining dough.

Bake for 10 minutes, or until the cookies look a little dry. Immediately transfer the cookies to a wire rack to cool.

> *You can use your leftover blackstrap molasses to make:*
>
> Blackstrap Vegan Bangers and Mash with Onion Gravy on page 125
> Simple Korean Kimchi BBQ Burgers on page 187
> Jerk "Chicken" Pasta Salad on page 98

Chocolate Chip and Banana Brownie Cookies

Chocolate chip and banana brownie cookies...I wish I knew how to quit you. You're the perfect potluck recipe, but you tap into my selfish soul and drive me to bring hummus instead so I can have all these soft, chocolaty cookies for myself.*

MAKES 24 COOKIES   **$0.18 PER SERVING**

1 cup all-purpose flour

½ cup cocoa powder

½ teaspoon baking soda

½ teaspoon sea salt

½ cup vegan margarine

1½ cups sugar

1 banana

½ teaspoon ground flaxseed

1 teaspoon vanilla extract

⅔ cup vegan chocolate chips

Preheat the oven to 325°F. Line a cookie sheet with aluminum foil.

In a large bowl, whisk together the flour, cocoa powder, baking soda, and salt.

In a separate large bowl, blend the vegan margarine, sugar, banana, flaxseed, and vanilla with an electric handheld mixer until creamy. Then, using a rubber spatula, add the banana mixture to the flour mixture, scraping the sides of the bowl. Use the mixer to blend the cookie dough, scraping down the sides to get any flour that sticks. Using a large spoon, fold in the chocolate chips. Warning: Your dough will be very soft, but it's going to be okay.

Roll 1 tablespoon of the dough into a ball, then gently press it into a disk. Place the finished cookie on the lined cookie sheet. Your dough will be kind of sticky, so don't press too hard or it will stick to your hands. Depending on the size of your cookie sheets, you may have to bake the cookies in batches.

Bake the cookies for 15 minutes, or until they look a little dry on top. These cookies are best when chewy, in my opinion, so you don't want to overbake them.

Let the cookies cool to room temperature before gobbling three or four down with a tall glass of almond milk.

> **You can use any leftover vegan chocolate chips to make:**
>
> Peanut Butter Cup Pie on page 264
> Cookie Pizza on page 276
> S'mores Cookie Bars on page 260

---

* Not that I would ever do that. Bringing hummus to a vegan potluck is unforgivable.

Carrot Cake Cookies

During World War II, carrot cake grew in popularity as a way to get kids to eat more vegetables and diversify their diet. But it wasn't until the health food craze of the 1970s that Americans truly embraced this now-classic bakery standby. This cookie is inspired by some carrot cookie recipes I found in British rations cookbooks from 1941 to 1943. We added more spices and sugar to liven it up a bit—and of course made it vegan.

MAKES 1 DOZEN COOKIES **$0.33 PER SERVING**

1 cup all-purpose flour

1 teaspoon ground cinnamon

¼ teaspoon grated nutmeg

Pinch of ground allspice

1 teaspoon baking powder

1 teaspoon baking soda

½ teaspoon sea salt

½ cup vegan margarine

½ cup packed brown sugar

3 tablespoons almond milk

1 tablespoon applesauce

1 teaspoon ground flaxseed

1 teaspoon vanilla extract

½ cup grated carrots

½ cup raisins

½ cup quick-cooking oats

¼ cup crushed raw walnuts

Preheat the oven to 325°F. Line a cookie sheet with aluminum foil.

In a large bowl, whisk together the flour, cinnamon, nutmeg, allspice, baking powder, baking soda, and salt.

In a separate bowl, blend together the vegan margarine, brown sugar, almond milk, applesauce, flaxseed, and vanilla with an electric handheld mixer until smooth. Blend the margarine mixture into the flour mixture. Use a rubber spatula to scrape down the sides of the bowl.

Use a large knife to dice the grated carrots into small bits. Using a large spoon, fold the carrots, raisins, oats, and walnuts into the cookie batter.

Gently roll the cookie dough into balls about the size of your palm, then place them on the lined cookie sheet.

Bake for 15 to 20 minutes or until the cookies are a light golden color.

You can use any leftover flaxseed to make:

Pumpkin Pie Muffins on page 46

Beet "Boudin" Balls with Garlic Aioli on
    page 206

Banana Churro Waffles on page 44

Salted Caramel Skillet Cake on page 250

Chocolate Chip and Banana Brownie
    Cookies on page 281

Lavender and Vanilla Cupcakes on
    page 308

White Wedding Cupcakes on page 310

Lemon and Lavender Cookies

It's a daring move to add culinary lavender to a cookbook about budgeting. We wanted to show people how to create a sustainable and affordable kitchen system in a new and interesting way. So why pull punches and deliver the expected, right? Surprisingly, culinary lavender can be an inexpensive way to make your special occasion special. We were able to get almost 4 cups for $5 at a bulk spice store—which is way more than you'd need to make both this recipe and the Lavender and Vanilla Cupcakes on page 308. The only catch is, you have to like floral flavors. If they're not for you, you can always skip the lavender and just enjoy lemon sugar cookies at your next bridal or baby shower, or whatever special event you might want to celebrate.

MAKES 18 COOKIES   **$0.34 PER SERVING**

1½ cups powdered sugar

1 cup vegan margarine

¼ cup almond milk

Grated zest of 1 lemon

1 teaspoon vanilla or lemon extract

2¼ cups all-purpose flour

2 tablespoons cornstarch

1 teaspoon baking soda

1 teaspoon cream of tartar

2 tablespoons dried culinary lavender, crushed

3 tablespoons granulated sugar

In a large bowl, blend the powdered sugar, vegan margarine, almond milk, lemon zest, and vanilla with an electric handheld mixer until smooth. Then gradually mix in the flour, cornstarch, baking soda, and cream of tartar and blend into a soft dough. It will form small pebbles at first, but as you continue blending it will become a dough. Be patient.

With a large spoon, mix in the crushed lavender until it is evenly spread throughout the dough. Cover the bowl with foil and refrigerate for 1 hour.

Preheat the oven to 375°F.

Use a soup spoon to scoop out the chilled dough. Form the cookies by hand into smooth patties smaller than your palm and place them on an unlined cookie sheet. Sprinkle the granulated sugar over the cookies. Bake for 5 to 7 minutes, or until a light golden brown crust forms around the edge of the cookie. Remove from the oven and let cool on a wire rack.

> *You can use any leftover cream of tartar to make:*
>
> Snowball Cupcakes on page 258
> Fresh Fruit Pizza on page 277

Potlucks and Parties

Potlucks hold a very special place in the vegan community. No other group I can think of gets together to share food with such excitement and regularity as the vegans. I belonged to a sewing circle in college,[†] and the vegans in this group kept us all well fed. Gradually, what started as a monthly meeting of knitters and crafty ladies expanded into a huge vegan potluck, with non-crafty roommates and significant others joining us regularly to share zucchini breads and tofu scrambles.

The recipes and potluck themes that follow are to help you plan your own parties. You can either make the central recipe yourself and ask your guests to bring some of the complementary recipes listed underneath, or go stone-soup style and ask your guests to bring the supporting ingredients—like taco or baked potato toppings—to help make hosting your event even more affordable.

[†] What? I was a women's studies major in Olympia in the nineties—are you really that surprised?

Cruelty-Free Crawfish Boil

The crawfish boil is a big thing in the South. It's basically like a fish fry or barbecue, but the central component is a pot of boiling crawfish and/or shrimp, usually with potatoes and corn mixed in. The crawfish boil tends to be the star of a large potluck party with a cooler full of beer and a table full of pies and potato salads. With the rise in popularity of Cajun and Creole food, these events are becoming popular all over the United States. Food bloggers from L.A. to N.Y. are hosting them in their backyards and on their rooftops, using crawfish flown in from the Gulf Coast. Our crawfish boil uses May-Wah's shrimp balls and vegan prawns to capture the spirit of the dish—but in a kinder fashion. It's also much easier and cleaner! You can make this year-round and enjoy a little faux summer in the middle of the coldest, harshest northern winter. And don't forget to serve cold beers, lemonade, and/or bourbon on the side—because no matter what, we're gonna have some "big fun," Bayou-style.

MAKES 4 TO 6 SERVINGS   **$2.85 PER SERVING**

- 1 pound whole small red potatoes
- 2 to 3 ears fresh corn, broken in half
- 2 teaspoons sea salt
- 1½ cups May-Wah frozen vegan prawns, defrosted
- 1½ cups May-Wah frozen shrimp balls, defrosted
- 2 tablespoons chopped fresh parsley
- 2 lemons

Sauce

- ½ cup vegan margarine
- 3 cloves garlic, minced

- 3 to 4 tablespoons hot sauce
- ¼ cup beer
- ¼ cup lemon juice
- 2 tablespoons plus 2 teaspoons Tony Chachere's Original Creole Seasoning
- ¼ red onion, diced
- ½ teaspoon ground cumin
- Pinch of celery seed
- Dash of vegan liquid smoke

Preheat the oven to 325°F.

In your largest Dutch oven or stockpot, boil enough water to cover the potatoes and corn. Once the water reaches a rolling boil, toss in the potatoes, corn, and salt. Cover and boil for 15 to 20 minutes, or until the potatoes are tender. Drain the vegetables, then return them to the warm pot and set aside off the heat.

Meanwhile, place the vegan prawns and shrimp balls in a glass baking dish and bake, uncovered, for 5 minutes, then toss with a spatula to make sure they cook evenly. Toss them every 5 minutes while cooking to make sure they don't stick. After 15 minutes, the vegan seafood should be warmed all the way through and have a firm but thin "skin" on the outside. Remove from the oven.

Toss the vegan seafood into the pot with the vegetables and leave uncovered.

Make the sauce: In a saucepan, melt the vegan margarine over medium heat. Whisk in the remaining sauce ingredients until smooth and bring the mixture to a boil. Once the sauce begins to bubble, remove it from the heat.

Pour the sauce over the vegetables and vegan seafood, then toss with a large spoon until evenly coated. Sprinkle the parsley over the top before serving with lemon wedges on the side.

SUGGESTIONS FOR OTHER DISHES YOUR FRIENDS CAN BRING:

Savannah Pecan Pie on page 266

Green Bean, Olive, and Roasted Potato Salad on page 86

French Potato Salad on page 88

Baked Creole Carrot Chips on page 112

Rustic Pesto and Heirloom Tomato Tart on page 117

Slow-Cooker Tempeh Jambalaya on page 213

Cajun Nachos on page 129

Beet "Boudin" Balls and Garlic Aioli on page 206

A variety of hot sauces

Vegan Seafood

Vegan seafood has come a long way from the eraser-head vegan "scallops" that came in a can back in the nineties. Today, there are a few different options out there for great vegan seafood, including Gardein, Sophie's Kitchen, Match Vegan Meats, and May-Wah. These brands offer a variety of choices ranging from shrimp to breaded crab cakes. Most use natural vegan flavors like seaweed to add that briny or "fishy" flavor, and many are soy-free, relying on ingredients like tapioca and yam flour. We recommend you experiment with what's available in your area to figure out which brands and products you prefer. If you're one of those unlucky folks that doesn't have access to vegan seafood in your area, but you miss it, we recommend filling out customer comment cards or asking your local grocery store or co-op to carry these products. Getting your friends to do this too can send a powerful message to the grocery providers in your community that there's a need and desire for vegan products—hopefully they'll listen and become more vegan-friendly. This tried-and-true method of grassroots outreach is how cities and towns all over the United States have become more vegan-friendly!

Butternut Squash and Beer Poutine Party

Canada is famous for many awesome things: beer, hockey, maple syrup, baby seals, geese, and publicly funded healthcare. They're not really all that famous for their cuisine, though—which is a shame, because in Canada you can get vegan hot dogs and sausages from street carts, and it's also the home of one of the best potato dishes of all time: poutine. This French-Canadian dish consists of French fries served with a light brown gravy and cheese curds. In this recipe, we've added butternut squash, nutritional yeast, and beer to the gravy to create something so amazing we're now serving it every Thanksgiving. We recommend this recipe as the base for a Super Bowl Sunday potluck or a Top Chef season finale party—anything with lots of cheering and camaraderie.

MAKES 6 TO 8 SERVINGS · **$1.95 PER SERVING**

Butternut and Beer Gravy

1 butternut squash, peeled, seeded, and cubed

2 small carrots, diced

2 tablespoons olive oil

1 small red onion, diced

3 dashes of vegan liquid smoke

1 cup of your favorite beer

2 tablespoons nutritional yeast

3 cloves garlic, minced

2 tablespoons soy sauce or Bragg's Liquid Aminos

½ cup almond milk

1 cup vegan beef broth or vegetable broth (we recommend Better Than Bouillon)

1 teaspoon smoked paprika

½ teaspoon dried rosemary

1 teaspoon dried thyme

2 teaspoons rubbed sage

1 teaspoon garlic powder

Fries and Toppings

2 (20-ounce) bags frozen French fries

1 (16-ounce) package extra-firm tofu, drained and crumbled

2 teaspoons onion powder

5 to 6 green onions, diced

Crushed black peppercorns, for sprinkling

· ·

Make the butternut and beer gravy: Preheat the oven to 425°F.

Toss the squash and carrots with the olive oil in a large baking dish, then roast for 40 minutes, or until the carrots are tender. Check on them a few times while roasting, and use a spatula to flip the vegetables to make sure they cook evenly.

Once the vegetables are tender, remove them from the oven. Leave the oven on.

Combine all the gravy ingredients in a large Dutch oven or stew pot and bring to a boil over medium heat. When the gravy begins to boil, use an immersion blender to puree the vegetables into a smooth gravy.

Make the fries and toppings: Bake the fries according to the instructions on the package.

In a small bowl, toss the crumbled tofu with the onion powder.

Once the fries are crispy, place them on a serving dish, with the gravy, tofu crumbles, green onions, and crushed pepper in separate bowls on the side so your guests can make up their own dishes.

The perfect way to eat this dish is to top the French fries with gravy, tofu crumbles, green onions, and pepper; but some prefer to dip their fries in the gravy. Their radical poutine agenda is harmless; just let your guests go wild.

SUGGESTIONS FOR OTHER DISHES YOUR FRIENDS CAN BRING:

Club Sandwich Salad with Dijon Mustard Dressing on page 80

Blackstrap Vegan Bangers and Mash with Onion Gravy on page 125

Bubbie's Polish Potato Pierogies on page 137

Irish Stout Stew on page 157

Betty's Wartime Walnut Burger on page 189 (made into sliders)

Salted Caramel Skillet Cake on page 250

Canadian beers, ginger ale, and soda

Baked Potato Bar

Five or so years ago, we attended a PETA office holiday party where they had a baked potato bar—and we're still talking about it today. This simple party idea might seem too basic to be any fun; but honestly, it's hard to find a person on this planet that doesn't enjoy a good baked potato. Seriously. You can't trust someone who hates potatoes. They're an awesome vegetable.

MAKES 6 SERVINGS   **$2.84 PER SERVING**

6 large russet potatoes

2 tablespoons olive oil

5 to 6 mushrooms, sliced

2 tablespoons white wine

1 (8-ounce) package vegan sour cream

⅓ cup minced fresh chives

⅓ cup vegan bacon bits

½ cup shredded vegan cheddar cheese (we recommend Daiya)

¾ cup broccoli florets, steamed

1 cup almond milk, plus a little more, if sauce reduces too much

1 teaspoon soy sauce or Bragg's Liquid Aminos

1 teaspoon garlic powder

½ teaspoon onion powder

½ cup nutritional yeast

¼ teaspoon ground turmeric

Dash of vegan liquid smoke

Salt and ground black pepper

Cheese Sauce

¼ cup vegan margarine

¼ cup whole wheat flour

Preheat the oven to 425°F.

Scrub the potatoes and cut a slit down one side. Wrap the potatoes in aluminum foil and place them in the oven to bake.

Meanwhile, heat the olive oil in a cast-iron skillet or frying pan over medium heat. Toss in the mushroom slices and pour the white wine over the top. Use a spatula to flip the mushrooms a few times to make sure they cook evenly. Once the mushrooms are tender, remove from the heat and cover with a lid to keep warm.

Make the cheese sauce: In a saucepan, melt the margarine over medium heat. Whisk in the flour and reduce the heat to low. Whisk in the remaining sauce ingredients except the salt and pepper. Once the sauce begins to bubble, give it a taste test and season with salt or pepper as needed.

If the sauce reduces too much while the potatoes are baking, mix in a little more almond milk.

Once the potatoes are tender, place them on an oven-safe serving plate on your buffet table. Place the vegan sour cream, chives, vegan bacon bits, vegan cheddar cheese, and steamed broccoli in individual small bowls.

Give the cheese sauce one last taste test before serving and adjust the flavor as needed with salt, pepper, or almond milk. Pour the warm cheese sauce into a gravy boat or a bowl large enough that you can serve the sauce with a ladle.

Let your guests go nuts and load up their potatoes.

SUGGESTIONS FOR OTHER DISHES YOUR FRIENDS CAN BRING:

Kale Caesar Salad on page 78

Roasted Red Pepper and Lentil Soup on page 91

Chipotle Avocado Sandwiches (cut into mini sandwiches) on page 106

Sweet Beet Mix on page 113

Swiss Chard Rolls with Domestic Goddess Sauce on page 139

Pink Lemonade Cupcakes on page 254

Additional toppings like chili

Mezze Platter

When we visited Istanbul, we ate at a cute little lunch counter across from the Hagia Sofia. When I asked, "What doesn't have meat, dairy, eggs in it?" the guy behind the counter looked at me like I was bonkers and said, "All this." He gestured to the wide variety of stuffed peppers, pilafs, tabbouleh salad, hummus, olives, stuffed mushrooms, grape leaves, baba ghanoush, and falafel balls. The look on my face must have been a little like Charlie's when he first saw the chocolate river in Willy Wonka's factory. This recipe will make enough Roasted Red Pepper Hummus, Fire-Roasted Baba Ghanoush, Tabbouleh Salad, and Sesame Falafel Balls for you to share with some of your favorite people while talking about your favorite things. For us, that's visiting Istanbul.

MAKES 8 TO 10 SERVINGS   **$3.25 PER SERVING**

. . . .

Platter

1 recipe Fire-Roasted Baba Ghanoush
(page 293)

1 recipe Roasted Red Pepper Hummus
(page 293)

1 recipe Tabbouleh Salad (page 294)

1 recipe Sesame Falafel Balls (page 294)

20 pitas, toasted and cut into wedges

1 cup olive mix

. . . .

Make your baba ghanoush, hummus, and tabbouleh first. Put them in the fridge to chill and marry flavors while you make your falafel balls. Once you've made all the components of your platter, you're ready to serve your guests. Arrange your mezze platter by placing your tabbouleh salad in the center of a very large platter or platters and putting your falafel balls on top. Then using a large spoon arrange your baba ghanoush and hummus around the outside of your tabbouleh leaving two open spots for your pita wedges and olives.

If you don't have a platter large enough to serve your entire mezze platter, you can always put your salad, falafel balls, spreads, pita wedges, and olives in five to six medium sized bowls. This might also be a good approach if you have some picky eaters coming to your party. Some folks don't like it when their foods touch. This is their way.

Fire-Roasted Baba Ghanoush

1 large eggplant

2 cloves garlic

Dash of vegan liquid smoke

⅓ cup fresh parsley

¼ cup tahini

Grated zest and juice of 1 lemon

Using barbeque tongs or a large skewer and oven mitts, roast the eggplant whole over an open flame for 15 minutes, either on your stovetop or a grill. You can also bake it in the oven at 425°F for 15 minutes, but that's not as much fun. The eggplant is done when the skin has turned crispy and black.

Cut off the top and bottom of the roasted eggplant, then cut it into cubes. Toss the cubes in a food processor with all the remaining ingredients and blend until smooth.

Transfer to an airtight container and refrigerate.

Roasted Red Pepper Hummus

3 cups cooked garbanzo beans or 2½ cans of garbanzo beans, drained and rinsed

⅓ cup roasted red peppers in oil

1 teaspoon smoked paprika

1 clove garlic, minced

1 teaspoon soy sauce or Bragg's Liquid Aminos

½ teaspoon red pepper flakes

½ cup tahini

Juice of 1 lemon

½ teaspoon ground cumin

2 tablespoons fresh parsley

¼ cup olive oil, plus more for drizzling

Toss all the ingredients in a food processor and process until creamy. Move to an airtight container and refrigerate.

Drizzle 1 to 2 tablespoons of olive oil over the top before serving.

(continued)

Tabbouleh Salad

1 cup bulgur wheat

1 cup boiling water

1 teaspoon soy sauce or Bragg's Liquid Aminos

Grated zest of 1 lemon

Juice of 2 lemons

⅓ cup olive oil

1 teaspoon crushed black peppercorns

½ red onion, diced

2 cloves garlic, finely minced

4 to 5 green onions, diced

2 Roma or Campari tomatoes, diced

1 cucumber, diced

1½ cups chopped fresh parsley

½ cup chopped fresh mint

Sea salt and ground black pepper

Prepare your bulgur by combining your bulgur and boiling water in a large bowl. Mix with a large wooden spoon and let stand for 20 minutes. Once your bulgur is tender, drain any extra water.

While the bulgur is soaking, in a small bowl, whisk together the soy sauce, lemon zest, lemon juice, olive oil, crushed pepper, red onion, and garlic.

Place your tender bulgur in a large bowl and pour the dressing over it. Mix in the green onions, tomatoes, cucumber, parsley, and mint. Stir until completely combined, then give it a taste test and add salt and ground pepper as needed.

Transfer the tabbouleh to an airtight container and refrigerate.

Sesame Falafel Balls

1 (15-ounce) can garbanzo beans, drained and rinsed, or 1½ cups cooked dry garbanzo beans

2 tablespoons garbanzo bean flour

1 small red onion, diced

⅓ cup fresh parsley

3 cloves garlic, minced

1½ teaspoons soy sauce or Bragg's Liquid Aminos

1 teaspoon sesame oil

½ teaspoon ground turmeric

1 teaspoon smoked paprika

2 teaspoons ground cumin

2 teaspoons sesame seeds

1 teaspoon whole coriander seeds, ground

½ teaspoon crushed black peppercorns

Pinch of cayenne pepper

Pinch of ground cardamom

Vegetable oil, for frying

Toss all the ingredients except the oil for frying in your food processor and puree into a firm paste. You're going to form it into balls, so you don't want the falafel mixture to be too soft. But if the mixture is too firm for your food processor to blend, stop the food processor and remove the bowl. Use a rubber spatula to scrape down the sides and fold the top ingredients in. Then put the bowl back on the motor and process until smooth, but not too soft.

Move the falafel mixture into a bowl, cover with plastic wrap, and refrigerate for 1 hour.

Fill a soup pot or Dutch oven halfway with oil and heat the oil over high heat. If you have a deep-fry thermometer, your oil will be ready to use when it's around 350 degrees.

While the oil is heating, remove the falafel mixture from the fridge. Roll into balls about the size of your palm and place them on a plate near the stove.

Using a slotted spoon, carefully drop the falafel balls in the hot oil a few at a time. Don't overcrowd them. Use a slotted spoon to roll the falafel balls in the oil to make sure they cook evenly. Once the falafel balls turn a dark brown, use the slotted spoon to transfer them to a paper towel–lined plate to soak up any extra oil.

Repeat until you've fried up all the falafel mixture into crispy little nommy sesame balls.

SUGGESTIONS FOR OTHER DISHES YOUR FRIENDS CAN BRING:

Lemon-Tahini Fattoush on page 71

Green Bean, Olive, and Roasted Potato Salad on page 86

Roasted Red Pepper and Lentil Soup on page 91

Greek Garbanzo Bean Salad Pitas on page 109

Turkish Pizza—Lahmacun on page 163 (cut into small pieces)

Vegan Gyros on page 219

Swiss Chard Rolls with Domestic Goddess Sauce on page 139

Chai Spice Cheesecake on page 272

Lemonade and a variety of teas

Slow-Cooker Taco Party

Here are the Dos and Don'ts of a good taco party:

DO:

> Enjoy Mexican and Latin-American foods.

> Explore new salsas and peppers. Mexico and Latin America are pretty big places. You might not have enough money for a plane ticket, but you might be surprised by what you'll find in your local grocery store.

DON'T:

> Wear costumes—particularly anything that portrays what some people think of as "stereotypical Mexican." Items to avoid include sombreros, fake mustaches, and anything having to do with crossing borders or alluding to illegal immigration at all. Seriously. No one will think you're funny.

> Serve Doritos. Some are vegan, but not even those belong at a grown-up party.

MAKES 20 TO 24 SERVINGS   **$1.01 PER SERVING**

Filling

2 (15-ounce) cans black beans, drained and rinsed, or 3 cups cooked dry black beans

2 (15-ounce) cans kidney beans, drained and rinsed, or 3 cups cooked dry kidney beans

1 tablespoon olive oil

1 red onion, diced

2 cloves garlic, minced

1 green bell pepper, diced

2 tomatoes, diced

1 jalapeño, seeded and diced (more or less, depending on how hot you like it)

1 tablespoon chili powder

½ to 1 teaspoon cayenne pepper (more or less, depending on how hot you like it)

1 teaspoon ground cumin

½ teaspoon smoked paprika

1 teaspoon dried oregano

1 cup vegan beef broth or vegetable broth (we recommend Better Than Bouillon)

1½ cups brown rice, cooked

Fixings

2 (7-ounce) boxes hard taco shells (10 to 12 shells per box)

2 cups of your favorite salsa (you can always use the recipe of Pineapple Salsa from the Aloha Dogs on page 175)

1½ cups shredded vegan cheddar cheese (we recommend Daiya)

2 avocados, pitted, peeled, and diced

¼ cup sliced pitted black olives

¼ cup chopped fresh cilantro

Make the filling: Toss all the filling ingredients in a slow cooker and mix with a large wooden spoon. Set the slow cooker to high and cover. Simmer for 15 minutes or until the filling bubbles, then reduce the heat to low.

Make the fixings: While the filling is cooking, heat the taco shells following the instructions on the package and put your fixings in separate bowls on the buffet table with spoons and forks so guests can build their own tacos. Put the taco shells out right before serving.

To serve the tacos, bring your slow cooker to the buffet table and keep it on low. Have a large spoon available so you can stir the filling every once in a while and so your guests can fill their tacos from the slow cooker, then top them off with their choice of fixings.

SUGGESTIONS FOR OTHER DISHES YOUR FRIENDS CAN BRING:

Chipotle Avocado Sandwiches on page 106 (cut into small pieces)

Cuba Libre Cake on page 248

Chipotle Chicken Chilaquiles on page 208

Pineapple Salsa, from Aloha Dogs on page 175

Chips, guacamole, and a variety of salsas

Mexican sodas, beers, and Agua Fresca, below

A blender and ingredients to make both alcoholic and virgin margaritas

Watermelon Agua Fresca

One of the most popular beverages all over Mexico and most of Latin America is called agua fresca. It's basically a sweetened fruit juice over crushed ice that melts in the heat while you drink it to create a refreshing cold beverage. This recipe is one of the simplest to make—especially in the summer when watermelon is in season! It should serve eight people at about $0.20 per serving.

8 cups chopped watermelon
Juice of 2 limes
2 cups crushed ice
2 tablespoons agave nectar

Depending on the size of your blender, you may have to make this in batches.

Toss all the ingredients in the blender and mix until the watermelon is pureed. This should take about 30 seconds.

Serve cold.

The DIY Wedding

The idea of a "Do-It-Yourself" wedding might seem like something that only exists among Brooklyn hipsters, but the truth is the multimillion-dollar wedding-industrial complex we've all come to accept as "normal" is relatively new. In fact, there's a statistical likelihood your grandma was a DIY bride. During World War II and the Korean War, most weddings took place at the bride's home, with family members on both sides contributing food and decorations. Oftentimes these weddings were planned around a serviceman's furlough home between basic training and being shipped overseas. It's hard to imagine a more bittersweet event.

But if you take the time to study the faces of the newlyweds in photos from these wartime weddings, you won't see anyone concerned that the bride's wearing her nicest suit with a corsage pinned to the lapel instead of carrying a bouquet of flowers, or wearing a little hat instead of a veil. In fact, many of the candid shots show young men grinning ear to ear as they look at their new wives. They're just two people happy to have each other, and to have a life together to look forward to after the war.

Here are a few tips to keep in mind if you're considering a DIY wedding:

> Are you planning a small wedding? Anything larger than thirty people[‡] will definitely require you to get some help, even if it's just enlisting an army of friends. If you're not the type of person who will enjoy baking and decorating a hundred cupcakes with your girlfriends the night before your wedding, you should rethink this.

> Are you able to maintain realistic expectations? Even when you hire professional caterers and florists for your big day, things don't always look the same in real life as they do in magazines. This goes double for DIY projects. Be kind to yourself, and if it's really going to bother you if the frosting doesn't match the bridesmaids' dresses perfectly, you need to think twice about whether it's worth the money to have a pro do it.

> Serving a sit-down meal requires servers. So unless you have friends willing to play this role, buffet-style usually works best for the DIY-wedding meal. If your dream wedding includes a sit-down dinner, rather than a simple cocktail hour with a buffet table of hors d'oeuvres, this is going to call for more manpower than your usual DIY event.

---

‡ We had about fifty at ours in 2009.

> Are you the kind of person who enjoys doing things yourself? Be honest. Because if you're not, this won't end up being the "Happiest Day of Your Life."

The collection of recipes in this section is inspired by some of the wonderful weddings we've been in and attended—including our own. We've tried to provide a variety of recipes, with tips on how to serve them, to help you plan out your big day. Like all the recipes in this book, each recipe lists how many servings it will make and what each serving will cost, but you'll need to do the math to figure out how many batches you'll have to make to feed your guest list, and what that's going to cost you.

Strawberry Salad

We live in New York, where same-sex marriage is now legal, and a few months ago our friends Jasmin Singer and Mariann Sullivan—the two lovely ladies behind the blog Our Hen House—finally made honest women out of each other and were married in a small, private civil ceremony. After the ceremony, Jasmin told me they were thinking about maybe having a "celebration type of a thing," but she was very noncommittal. That's why, when we were invited to the belated reception, I admit the Italian mother in me was like, "It's about time! What is this, Braveheart? We're all getting secretly married in the woods now? I wonder if I should bring a lemon cake?" and the Jewish mother in me was like, "So what can I bring to feed everyone, besides the lemon cake? People can't live on cake, you crazy Italian."[§] This recipe is what I brought to their DIY potluck reception instead of cake. It was a crowd-pleaser with even the most health-conscious guests, and it was not only easy to throw together but also looked very pretty on the buffet table. All three of those things are big positives for a vegan DIY-wedding event.

MAKES 8 TO 10 SERVINGS　　　　　　　　　　　**$0.93 PER SERVING**

Orange, Agave, and Mustard Dressing

3 tablespoons agave nectar

3 tablespoons Dijon mustard (less, if you like things sweeter)

3 tablespoons orange juice with pulp

Strawberry Salad

½ cup cubed peeled raw jicama

3 kiwifruit, peeled and sliced (optional)

1½ cups hulled and halved raw strawberries

¾ cup halved black or red seedless grapes

¼ cup torn fresh mint leaves

4 to 6 cups baby spinach leaves

Make the orange, agave, and mustard dressing: In a small bowl, whisk together all the dressing ingredients. Cover and refrigerate for about 20 minutes.

Once your dressing is chilled, toss all of your salad ingredients in a large bowl and then drizzle your dressing over the top right before you serve.

[§] I was very conflicted over the whole process of making food for such an important event.

Chilled Cucumber and Avocado Soup

I actually made this soup with a pot of Earl Grey tea to enjoy while I watched one of the wedding episodes of Downton Abbey. Although cucumber soup is originally a Polish dish, something about chilled cucumber soup just says "British" to me, and I wanted to add some Anglophile cuisine to our Italian- and French-heavy home. This soup is a wonderful addition to any DIY wedding because you don't have to worry about keeping it warm—just cold, which is way easier. The most expensive ingredient is going to be the avocados, so use the tips on page 13 to make sure the avocados you buy aren't spoiled.

MAKES 10 SERVINGS   **$1.56 PER SERVING**

6 to 7 cucumbers

2 green bell peppers, seeded and sliced

2 avocados, halved, pitted, and peeled

2 yellow onions, chopped

8 stalks celery, chopped

2 cloves garlic, minced

2 teaspoons ground cumin

1 tablespoon sea salt

½ cup fresh basil leaves

½ cup fresh parsley leaves

2 tablespoons chopped fresh dill

2 tablespoons chopped fresh mint leaves

2 tablespoons chopped fresh chives

Sea salt and crushed black peppercorns

Slices of cucumber, fresh herbs, olive oil and/or Sriracha, for garnish

Working in batches, in a food processor or blender, puree all the ingredients, then combine in a large, chilled bowl. Give the soup a taste test and add salt or black pepper as needed. Cover with plastic wrap and refrigerate until ready to serve.

Serve cold, garnished with slices of cucumber, fresh herbs, olive oil, and/or Sriracha.

Veg Manchurian

When our friends Pulin and Christina were married in 2013, we were ridiculously excited. Not just for our friends—two wonderful people and dedicated advocates for animals—but because our friends know good vegan food. Pulin is Indian American, and when we learned their wedding would include several modern takes on the traditional Hindi wedding ceremony, we got even more excited—who doesn't love Indian food? It was a beautiful ceremony that celebrated Indian culture through song and dance. Of course, Pulin opted out of the tradition where the groom rides to the event on an elephant or horse. We were proud to be part of his baraat, or wedding procession. This recipe was one of our favorite recipes from the reception. It's originally a Chinese dish that became popular in India through the Chinese communities that settled in Kolkata (once known as Calcutta) more than a hundred years ago. During that time, dishes such as veg Manchurian were slowly adopted and adapted by Indian homes to create a new kind of Indian-Chinese fusion cuisine that is still popular today. This dish of vegan "meatballs" in a spicy sauce is usually served as an appetizer, and would be a wonderful addition to any DIY wedding.

MAKES 4 TO 6 SERVINGS **$0.59 PER SERVING**

Vegan Meatballs

Vegetable oil, for frying

2 tablespoons all-purpose flour

2 tablespoons garbanzo bean flour

1 tablespoon rice flour

1 teaspoon onion powder

1 teaspoon crushed black peppercorns

3 green onions, diced

2 cups coleslaw mix, diced smaller

1 tablespoon ginger paste

1 teaspoon soy sauce or Bragg's Liquid Aminos

¼ cup vegetable broth (we recommend Better Than Bouillon)

Sauce

¼ cup green onions, diced

2 cloves garlic, minced

½ teaspoon ginger paste

2 teaspoons soy sauce or Bragg's Liquid Aminos

1 to 2 teaspoons Sriracha or Thai chili sauce (more or less, depending on how hot you like it)

3 tablespoons tomato paste

1 teaspoon packed brown sugar

¼ cup vegetable broth (we recommend Better Than Bouillon)

1 tablespoon plus 1 teaspoon sesame oil

2 sliced green chilies (optional)

Fresh cilantro leaves, to sprinkle over the top

Fill a soup pot or Dutch oven halfway with oil and heat over high heat. If you have a deep-fry thermometer, your oil is ready when it's 350 degrees.

In your largest bowl, use a large spoon to mix together the all-purpose flour, garbanzo bean flour, rice flour, onion powder, black pepper, green onions, and coleslaw mix.

In a separate bowl, whisk together the ginger paste, soy sauce, and vegetable broth. Pour the vegetable broth mixture into the flour mixture, then combine with your hands to make a thick dough. Use your hands to form the dough into balls smaller than your palm. If your dough is too soft, add a little more flour ¼ teaspoon at a time until your dough can remain formed into a ball.

Use a slotted spoon to carefully drop a few of the dough balls into the hot oil without crowding the oil. Use a slotted spoon to roll the dough balls in the oil a few times so they cook evenly. Once the dough balls are a dark golden color, they're done. Use the slotted spoon to transfer the fried dough balls to a paper towel–lined plate to soak up any extra oil. Repeat until you have fried all of the dough. While you're frying your balls, make your sauce.

Make the sauce: In a saucepan, combine all the sauce ingredients except the cilantro leaves and bring to a boil over medium heat, stirring occasionally. Reduce the heat to maintain a simmer.

Once all the dough balls have been fried, pour the sauce into your deepest cast-iron skillet or wok and toss in all the fried dough balls. Heat over medium heat until the sauce begins to bubble, then remove from the heat.

Serve hot, with cilantro sprinkled over the top.

Fresh Herb and Heirloom Tomato Salad

Back in 2011, our friends Rob and Anjali were married in San Luis Obispo, California, in one of the most beautiful DIY weddings I've ever attended. The event took place at a little yellow ranch house nestled among rolling buff-colored hills, with a fire pit, outdoor dance floor, and small jewel-toned glass lanterns hanging from the trees. The flowers came from the farmers' market and had been arranged the night before. The favors were small booklets containing a collection of recipes from both Rob's and Anjali's families, plus a bottle of homemade Thai chili sauce. The sit-down courses included a fresh tomato salad and vegetable dishes made using the remarkable locally grown produce of the area. The bride and her bridesmaids even baked pies to cut and serve instead of a cake. After the dancing died down, several of us gathered around the fire pit to make s'mores (some with vegan marshmallows) under the spectacular starry sky and talk until we just couldn't stay awake any longer. It was the DIY wedding that I'd wish for everyone, and this simple and colorful salad recipe was inspired by that lovely night.

MAKES 8 TO 10 SERVINGS **$2.01 PER SERVING**

3 pounds heirloom tomatoes of different sizes and colors, thinly sliced

2 red onions, thinly sliced

4 green onions, diced

Fresh Herb Dressing

Juice of 3 lemons

¼ cup olive oil

3 tablespoons chopped fresh mint leaves

¼ cup chopped fresh basil leaves

¼ cup chopped fresh parsley

1 teaspoon sea salt

1 teaspoon crushed black peppercorns

2 cloves garlic, minced

For each serving of salad, arrange the tomatoes and red onions on a cold plate so they look pretty. Sprinkle the green onions over the tomatoes.

Make the fresh herb dressing: Blend all the dressing ingredients in a food processor until smooth. Transfer to an airtight container and refrigerate until ready to serve.

Keep the salad chilled for as long as possible before serving. Drizzle the dressing over tomatoes and onions just before you serve.

Honeydew Skewers

One trap many vegans fall into when choosing food for their wedding is feeling like they have to choose between "healthy" and "affordable." This recipe is both. Honeydew melon is particularly inexpensive when it's in season between August and October. And because of its light green hue, it'll go with most wedding color schemes.

MAKES 10 TO 12 SERVINGS　　　　　　　　　　　　　　　　**$0.36 PER SERVING**

3 pounds honeydew melon, cut into 1-inch cubes

¾ cup orange juice with pulp

Juice from 1 lime

Peel from 1 lime, grated

¼ cup fresh mint leaves

Cut the melon into cubes. Put 5 to 6 melon cubes on a bamboo skewer and repeat until you have skewered all the cubes. Place the skewers in a large, shallow dish.

In a blender or food processor, combine all the remaining ingredients and process until the mint is in small pieces, but not liquefied.

Pour the juice blend over the skewers and roll them until the melon is completely coated.

Arrange the skewers on a serving plate and cover with plastic wrap. Refrigerate until ready to serve.

Chocolate Strawberry Cheesecake Cups

Strawberries dipped in chocolate are a romantic standby that are easy to make, inexpensive, and impressive all at the same time. These little cheesecake cups are a great way to show even your most stubborn guest that anything can be made vegan. The toughest part of this recipe can be locating enough beautiful strawberries. We recommend trying your local farmers' market, where it's a little more socially acceptable to search through the pint boxes to check for any spoiled strawberries.

The cupcakes need to be refrigerated overnight, so be sure to plan ahead. (Not that you want to be baking on your wedding day, anyway!)

MAKES 12 SERVINGS   **$1.95 PER SERVING**

Crust
2 cups crushed graham crackers

2 tablespoons sugar

2 tablespoons vegan margarine, melted

½ teaspoon applesauce

Filling
3 (8-ounce) packages vegan cream cheese

⅓ cup sugar

1 tablespoon applesauce

2 teaspoons egg replacer (we recommend Ener-G or Beyond Eggs)

1 tablespoon all-purpose flour

1 ripe strawberry, destemmed and pureed

Chocolate-Dipped Strawberry Topping
1 (12-ounce) package vegan chocolate chips

12 ripe strawberries with stems attached

Preheat the oven to 300°F. Line a 12-cup cupcake tin with paper liners.

Make the crust: In a large bowl, mix all the crust ingredients with a large spoon, then press a little more than 1 tablespoon of the crust mixture into the bottom of each paper liner.

Make the filling: In a large bowl, blend all the filling ingredients with an electric hand-held mixer until smooth and very light pink. Spoon a little more than 3 tablespoons of the filling into each cupcake cup. Use a spoon to spread the filling so each cup has a smooth top.

Bake for 20 to 25 minutes, or until the edges are firm. Don't worry if the center looks undone. Turn off the oven and leave the cups in the warm oven for 20 minutes. Let cool in the pan on a wire rack for another 30 minutes. Cover the pan with plastic wrap and refrigerate overnight.

Make the chocolate-dipped strawberry topping: Three hours before serving, melt the chocolate chips following the instructions on the package. One at a time, carefully dip the strawberries in the melted chocolate while holding on to the stem.

Take the cheesecake cups out of the refrigerator. Carefully remove them from the cupcake pan and place them on a serving plate.

Place a chocolate-covered strawberry on top of each cheesecake cup.

Rewrap the serving plate with plastic wrap and refrigerate for at least 2 hours or until ready to serve.

Enjoy cold with a glass of Champagne and someone to slow dance with.

Lavender and Vanilla Cupcakes

The second question most brides and grooms must answer after the official "Will you marry me?" is "What are your colors going to be?" These days, weddings are planned around themes and color schemes, and one of the most popular colors is purple. Violet hues provide a wide variety of flowers and bridesmaids' dresses to choose from that don't fall into the trap of being "dated" in five years. My sister-in-law and two of my best friends had purple weddings, and each one was a lovely representation of the bride's taste.

We wanted to include something purple in this section for all those lavender-loving folks out there. The glaze for these cupcakes does have a slighty floral taste, which is something I love, but for some it is new and unusual. Please keep that in mind, and maybe offer both these and the White Wedding Cupcakes on page 310 if you know you'll have picky eaters at the reception. If you're looking to carry the lavender theme throughout, we recommend having the Lemon and Lavender Cookies on page 284 with tea after your food service as a way to wind down the night.

MAKES 18 CUPCAKES　　　　　　　　　　　　　　　　**$0.29 PER SERVING**

Vanilla Cupcakes

Baking spray

1½ cups all-purpose flour

1 cup granulated sugar

1½ teaspoons baking powder

½ teaspoon sea salt

½ cup vegan margarine

1 tablespoon applesauce

1½ teaspoons ground flaxseed

1 teaspoon coconut milk, from a carton, not a can

1½ teaspoons vanilla extract

Lavender Glaze

1 cup coconut milk, from a carton, not a can

1 tablespoon plus 2 teaspoons dried culinary lavender buds, crushed

2 cups powdered sugar, or more as needed

Lavender buds or edible flowers, for garnish

Make the vanilla cupcakes: Preheat the oven to 350°F. Prepare two cupcake pans by coating 18 cups with baking spray.

In large bowl, whisk together the flour, granulated sugar, baking powder, and salt.

In a separate bowl, blend the vegan margarine, applesauce, flaxseed, coconut milk, and vanilla with an electric handheld mixer. Using a rubber spatula, scrape all the margarine mixture into the flour mixture and blend with an electric handheld mixer into a creamy batter.

Use a ladle to fill the cupcake cups two-thirds of the way with batter.

Bake for about 20 minutes, or until the cupcakes are a light golden brown and a bamboo skewer inserted into the center of a cupcake comes out clean.

Meanwhile, make the lavender glaze: In a saucepan, heat the coconut milk and lavender over medium heat, stirring constantly. Once the coconut milk begins to bubble, reduce the heat to maintain a low simmer. Once you can smell a light floral fragrance from the coconut milk, remove the saucepan from the heat.

Pour 2 cups of the powdered sugar into a small bowl. Whisk the lavender-infused coconut milk into the powdered sugar a little bit at a time until it becomes a thick glaze. Add a little more or a little less powdered sugar to achieve the consistency you prefer.

Let the cupcakes cool to room temperature before glazing. One at a time, dip the top of a cooled cupcake into the glaze, and then slowly twist the cupcake to get an even coating. Place the cupcake on a sheet of parchment paper to set. Repeat with all the remaining cupcakes.

Before the glaze sets, sprinkle with some lavender buds or place an edible flower on the top to decorate.

White Wedding Cupcakes

I was one of those brides who didn't want a wedding. I wanted to run away with the man I love to a far-off place where we could meet all our loved ones in front of a justice of the peace, then go out afterward for vegan gelato or dim sum or whatever the local cuisine was. But once I accepted that we were going to have this thing, I was determined to host the best party possible. That meant there had to be good food. This recipe is an adaption of the cupcakes we had at our Boston wedding in 2009. They're a sweet, snowy-white treat, and easy to decorate a hundred of because they don't require perfect frosting peaks or really any cake-decorating skills whatsoever. We recommend creating an assembly line, where one person is in charge of frosting, another person is in charge of coating the frosting in coconut, and a third person waits in the wings to whisk off the plates of ivory-colored cupcakes to the fridge for storage until you're ready to serve them.

MAKES 18 CUPCAKES   **$0.67 PER SERVING**

Coconut-Banana Cupcakes

2¼ cups all-purpose flour

2¼ teaspoons baking powder

Pinch of sea salt

1 ripe banana

1 tablespoon applesauce

2 teaspoons ground flaxseed

1 cup granulated sugar

¾ cup olive oil

1 (14-ounce) can coconut milk

¼ cup almond milk

1 teaspoon vanilla extract

Coconut-Vanilla Frosting

6 cups powdered sugar

⅔ cup vegan margarine, at room temperature

1 teaspoon ground cardamom (optional)

4 teaspoons vanilla extract

5 tablespoons almond milk

1½ cups shredded raw coconut

Make the coconut-banana cupcakes: Preheat the oven to 350°F. Line two 12-cup cupcake tins with paper liners.

In a large bowl, whisk together the flour, baking powder, and salt.

In a separate bowl, blend the banana, applesauce, flaxseed, granulated sugar, and olive oil together using an electric handheld mixer. Gradually blend in the flour mixture ½ cup at a time.

Gradually blend in the coconut milk, almond milk, and vanilla with the handheld mixer until the batter is creamy.

Using a ladle, fill the cupcake cups three-quarters of the way with batter.

Bake for 20 minutes, or until a bamboo skewer inserted into the center of a cupcake comes out clean.

Meanwhile, make the coconut-vanilla frosting: In a large bowl, blend the powdered sugar, vegan margarine, and cardamom (if using) with an electric handheld mixer until the mixture resembles small pebbles. Gradually mix in the vanilla and almond milk. If the frosting is too thin, add a little more powdered sugar; if the frosting is too thick, add more almond milk, 1 teaspoon at a time.

Let the cupcakes cool to room temperature before frosting.

Fill a frosting gun or pastry bag with the frosting, then pour the shredded coconut in a shallow dish. To decorate, use the frosting gun to create equal-size peaks on each cupcake, then gently roll the icing in the shredded coconut until covered.

Serve at room temperature, with some Billy Idol and a sneer.

CONCLUSION

In her book *My Life in France*, Julia Child wrote: "Upon reflection, I decided I had three main weaknesses: I was confused (evidenced by a lack of facts, an inability to coordinate my thoughts, and an inability to verbalize my ideas); I had a lack of confidence, which caused me to back down from forcefully stated positions; and I was overly emotional at the expense of careful, 'scientific' thought. I was thirty-seven years old and still discovering who I was."

I was thirty-seven when we started this cooking project and can say with sincere conviction that I thought I knew who I was, only to discover that I was no different than Julia when she arrived in France. I was confused by what to do when life didn't go as planned. My confidence and in many ways my identity was bruised by the realization that becoming a mother might not be possible for me, and I was prone to terrible bouts of self-doubt. To sum it up, when I started writing this book, I was in that familiar turmoil Julia described. This realization might have been the biggest

blow of all. I mean, how many of us imagine ourselves feeling like this at thirty-seven? Especially when we had found such confidence and happiness at thirty-five.

Julia decided she was going to master the art of French cooking. We decided we were going to create a cooking project that would master our finances, kitchen, and diet, without compromising our lifestyle and ethics. Bit more wordy than Julia's mission, but to us it was more noble, because we wanted to prove that being vegan wasn't a luxury or a privilege but a sustainable lifestyle. Although we had set out on different courses, I was able to find the best parts of myself again—much like that Francophile amazon.

We wrote this book to do more than just share vegan recipes and pantry tips. We wanted to be able to share how we overcame some of the struggles in our life and where we found the inspiration to do so. It might sound dramatic to say that reducing the amount of food and money we were wasting changed my whole life, but it did. Being able to take control of your life and seeing the positive and tangible results can be more than empowering…it's freaking awesome! I can describe the thrill of seeing our grocery bills shrink while our savings flourished. I can try to capture the feeling of accomplishment that comes with ending a week with a clean fridge because we've used all our produce and eaten all our leftovers—rather than just throwing out what had spoiled. But until you find those feelings for yourself…words just don't do it justice.

So we tried to give you what you'd need to find your own solutions to the problems you might be facing in the kitchen. We wanted to challenge the myth that going vegan was actually more expensive than eating a meat-based diet, and we wanted to empower our readers to enjoy a compassionate lifestyle without feeling like they were sacrificing convenience. We also wanted to eat delicious food and quote classic movies and talk about our favorite TV shows. And not to be too much of a cornball, but we wanted to share with you the importance of never giving up hope.

As I'm typing this, we are thirty-four weeks pregnant with a little girl. We debated including this fact in the book, because things could always go wrong again; and no matter how advanced and educated our society has become, whenever a woman loses a baby there's a lingering unasked question: "What did she do wrong?" The truth is that 20 to 30 percent of pregnancies end in miscarriage, and a staggeringly small percentage of those are due to actions by the mother. Yet in a society where we claim we no longer think a woman's primary goal in life is to have children, women who lose babies—or decide not to have them at all—are often openly judged or treated as if there's something wrong with them.

My way of dealing with the loss of our daughter Piper is to talk openly about it and not contribute to this stigmatization. I wanted to share our good news with you all, while accepting that nothing should be taken for granted. I wanted to show that, even though I stand by my statement in the introduction that life isn't fair, we do have the power to make choices that make the world a better place for others. We can push back against social stigmas and expectations; we can reduce how much food we use, waste, and consume; or we can simply choose a more compassionate lifestyle that doesn't contribute to the suffering of others.

We can be the change in the world that Gandhi talked about—and we can start today by making vegan waffles.

INDEX

*Note: Page numbers in **bold** indicate recipe category tables of contents.*

A

agave nectar
  about, 81; leftover, recipes for, 40, 122, 179
  Agave Chili Dipping Sauce, 121–122
  Orange, Agave, and Mustard Dressing, 300
almonds. *See* nuts and seeds
Aloha Dogs, 175–176
Aloo Saag, 235
apples
  about: applesauce, 253; leftover applesauce, recipes for, 190; storing, 12
  Apple-Sage Tempeh Sausage over Savory Polenta, 133–134
  Humble Apple Pie, 267–268
apricots, storing, 10–11
Arancini (Fried Risotto Balls), 136
artichokes
  Groove Is in the Artichoke Salad, 72
  Leftover Recipe: Pan-Fried Artichoke Hearts and Sauce, 227
  Pasta with DIY Marinara, 226
asparagus
  about: storing, 9
  Leftover Recipe: Primavera Pizza, 240
  Pasta with Asparagus and Green Onion Pesto, 200–201
  Savory Crêpes with Easy "Hollandaise" Sauce, 42–43
avocados
  about: leftover, recipe for, 37; storing, 13
  Avocado and Grapefruit Salad with Cilantro Dressing, 81
  BLT Pancake Stacks, 36–37
  Chilled Cucumber and Avocado Soup, 301
  Chipotle Avocado Sandwiches, 106
  Slow-Cooker Taco Party, 296–297

B

baba ghanoush, 293
bacon bits, vegan. *See also* tempeh
  about, 156
  Baked Potato Bar, 290–291
  Brinner Lasagna, 169–170
  Vegan Bacon and Broccoli Quiche, 59
  Vegan Bacon and "Egg" Enchiladas, 55–56
  Vegan Bacon Ranch Dipping Sauce, 165
  Vegan Bacon, White Bean, and Spinach Risotto, 155–156
Baked Creole Carrot Chips, 112
Baked Potato Bar, 290–291
Baked Strapatsada—Greek Baked "Egg" Cups, 53–54
Balsamic and Black Pepper Dressing, 72
bananas
  about: storing, 12
  Banana Churro Waffles, 44
  Chocolate Chip and Banana Brownie Cookies, 281
  Coconut-Banana Cupcakes, 310–311
  Green Tea and Pear Smoothie, 30
barley, in Mason Jar Farmers' Market Salad, 82
basil
  about: fresh, 103; leftover leaves, recipes for, 204; storing, 14
  Pesto, 117–118
BBQ Sauce, 187–188
beans and legumes. *See also* green beans
  about: canned vs. dry, 17; dangerous/toxic beans, 19; peas and lentils in two steps, 18; preparing dry, 17–19; quick-soak method, 18–19; saving money on, 17; storing, 8
  Betty's Wartime Walnut Burger, 189–190
  Chickpea à la King Skillet, 123–124
  Chili-Stuffed Sweet Potatoes, 167–168
  Cincinnati Chili, 177
  Cowboy Quinoa Chili, 241
  Greek Garbanzo Bean Salad Pitas, 109
  Green Gunpowder Gumbo Skillet, 131–132
  Mason Jar Farmers' Market Salad, 82
  Mexican Stuffed Zucchini, 146–147
  Pasta with Asparagus and Green Onion Pesto, 200–201
  Pomegranate and Brown Rice Salad, 223
  Red Beans and Rice Salad, 75
  Ribollita Soup, 103
  Roasted Beet and Lentil Salad, 73–74
  Roasted Garlicky Garbanzos, 84

beans and legumes (*cont.*)
Roasted Red Pepper and Lentil Soup, 91
Roasted Red Pepper Hummus, 293
Samosa Pizza, 161–162
Sesame Falafel Balls, 294–295
Simple Spanish Rice Bake, 232
Slow-Cooker Taco Party, 296–297
Slow-Cooker Tempeh Jambalaya, 213
Sweet Potato and Black Bean Tacos, 182
Tuscan Eggplant and White Bean Sandwiches, 110
Vegan Bacon, White Bean, and Spinach Risotto, 155–156
beef, vegan. *See also* seitan
Beefless Brussels Sprout Shepherd's Pie, 183–184
Irish Stout Stew, 157–158
beets
about, 207; storing, 10
Beet "Boudin" Balls with Garlic Aioli, 206–207
Ratatouille Rice Bake, 153–154
Roasted Beet and Lentil Salad, 73–74
Roasted Red Flannel Hash, 38
The Sweet Beet Mix, 113
beignets, 215
berries
about: storing, 11
Easy Mixed Berry Muffins, 45
Fresh Blueberry Blintzes, 51–52
Fresh Fruit Pizza, 277
Strawberry Salad, 300
Betty Crocker Cooking School of the Air, The, 3
Bisquick, vegan, recipes for, 34
blackstrap molasses
about, 99
recipes for using, 126
Blackstrap Vegan Bangers and Mash with Onion Gravy, 125–126
blintzes, fresh blueberry, 51–52
BLT Pancake Stacks, 36–37
blueberries. *See* berries
book background and overview, 1–4, 313–314
Bragg's Liquid Aminos
about, 148–149
recipes for using, 56, 148–149
breads. *See also* pancakes and waffles; pizza
Cheezy Croutons, 85
Cinnamon Peach Skillet Rolls, 47–48
Easy Mixed Berry Muffins, 45
Leftover Recipe: Curry Spinach and Potato Biscuits, 236
Leftover Recipe: Hestia's Biscuits, 222
Leftover Recipe: Pomegranate and Brown Rice Cabbage Rolls, 224
Leftover Recipe: Savory Pumpkin Biscuits, 218
Monkey Bread, 274–275
Orange Drop Doughnuts, 49–50
Pumpkin Pie Muffins, 46

breakfast, 25–64. *See also* pancakes and waffles
about: overview of recipes, 25; storing cereals, 8
Baked Strapatsada—Greek Baked "Egg" Cups, 53–54
Cinnamon Peach Skillet Rolls, 47–48
Clementine and Coconut Smoothie, 31
Easy Mixed Berry Muffins, 45
Emily Dickinson Porridge, 27
Fresh Blueberry Blintzes, 51–52
Ginger-Plum Oatmeal, 26
Granola Grrrl Bars, 29
Green Tea and Pear Smoothie, 30
Mexican Coffee, 63
Orange Drop Doughnuts, 49–50
PB&J Granola Bars, 28
Pumpkin Pie Muffins, 46
Pumpkin Spice Latte, 64
Roasted Red Flannel Hash, 38
Rosemary Potato Frittata, 60
Savory Crêpes with Easy "Hollandaise" Sauce, 42–43
Smoky Butternut Squash Scramble, 57–58
Tofu à la Goldenrod, 61–62
Vegan Bacon and Broccoli Quiche, 59
Vegan Bacon and "Egg" Enchiladas, 55–56
Virgin Crêpes Suzette, 39–40
broccoli
about: storing, 9
Baked Potato Bar, 290–291
Spinach and Broccoli Stuffed Shells, 205
Vegan Bacon and Broccoli Quiche, 59
broths. *See* soups and stews
brown sugar, leftover uses, 26, 275
Brussels sprouts
Beefless Brussels Sprout Shepherd's Pie, 183–184
Roasted Pear, Walnut, and Brussels Sprout Tacos, 197
Budapest Burgers (leftover recipe), 230
budget and thriftiness. *See also leftover references*; pantry, practical
Betty Crocker and, 3
club card savings, 19–20
coffee shop drink prices and, 62
condensed broths and, 8
couponing and, 19–20
four-step strategy, 2–3
lifestyle change tips, 271
maximizing shelf life for. *See* storing ingredients
meal perspective for, 15
pots, pans and, 6
reading price tags and, 19–20
sustainability and, 2
this book and, 2–4, 313–314
using what you have and, 15
vegan diet and, 15–17
war times, Great Depression and, 2–3, 23, 36, 105, 199, 238, 245, 267, 280, 282, 298
waste cost to avoid, 17

bulgur wheat
  Swiss Chard Rolls with Domestic Goddess Sauce, 139–140
  Tabbouleh Salad, 294
burgers. *See* sandwiches

C

cabbage
  about: storing, 9–10
  Green Shchi—Russian Cabbage Soup, 92
  Leftover Recipe: Pomegranate and Brown Rice Cabbage Rolls, 224
  Thai Vegan Chicken Slaw, 69–70
  Veg Manchurian, 302–303
Cajun Nachos, 129–130
cakes. *See* sweet treats
Caldo Verde—Portuguese Soup, 93–94
calzones, 165–166, 228
capers leftovers, recipes for, 78, 130
cardamom
  about, 196
  leftover, recipes for, 257
carrots
  about: leftover, recipes for, 94; storing, 10; World War II and, 94
  Baked Creole Carrot Chips, 112
  Carrot Cake Cookies, 282–283
cast-iron skillets, 6
cauliflower
  about: storing, 9
  Buffalo Cauliflower Calzones with Vegan Bacon Ranch, 165–166
  Cauliflower Fettuccine Alfredo, 238
  Leftover Recipe: Pasta Primavera, 239
  Yankee Doodle Macaroni, 191–192
cereals. *See* breakfast
Chai Spice Cheesecake, 272–273
cheese, vegan
  about, 151; cost considerations, 16; leftover cheddar cheese, recipes for, 106, 170; leftover cream cheese, recipes for, 33; leftover mozzarella cheese, recipes for, 108, 205; leftover Parmesan, recipes for, 84
  Baked Potato Bar, 290–291
  Chai Spice Cheesecake, 272–273
  Cheese Sauce, 290–291
  Cheez Sauce, 193
  Cheezy Croutons, 85
  Chef's Pasta Salad, 97
  Chocolate Strawberry Cheesecake Cups, 306–307
  Cincinnati Chili, 177
  Cream Cheese Drizzle, 32–33
  Cream Cheese Topping, 46
  Lasagna Sandwiches featuring Italian Tempeh Sausage, 107–108

  Mexican Stuffed Zucchini, 146–147
  pasta with. *See* pasta
  pizza with. *See* pizza
  Rosemary Potato Frittata, 60
  sandwiches/tacos with. *See* sandwiches; tacos
Chef's Pasta Salad, 97
cherries
  about: storing, 11
  Cherry Glaze, 254–255
  PB&J Granola Bars, 28
chicken, vegan
  Cajun Nachos, 129–130
  Chipotle Chicken Chilaquiles, 208–209
  Chop Suey Noodles, 178–179
  Fajita Pizza, 160
  Jerk "Chicken" Pasta Salad, 98–99
  Leftover Recipe: Vegan Pollo Gumbo, 233
  Rosemary Chicklins and Dumplins Stew, 127–128
  Thai Vegan Chicken Slaw, 69–70
Child, Julia
  cake quote, 245
  inspiration from, 3, 39, 41, 313
  introspection, 313
  Julia's Kitchen Wisdom by, 3
  kitchen of, 41
  on vegetarianism, 41
Child, Lydia Maria, 143
Chili. *See* soups and stews
Chilled Cucumber and Avocado Soup, 301
Chipotle Avocado Sandwiches, 106
Chipotle Chicken Chilaquiles, 208–209
chocolate
  about: leftover chips, recipes for, 281; leftover cocoa, recipes for, 259
  Chocolate Chip and Banana Brownie Cookies, 281
  Chocolate Strawberry Cheesecake Cups, 306–307
  Cookie Pizza, 276
  Granola Grrrl Bars, 29
  S'mores Cookie Bars, 260–261
  Snowball Cupcakes, 258–259
Chop Suey Noodles, 178–179
churro waffles, 44
cilantro
  about, 147; recipes with, 147; storing, 14
  Cilantro Dressing, 81
Cincinnati Chili, 177
Cinnamon Peach Skillet Rolls, 47–48
Cinnamon Roll Pancakes, 32–33
citrus
  about: storing, 10
  Avocado and Grapefruit Salad with Cilantro Dressing, 81
  Clementine and Coconut Smoothie, 31
  Greek Lemon Dressing, 109
  Lemon and Lavender Cookies, 284
  Lemon-Tahini Dressing, 71

citrus (*cont.*)
    Lemon-Tahini Fattoush/Dressing, 71
    Lime and Pepper Dressing, 76
    Orange, Agave, and Mustard Dressing, 300
    Orange Drop Doughnuts, 49–50
    Orange Spice USO Cake, 252–253
    Pink Lemonade Cupcakes, 254–255
    Virgin Crêpes Suzette, 39–40
Club Sandwich Salad with Dijon Mustard Dressing, 80
coconut
    about: leftover, recipes for, 31; leftover oil, reci-
        pes for, 29; leftover shredded, recipes for, 27;
        milk, 250–251; oil, 270; toasting, 27
    Clementine and Coconut Smoothie, 31
    Coconut-Banana Cupcakes, 310–311
    Emily Dickinson Porridge, 27
    Granola Grrrl Bars, 29
    Mango Coconut Pie, 269–270
    Snowball Cupcakes, 258–259
    Tom Kha Gai—Spicy Coconut Soup, 89–90
    White Wedding Cupcakes, 310–311
coffee. *See* drinks and smoothies
community supported agriculture (CSA) program, 23
cookies. *See* sweet treats
corn and polenta
    about: leftover frozen, recipes for, 100
    Apple-Sage Tempeh Sausage over Savory Polenta,
        133–134
    Cajun Nachos, 129–130
    Cruelty-Free Crawfish Boil, 286–287
    Leftover Recipe: Corn Beignets, 215
    Pan-Seared Corn and Quinoa Salad, 76–77
coupons, finding/using, 19–20
Cowboy Quinoa Chili, 241
cream cheese. *See* cheese, vegan
cream of tartar, recipes to use, 284
Creole seasoning, recipes for, 112
crêpes
    Fresh Blueberry Blintzes, 51–52
    Savory Crêpes with Easy "Hollandaise" Sauce,
        42–43
    Virgin Crêpes Suzette, 39–40
Crocker, Betty, 3, 189, 199
croutons, cheezy, 85
Cruelty-Free Crawfish Boil, 286–287
CSA (community supported agriculture) program, 23
cucumbers, in Chilled Cucumber and Avocado
    Soup, 301
cupcakes. *See* sweet treats; wedding, DIY
curry powder, about, 113

D

desserts. *See* sweet treats
Dickinson, Emily, 27
Dijon mustard leftovers, recipes for, 80

Dill Dressing, 73
dinner, 115–210. *See also* pizza
    about: overview of recipes, **115–116**
    Aloha Dogs, 175–176
    Angel Hair Pasta with Garlic and Rosemary
        Mushrooms, 202
    Apple-Sage Tempeh Sausage over Savory Polenta,
        133–134
    Beefless Brussels Sprout Shepherd's Pie, 183–184
    Beet "Boudin" Balls with Garlic Aioli, 206–207
    Betty's Wartime Walnut Burger, 189–190
    Blackstrap Vegan Bangers and Mash with Onion
        Gravy, 125–126
    Brinner Lasagna, 169–170
    Bubbie's Polish Potato Pierogies, 137–138
    Cajun Nachos, 129–130
    Chickpea à la King Skillet, 123–124
    Chili-Stuffed Sweet Potatoes, 167–168
    Chimichurri Rice Casserole, 148–149
    Chipotle Chicken Chilaquiles, 208–209
    Chop Suey Noodles, 178–179
    Cincinnati Chili, 177
    Green Gunpowder Gumbo Skillet, 131–132
    Irish Stout Stew, 157–158
    Lasagna Bolognese, 119–120
    Mac and Cheez Pie, 173–174
    Mexican Stuffed Zucchini, 146–147
    Pan-Seared Black Tea and Pepper Tofu, 186
    Pan-Seared Tofu with Arugula, Capers, and
        Tomatoes, 210
    Pasta with Asparagus and Green Onion Pesto,
        200–201
    Quinoa Taco Casserole, 152
    Ratatouille Rice Bake, 153–154
    Roasted Pear, Walnut, and Brussels Sprout Tacos,
        197
    Rosemary Chicklins and Dumplins Stew, 127–128
    Rustic Pesto and Heirloom Tomato Tart, 117–118
    Sesame and Soy Marinated Mushroom Steaks,
        198
    Simple Korean Kimchi BBQ Burgers, 187–188
    Sloppy Joel Pie, 171–172
    Spinach and Broccoli Stuffed Shells, 205
    Spinach and Tempeh Pastitsio, 180–181
    Steamed Sesame Seitan Dim Sum, 141–142
    Sweet Potato and Black Bean Tacos, 182
    Swiss Chard Rolls with Domestic Goddess Sauce,
        139–140
    Tater Tot Pie, 150–151
    Tofu, Green Beans, and Cashews, 185
    Tofu Spring Rolls with Agave Chili Sauce, 121–122
    Tofu Vindaloo, 195–196
    Tuesday Night Dinner, 203–204
    Vegan Bacon, White Bean, and Spinach Risotto,
        155–156
    Vegan BLT Mac and Cheez, 193–194

Wild Mushroom Risotto, 135–136
Yankee Doodle Macaroni, 191–192
Yankee Pot Roast Dinner, 144–145
dressings. See sauces and dressings
drinks and smoothies
    about: coffee shop drink prices and, 62
    Clementine and Coconut Smoothie, 31
    Green Tea and Pear Smoothie, 30
    Mexican Coffee, 63
    Pumpkin Spice Latte, 64
    Watermelon Agua Fresca, 297
dry goods, storing, 8

E

eggplant
    Fire-Roasted Baba Ghanoush, 293
    Ratatouille Rice Bake, 153–154
    Tuscan Eggplant and White Bean Sandwiches, 110
eggs
    Ener-G replacer recipes, 50, 255
    tofu instead of. See tofu
Emily Dickinson Porridge, 27
enchiladas, vegan bacon and "egg," 55–56
equipment
    pots and pans, 6
    spice rack, 7

F

Fajita Pizza, 160
falafel balls, 294–295
farmers' markets, 83
Fire-Roasted Baba Ghanoush, 293
flaxseed leftovers, recipes for, 45, 48, 283
flours, storing, 8. See also vital wheat gluten
French Potato Salad, 88
frittata, rosemary potato, 60
frostings and glazes. See also sweet treats
    Cherry Glaze, 254–255
    Coconut-Vanilla Frosting, 310–311
    Cola Frosting, 248–249
    Lavender Glaze, 308–309
    Maple Frosting, 256–257
fruit. See also specific fruit
    about: buying seasonal, 21–22; citrus, 10; fresh, by month, 22; stone fruit, 10–11; storing fresh, 10–13
    Fresh Fruit Pizza, 277
frying oil, saving, 50

G

gardens, growing, 23
Garlic Aioli, 206–207
ginger
    about: leftover paste, recipes for, 162, 198

Ginger-Miso Dressing, 69–70
    Ginger-Plum Oatmeal, 26
gluten. See vital wheat gluten
graham crackers, 261
grains, storing, 8. See also vital wheat gluten
Granola Grrrl Bars, 29
grapefruit. See citrus
Great Depression, food economy and, 3, 38, 127, 247, 250, 267
Greek Garbanzo Bean Salad Pitas, 109
Greek Lemon Dressing, 109
green beans
    Chimichurri Rice Casserole, 148–149
    Green Bean, Olive, and Roasted Potato Salad, 86
    Tofu, Green Beans, and Cashews, 185
green leafy vegetables, storing, 9–10. See also cabbage; kale; spinach
Green Shchi—Russian Cabbage Soup, 92
Green Tea and Pear Smoothie, 30
grocery shopping. See budget and thriftiness; shopping strategy
Groove Is in the Artichoke Salad, 72
gumbo, 131–132, 233
gyros, vegan, 219–220

H

hash, roasted red flannel, 38
herbs and spices
    about: buying spice rack, 7; cardamom, 196; curry powder, 113; fresh basil, 103; fresh mint, 71; liquid smoke, 91; saving money on fresh herbs, 14; smoked paprika, 58; storing fresh herbs, 13–14; turmeric, 62
    Fresh Herb and Heirloom Tomato Salad, 304
Honeydew Skewers, 305
hummus, 293
Hungarian Goulash Stew, 229

I

ingredients. See pantry, practical; shopping strategy
Irish Stout Stew, 157–158

J

jambalaya, 213
Jerk "Chicken" Pasta Salad, 98–99
Julia's Kitchen Wisdom (Child), 3, 39, 88

K

kale
    about: storing, 9–10
    Kale Caesar Salad, 78
    Sesame Miso Kale Chips, 111
kiwifruit, 277, 300

L

Lahmacun—Turkish Pizza, 163–164
lavender
    Lavender and Vanilla Cupcakes, 308–309
    Lemon and Lavender Cookies, 284
leftover recipes, 211–244
    about: optimizing strategies, 2; overview of,
        211–212
    Aloo Saag, 235
    Cauliflower Fettuccine Alfredo, 238
    Cowboy Quinoa Chili, 241
    Hungarian Goulash Stew, 229
    Leftover Recipe: Budapest Burgers, 230
    Leftover Recipe: Cahoots Quiche, 243
    Leftover Recipe: Corn Beignets, 215
    Leftover Recipe: Curry Spinach and
        Potato Biscuits, 236
    Leftover Recipe: Hermes' Pizza, 221
    Leftover Recipe: Hestia's Biscuits, 222
    Leftover Recipe: Indian Takeout Pizza, 237
    Leftover Recipe: Mayday Noodles, 231
    Leftover Recipe: Not-cho Everyday Chili Dogs, 244
    Leftover Recipe: Pan-Fried Artichoke Hearts and
        Sauce, 227
    Leftover Recipe: Pasta Primavera, 239
    Leftover Recipe: Pocket Calzones, 228
    Leftover Recipe: Pomegranate and Brown Rice
        Cabbage Rolls, 224
    Leftover Recipe: Primavera Pizza, 240
    Leftover Recipe: Pumpkin and Spinach Orzo, 217
    Leftover Recipe: Roasted Red Pepper Tamale Pie,
        242
    Leftover Recipe: Savory Pumpkin Biscuits, 218
    Leftover Recipe: Spanish Rice Quiche, 234
    Leftover Recipe: The Big Easy Tacos with Garlic
        Aioli, 214
    Leftover Recipe: Turkish Stuffed Peppers, 225
    Leftover Recipe: Vegan Pollo Gumbo, 233
    Pasta with DIY Marinara, 226
    Pomegranate and Brown Rice Salad, 223
    Pumpkin Curry Soup, 216
    Simple Spanish Rice Bake, 232
    Slow-Cooker Tempeh Jambalaya, 213
    Vegan Gyros, 219–220
leftovers, recipe lists (for specific ingredients)
    agave nectar, 40, 122, 179
    avocado, 37
    basil, 204
    Bragg's Liquid Aminos, 56
    brown sugar, 26, 275
    capers, 78
    carrots, 94
    cheese (cheddar), 106, 170
    cheese (cream), 33
    cheese (mozzarella), 108, 205
    cheese (Parmesan), 84
    cilantro, 168

    cocoa, 259
    coconut, 31
    coconut (oil), 29
    coconut (shredded), 27
    corn (frozen), 100
    Creole seasoning, 112
    Ener-G replacer, 50, 255
    flaxseed, 45, 48, 283
    ginger paste, 162, 198
    mint, 164
    mushrooms, 43, 158, 202
    mustard (Dijon), 80
    nutritional yeast, 54, 85, 194
    nuts (almond milk), 30, 44, 273
    nuts (cashews), 185
    nuts (walnuts), 59, 79, 276
    oats, 28, 268
    olives, 86
    onions (green), 74
    onions (red), 75
    parsley, 128
    peppers (jalapeño), 77, 176
    peppers (red), 72, 90
    pumpkin puree, 46
    quinoa, 152
    rice vinegar, 70
    sesame oil, 90, 188
    tortillas, 56
    vegan Bisquick, 34
    wine (red), 120
    Worcestershire sauce, 38, 172
lemons and limes. *See* citrus
lentils. *See* beans and legumes
lifestyle change tips, 271
liquid smoke, 91
lunch, 65–113. *See also* salads; soups and stews
    about: bringing to work lunch, 168; guide to
        lunch boxes, 87; overview of recipes, **65–66**;
        Rosie the Riveter and her lunch pail, 105
    Baked Creole Carrot Chips, 112
    Chipotle Avocado Sandwiches, 106
    Lasagna Sandwiches featuring Italian Tempeh
        Sausage, 107–108
    Roasted Garlicky Garbanzos, 84
    Sesame Miso Kale Chips, 111
    Sesame Peanut Noodles, 101–102
    Simple Soba Noodles, 100
    The Sweet Beet Mix, 113
    Tuscan Eggplant and White Bean Sandwiches, 110
lunch boxes
    guide to, 87
    Rosie the Riveter and, 105

M

Manchurian, veg, 302–303
mangoes
    Fresh Fruit Pizza, 277

Mango Coconut Pie, 269–270
Mason Jar Farmers' Market Salad, 82
Mayday Noodles (leftover recipe), 231
meat, faux
    cost considerations, 16
    recipes with. *See* beef, vegan; chicken, vegan;
        sausage, vegan; seafood, vegan; seitan; tempeh;
        tofu; Tofurky Deli Slices
meatballs, vegan, 302–303
Meatless Mondays, 199
melons
    about: storing, 11
    Honeydew Skewers, 305
    Watermelon Agua Fresca, 297
Mexican Coffee, 63
Mexican Stuffed Zucchini, 146–147
Mezze Platter, 292–295
mint
    fresh, 71
    leftover leaves, recipes for, 164
    storing, 14
miso
    Ginger-Miso Dressing, 69–70
    Sesame Miso Kale Chips, 111
molasses, blackstrap, 99, 280
Molasses Crinkle Cookies, 280
mushrooms
    about: leftover, recipes for, 43, 158, 202
    Angel Hair Pasta with Garlic and Rosemary
        Mushrooms, 202
    Savory Crêpes with Easy "Hollandaise" Sauce,
        42–43
    Sesame and Soy Marinated Mushroom Steaks,
        198
    Smoky Butternut Squash Scramble, 57–58
    Tuesday Night Dinner, 203–204
    Wild Mushroom Risotto, 135–136
mustard
    Dijon Mustard Dressing, 80
    Orange, Agave, and Mustard Dressing, 300

N

nachos, 129–130
noodles. *See* pasta
nutritional yeast recipes, 54, 85, 194
nuts and seeds
    about: cashews, 174, 185; leftover almond milk,
        recipes for, 30, 44, 273; leftover cashews, reci-
        pes for, 185; leftover walnuts, recipes for, 59,
        79, 276; peanut butter, 264–265; pine nuts, 118;
        pumpkin seeds, 201; walnuts, 197
    Betty's Wartime Walnut Burger, 189–190
    Domestic Goddess Sauce, 139
    Fire-Roasted Baba Ghanoush, 293
    Granola Grrrl Bars, 29
    Lemon-Tahini Fattoush, 71
    PB&J Granola Bars, 28

Peanut Butter Cup Pie, 264–265
Peanut Sauce, 101–102
Roasted Pear, Walnut, and Brussels Sprout Tacos,
    197
Savannah Pecan Pie, 266
Sesame Peanut Noodles, 101–102
Tofu, Green Beans, and Cashews, 185

O

oats
    about: leftover, recipes for, 28, 268
    Emily Dickinson Porridge, 27
    Ginger-Plum Oatmeal, 26
    Granola Grrrl Bars, 29
    PB&J Granola Bars, 28
oil (frying), saving, 50
oil, coconut, 270
okra, in Green Gunpowder Gumbo Skillet, 131–132
Olive Oil Piecrust, 263
olives
    about: kalamata, 109; recipes for leftovers, 86
    Greek Garbanzo Bean Salad Pitas, 109
    Green Bean, Olive, and Roasted Potato Salad, 86
onions and chives
    about: leftover, recipes for green onions, 74; left-
        over, recipes for red onions, 75; storing, 14
    Green Onion Pesto, 200–201
    Onion Gravy, 125–126
    Sriracha and Sweet Onion Stew, 104–105
oranges. *See* citrus
oregano, storing, 14

P

pancakes and waffles
    about: freezing and reheating, 35; recipes for left-
        over vegan Bisquick, 34
    Banana Churro Waffles, 44
    BLT Pancake Stacks, 36–37
    Cinnamon Roll Pancakes, 32–33
    Sweet Potato Pancakes, 34–35
Pan-Fried Artichoke Hearts and Sauce (leftover
    recipe), 227
Pan-Seared Black Tea and Pepper Tofu, 186
Pan-Seared Corn and Quinoa Salad, 76–77
Pan-Seared Tofu with Arugula, Capers, and Toma-
    toes, 210
pantry, practical
    about: overview of, 5
    assessing, purging existing stock, 5–6
    basic items to buy, 6–7
    condensed broths for, 8
    maximizing shelf life. *See* storing ingredients
    using what you have, 15. *See also leftover references*
paprika, smoked, 58
parsley, storing, 14
Parsnip and Peppercorn Soup, 95–96

parties. *See* potlucks and parties; wedding, DIY
pasta
  about: storing, 8
  Angel Hair Pasta with Garlic and Rosemary
    Mushrooms, 202
  Brinner Lasagna, 169–170
  Cauliflower Fettuccine Alfredo, 238
  Chef's Pasta Salad, 97
  Chop Suey Noodles, 178–179
  Cincinnati Chili, 177
  Jerk "Chicken" Pasta Salad, 98–99
  Leftover Recipe: Mayday Noodles, 231
  Leftover Recipe: Pasta Primavera, 239
  Leftover Recipe: Pumpkin and Spinach Orzo, 217
  Mac and Cheez Pie, 173–174
  Pasta with Asparagus and Green Onion Pesto,
    200–201
  Pasta with DIY Marinara, 226
  Sesame Peanut Noodles, 101–102
  Simple Soba Noodles, 100
  Spinach and Broccoli Stuffed Shells, 205
  Spinach and Tempeh Pastitsio, 180–181
  Tuesday Night Dinner, 203–204
  Vegan BLT Mac and Cheez, 193–194
  Yankee Doodle Macaroni, 191–192
PB&J Granola Bars, 28
peaches
  about: storing, 10–11
  Cinnamon Peach Skillet Rolls, 47–48
  Fresh Fruit Pizza, 277
peanuts and peanut butter. *See* nuts and seeds
pears
  about: storing, 12
  Green Tea and Pear Smoothie, 30
  Roasted Pear, Walnut, and Brussels Sprout Tacos,
    197
  Spiced Pear Cupcakes with Maple Frosting,
    256–257
pepperoni, vegan, 97
peppers
  about: handling jalapeños, 176; leftover, recipes
    for jalapeños, 77, 176; leftover, recipes for red
    peppers, 72, 90
  Baked Strapatsada—Greek Baked "Egg" Cups,
    53–54
  Chipotle Chicken Chilaquiles, 208–209
  Fajita Pizza, 160
  Leftover Recipe: Roasted Red Pepper Tamale Pie,
    242
  Leftover Recipe: Turkish Stuffed Peppers, 225
  Lime and Pepper Dressing, 76
  Ratatouille Rice Bake, 153–154
  Roasted Red Pepper and Lentil Soup, 91
  Roasted Red Pepper Hummus, 293
pierogies, 137–138
pies. *See* sweet treats

Pineapple Salsa, 175–176
pizza
  about: premade crusts, 159
  Buffalo Cauliflower Calzones with Vegan Bacon
    Ranch, 165–166
  Cookie Pizza, 276
  Fajita Pizza, 160
  Lahmacun—Turkish Pizza, 163–164
  Leftover Recipe: Hermes' Pizza, 221
  Leftover Recipe: Indian Takeout Pizza, 237
  Leftover Recipe: Pocket Calzones, 228
  Leftover Recipe: Primavera Pizza, 240
  Pizza Dough, 159
  Samosa Pizza, 161–162
  Vegan Cheese Party Pizza, 278–279
platter, for potlucks, 292–295
plums
  about: storing, 10–11
  Ginger-Plum Oatmeal, 26
polenta. *See* corn and polenta
pomegranates
  about: storing, 13
  Leftover Recipe: Pomegranate and Brown Rice
    Cabbage Rolls, 224
  Pomegranate and Brown Rice Salad, 223
potatoes. *See also* sweet potatoes
  about: storing, 10
  Aloo Saag, 235
  Baked Potato Bar, 290–291
  Bubbie's Polish Potato Pierogies, 137–138
  Caldo Verde—Portuguese Soup, 93–94
  Cruelty-Free Crawfish Boil, 286–287
  French Potato Salad, 88
  Fries and Toppings, 288–289
  Green Bean, Olive, and Roasted Potato Salad, 86
  Leftover Recipe: Curry Spinach and Potato Bis-
    cuits, 236
  Leftover Recipe: Indian Takeout Pizza, 237
  Mash, 125–126
  Roasted Red Flannel Hash, 38
  Rosemary Potato Frittata, 60
  Samosa Pizza, 161–162
  Tater Tot Pie, 150–151
  Yankee Pot Roast Dinner, 144–145
potlucks and parties, 285–297. *See also* wedding, DIY
  about: other dishes to bring, 287, 289, 291, 295,
    297; overview of, **246**, 285
  Baked Potato Bar, 290–291
  Butternut Squash and Beer Poutine Party, 288–289
  Cruelty-Free Crawfish Boil, 286–287
  Fire-Roasted Baba Ghanoush, 293
  Mezze Platter, 292–295
  Roasted Red Pepper Hummus, 293
  Sesame Falafel Balls, 294–295
  Slow-Cooker Taco Party, 296–297
  Tabbouleh Salad, 294

pots and pans, 6
price tags, reading, 19–20
pumpkin
    about: leftover puree recipes, 46; seeds, 201
    Leftover Recipe: Pumpkin and Spinach Orzo, 217
    Leftover Recipe: Savory Pumpkin Biscuits, 218
    Pumpkin Curry Soup, 216
    Pumpkin Pie Muffins, 46
    Pumpkin Spice Latte, 64

Q

quinoa
    about: leftover, recipes for, 152; toasting, 77
    Cowboy Quinoa Chili, 241
    Pan-Seared Corn and Quinoa Salad, 76–77
    Quinoa Taco Casserole, 152

R

radishes, storing, 10
raspberries. *See* berries
Ratatouille Rice Bake, 153–154
reading price tags, 19–20
receptions. *See* potlucks and parties; wedding, DIY
red beans. *See* beans and legumes
red peppers. *See* peppers
Ribollita Soup, 103
rice
    about: using leftover risotto, 136
    Arancini (Fried Risotto Balls), 136
    Chimichurri Rice Casserole, 148–149
    Granola Grrrl Bars, 29
    Green Gunpowder Gumbo Skillet, 131–132
    Leftover Recipe: Pomegranate and Brown Rice
        Cabbage Rolls, 224
    Leftover Recipe: Spanish Rice Quiche, 234
    PB&J Granola Bars, 28
    Pomegranate and Brown Rice Salad, 223
    Ratatouille Rice Bake, 153–154
    Red Beans and Rice Salad, 75
    Simple Spanish Rice Bake, 232
    Slow-Cooker Tempeh Jambalaya, 213
    Vegan Bacon, White Bean, and Spinach Risotto,
        155–156
    Wild Mushroom Risotto, 135–136
rice vinegar leftovers, recipes for, 70
Roasted Beet and Lentil Salad, 73–74
Roasted Garlicky Garbanzos, 84
Roasted Pear, Walnut, and Brussels Sprout Tacos,
    197
Roasted Red Flannel Hash, 38
Roasted Red Pepper and Lentil Soup, 91
Roasted Red Pepper Hummus, 293
Rosemary Chicklins and Dumplins Stew, 127–128
Rosemary Potato Frittata, 60
Rosie the Riveter and her lunch pail, 105

S
salads
    Avocado and Grapefruit Salad with Cilantro
        Dressing, 81
    Cheezy Croutons for, 85
    Chef's Pasta Salad, 97
    Club Sandwich Salad with Dijon Mustard Dress-
        ing, 80
    French Potato Salad, 88
    Fresh Herb and Heirloom Tomato Salad, 304
    Greek Garbanzo Bean Salad Pitas, 109
    Green Bean, Olive, and Roasted Potato Salad, 86
    Groove Is in the Artichoke Salad, 72
    Jerk "Chicken" Pasta Salad, 98–99
    Kale Caesar Salad, 78
    Lemon-Tahini Fattoush, 71
    Mason Jar Farmers' Market Salad, 82
    Pan-Seared Corn and Quinoa Salad, 76–77
    Pomegranate and Brown Rice Salad, 223
    Red Beans and Rice Salad, 75
    Roasted Beet and Lentil Salad, 73–74
    The Six Million Dollar Tofu "Egg" Salad, 67–68
    Strawberry Salad, 300
    Tabbouleh Salad, 294
    Thai Vegan Chicken Slaw, 69–70
Samosa Pizza, 161–162
sandwiches. *See also* tacos
    Aloha Dogs, 175–176
    Betty's Wartime Walnut Burger, 189–190
    Chipotle Avocado Sandwiches, 106
    Greek Garbanzo Bean Salad Pitas, 109
    Lasagna Sandwiches featuring Italian Tempeh
        Sausage, 107–108
    Leftover Recipe: Budapest Burgers, 230
    Leftover Recipe: Not-cho Everyday Chili Dogs, 244
    Pan-Seared Black Tea and Pepper Tofu for, 186
    Simple Korean Kimchi BBQ Burgers, 187–188
    Tuscan Eggplant and White Bean Sandwiches, 110
    Vegan Gyros, 219–220
sauces and dressings. *See also* frostings and glazes
    about: Sriracha, 102
    Agave Chili Dipping Sauce, 121–122
    Balsamic and Black Pepper Dressing, 72
    BBQ Sauce, 187–188
    Bolognese Sauce, 119–120
    Cheese Sauce, 290–291
    Cheez Sauce, 193
    Chimichurri Sauce, 148
    Cilantro Dressing, 81
    Dijon Mustard Dressing, 80
    Dill Dressing, 73
    DIY Marinara Sauce, 226
    Domestic Goddess Sauce, 139
    Easy "Hollandaise" Sauce, 42–43
    Enchilada Sauce, 55–56
    Garlic Aioli, 206–207

sauces and dressings (*cont.*)
Ginger-Miso Dressing, 69–70
Greek Lemon Dressing, 109
Green Onion Pesto, 200–201
Lime and Pepper Dressing, 76
Onion Gravy, 125–126
Orange, Agave, and Mustard Dressing, 300
Peanut Sauce, 101–102
Pesto, 117–118
Pineapple Salsa, 175–176
Spicy Aioli, 129
Tzatziki Sauce, 219
Vegan Bacon Ranch Dipping Sauce, 165
Vegan Béchamel Sauce, 180–181
sausage, vegan
Aloha Dogs, 175–176
Blackstrap Vegan Bangers and Mash with Onion
Gravy, 125–126
Brinner Lasagna, 169–170
Lasagna Sandwiches featuring Italian Tempeh
Sausage, 107–108
Leftover Recipe: Not-cho Everyday Chili Dogs, 244
Leftover Recipe: Pocket Calzones, 228
Leftover Recipe: Turkish Stuffed Peppers, 225
Tuesday Night Dinner, 203–204
Savannah Pecan Pie, 266
saving money. *See* budget and thriftiness; *leftover
references*; pantry, practical
Savory Crêpes with Easy "Hollandaise" Sauce, 42–43
seafood, vegan
about, 287
Cruelty-Free Crawfish Boil, 286–287
seasonal produce, 21–22
seitan. *See also* sausage, vegan
Beefless Brussels Sprout Shepherd's Pie, 183–184
Chimichurri Rice Casserole, 148–149
Hungarian Goulash Stew, 229
Lahmacun—Turkish Pizza, 163–164
Steamed Sesame Seitan Dim Sum, 141–142
Tater Tot Pie, 150–151
Sesame and Soy Marinated Mushroom Steaks, 198
Sesame Falafel Balls, 294–295
Sesame Miso Kale Chips, 111
sesame oil, recipes for, 90, 188
shopping strategy, 15–23. *See also* budget and
thriftiness
buying seasonal produce, 21–22
club card savings, 19
couponing, 19–20
CSAs and, 23
farmers' markets and, 83
reading price tags, 19–20
vegan diet and, 15–17
Simple Korean Kimchi BBQ Burgers, 187–188
Six Million Dollar Tofu "Egg" Salad, 67–68
skillets, 6

Sloppy Joel Pie, 171–172
Slow-Cooker Tempeh Jambalaya, 213
smoked paprika, about, 58
Smoky Butternut Squash Scramble, 57–58
smoothies
Clementine and Coconut Smoothie, 31
Green Tea and Pear Smoothie, 30
S'mores Cookie Bars, 260–261
Snowball Cupcakes, 258–259
soups and stews
about: recipes for leftover vegetable broth, 92
Caldo Verde—Portuguese Soup, 93–94
Chili-Stuffed Sweet Potatoes, 167–168
Chilled Cucumber and Avocado Soup, 301
Cincinnati Chili, 177
Cowboy Quinoa Chili, 241
Green Shchi—Russian Cabbage Soup, 92
Hungarian Goulash Stew, 229
Irish Stout Stew, 157–158
Parsnip and Peppercorn Soup, 95–96
Pumpkin Curry Soup, 216
Ribollita Soup, 103
Roasted Red Pepper and Lentil Soup, 91
Rosemary Chicklins and Dumplins Stew, 127–128
Sriracha and Sweet Onion Stew, 104–105
Tom Kha Gai—Spicy Coconut Soup, 89–90
sour cream, vegan, about/recipes with, 208–209
special occasions, overview of recipes, 245–**246**. *See
also* potlucks and parties; sweet treats;
wedding, DIY
spice rack, buying, 7
Spiced Pear Cupcakes with Maple Frosting, 256–257
spinach
about: storing, 9–10
Aloo Saag, 235
Baked Strapatsada—Greek Baked "Egg" Cups, 53–54
Green Onion Pesto, 200–201
Leftover Recipe: Curry Spinach and Potato Bis-
cuits, 236
Leftover Recipe: Indian Takeout Pizza, 237
Leftover Recipe: Pumpkin and Spinach Orzo, 217
Mason Jar Farmers' Market Salad, 82
Spinach and Broccoli Stuffed Shells, 205
Spinach and Tempeh Pastitsio, 180–181
Vegan Bacon, White Bean, and Spinach Risotto,
155–156
squash
about: storing, 11–12
Butternut Squash and Beer Poutine Party, 288–289
Mexican Stuffed Zucchini, 146–147
Smoky Butternut Squash Scramble, 57–58
Sriracha, about, 102
Sriracha and Sweet Onion Stew, 104–105
Steamed Sesame Seitan Dim Sum, 141–142
storing ingredients
about: maximizing shelf life, 8

dry goods, 8
fresh fruit, 10–13
fresh herbs, 13–14
fresh vegetables, 9–10
strawberries. *See* berries
sugar (brown), leftover uses, 26, 275
Sweet Beet Mix, 113
sweet potatoes
    about: perfect bring-to-work lunch, 168; storing, 10
    Chili-Stuffed Sweet Potatoes, 167–168
    Sweet Beet Mix, 113
    Sweet Potato and Black Bean Tacos, 182
    Sweet Potato Pancakes, 34–35
sweet treats, 247–284
    about: overview of, **246**, 247
    Carrot Cake Cookies, 282–283
    Chai Spice Cheesecake, 272–273
    Chocolate Chip and Banana Brownie Cookies, 281
    Chocolate Strawberry Cheesecake Cups, 306–307
    Cookie Pizza, 276
    Cuba Libre Cake, 248–249
    Fresh Fruit Pizza, 277
    Humble Apple Pie, 267–268
    Lavender and Vanilla Cupcakes, 308–309
    Lemon and Lavender Cookies, 284
    Mango Coconut Pie, 269–270
    Molasses Crinkle Cookies, 280
    Monkey Bread, 274–275
    Olive Oil Piecrust, 263
    Orange Spice USO Cake, 252–253
    Peanut Butter Cup Pie, 264–265
    Pink Lemonade Cupcakes, 254–255
    Salted Caramel Skillet Cake, 250–251
    Savannah Pecan Pie, 266
    S'mores Cookie Bars, 260–261
    Snowball Cupcakes, 258
    Spiced Pear Cupcakes with Maple Frosting, 256–257
    Vegan Cheese Party Pizza, 278–279
    Vegan Piecrust, 262
    White Wedding Cupcakes, 310–311
sweeteners
    agave nectar, 81
    blackstrap molasses, 99
    brown sugar leftover uses, 26, 275
Swiss chard
    about, 140
    Caldo Verde—Portuguese Soup, 93–94
    Swiss Chard Rolls with Domestic Goddess Sauce, 139–140

T

Tabbouleh Salad, 294
tacos
    Leftover Recipe: The Big Easy Tacos with Garlic Aioli, 214

Quinoa Taco Casserole, 152
    Roasted Pear, Walnut, and Brussels Sprout Tacos, 197
    Slow-Cooker Taco Party, 296–297
    Sweet Potato and Black Bean Tacos, 182
tamale pie, 242
tempeh
    about, 134
    Apple-Sage Tempeh Sausage over Savory Polenta, 133–134
    BLT Pancake Stacks, 36–37
    Lahmacun—Turkish Pizza, 163–164
    Lasagna Sandwiches featuring Italian Tempeh Sausage, 107–108
    Sloppy Joel Pie, 171–172
    Slow-Cooker Tempeh Jambalaya, 213
    Spinach and Tempeh Pastitsio, 180–181
Thai Vegan Chicken Slaw, 69–70
thriftiness. *See* budget and thriftiness; *leftover references*
thyme, storing, 14
toasting
    coconut, 27
    quinoa, 77
tofu
    about: freezing, 68
    Baked Strapatsada—Greek Baked "Egg" Cups, 53–54
    Chef's Pasta Salad, 97
    Green Gunpowder Gumbo Skillet, 131–132
    Leftover Recipe: Cahoots Quiche, 243
    Leftover Recipe: Spanish Rice Quiche, 234
    Pan-Seared Black Tea and Pepper Tofu, 186
    Pan-Seared Tofu with Arugula, Capers, and Tomatoes, 210
    Rosemary Potato Frittata, 60
    The Six Million Dollar Tofu "Egg" Salad, 67–68
    Smoky Butternut Squash Scramble, 57–58
    Tofu, Green Beans, and Cashews, 185
    Tofu à la Goldenrod, 61–62
    Tofu Spring Rolls with Agave Chili Sauce, 121–122
    Tofu Vindaloo, 195–196
    Tom Kha Gai—Spicy Coconut Soup, 89–90
    Vegan Bacon and Broccoli Quiche, 59
    Vegan Bacon and "Egg" Enchiladas, 55–56
Tofurky Deli Slices. *See also* sausage, vegan
    about: tempeh and, 134
    Chef's Pasta Salad, 97
    Club Sandwich Salad with Dijon Mustard Dressing, 80
Tom Kha Gai—Spicy Coconut Soup, 89–90
tomatoes
    about: storing, 12–13; sun-dried, 118
    Fresh Herb and Heirloom Tomato Salad, 304
    pizza with. *See* pizza
    Rustic Pesto and Heirloom Tomato Tart, 117–118
    sauces with. *See* sauces and dressings

tortilla recipes, 55–56, 182, 197
Tuesday Night Dinner, 203–204
Turkish Stuffed Peppers (leftover recipe), 225
turmeric, about, 62
Tuscan Eggplant and White Bean Sandwiches, 110

U

USO (United Service Organization), about, 252

V

vanilla cupcakes, 308–309
vegan diet
    cost comparison to non-vegan diet, 15–16
    ingredients to stock. *See* pantry, practical
    Meatless Mondays and, 199
    saving money on. *See* budget and thriftiness; *left-over references*
vegetables. *See also specific vegetables*
    about: buying seasonal, 21–22; flower buds/cru-ciferous, 9; fresh, by month, 22; growing your own, 23; roots and tubers, 10; storing fresh, 9–10
    soups with. *See* soups and stews
victory gardens, 23
vital wheat gluten
    about, 145; storing, 8
    Blackstrap Vegan Bangers and Mash with Onion Gravy, 125–126
    Leftover Recipe: Budapest Burgers, 230
    Vegan Gyros, 219–220
    Yankee Pot Roast Dinner, 144–145

W

waffles. *See* pancakes and waffles
Watermelon Agua Fresca, 297
wedding, DIY, 298–311
    about: overview of, **246**; tips for, 298–299
    Chilled Cucumber and Avocado Soup, 301
    Chocolate Strawberry Cheesecake Cups, 306–307
    Fresh Herb and Heirloom Tomato Salad, 304
    Honeydew Skewers, 305
    Lavender and Vanilla Cupcakes, 308–309
    Strawberry Salad, 300
    Veg Manchurian, 302–303
    White Wedding Cupcakes, 310–311
wheat gluten. *See* vital wheat gluten
White Wedding Cupcakes, 310–311
Wild Mushroom Risotto, 135–136
wine
    about: white, 181
    red, recipes for using, 120
    white, recipes for using, 181
Worcestershire sauce recipes, 38, 172
World War II, food economy and, 2–3, 23, 36, 105, 199, 238, 245, 267, 280, 282, 298

Y

Yankee Doodle Macaroni, 191–192
Yankee Pot Roast Dinner, 144–145

Z

zucchini. *See* squash

ACKNOWLEDGMENTS

This is a small "thank you" for some of the folks who helped turn our latest kitchen project into this book. These people dealt with experimental cooking, last minute canceled plans, teary-eyed venting, lots of typos and rewrites, carrying heavy bags of groceries on the subway and numerous other favors so this book could be possible: Ed and Linda Shannon, Laura Dail (our rainmaker and good friend), Sara Weiss, Karen Murgolo, Sarah Fitch Posey, Mylie Thompson, Leinana Two Moons, Sarah Morgan, Joel Bartlett, Libbe Blain, Michelle Schwegmann, Alka Chandna, Jennifer Chen, Diana Baroni, Amanda Englander, Doron Petersan, Seth Tibbot, Lisa Lange, Jasmin Singer, Mariann Sullivan, Anjali Prasertong, Sarah Sohn, Marisa Miller Wolfson, Chloe Jo Davis, Jenny Brown, Nicole Sopko, Dan Staackman, JL Fields, Erik Marcus, Shannon Radke, Jack Shepherd, Stephanie Corrigan, Ben Gould, Tanner Ringerud, Sean Fagen, Marta Holmberg, Scott Brewer, Ben Peterson, Josh Hooten, Ruby Hooten, Cassandra Cusack Curbelo, Elizabeth Castoria, Lisa Shapiro, Greg Rekas, Ivy Mcfadden, Pulin Modi, Christina Modi, Kristie Middleton, Erica Meier, Susanne Forte, Nick Patch, Barbara Sitmor, Emily Rems, The Hannah Banana Bakery, P.T. McNiff, Lisa Tulipani McNiff, Angie Snapp, and as always the folks over at *Veg-News* magazine.

ABOUT THE AUTHORS

Vanessa Rees

Though the cooking project that inspired this book began as a sad story, these days Annie and Dan Shannon are living happily ever after in Brooklyn, NY with their new daughter and their spoiled cats. Annie and Dan met in 2006 while advocating for animals at People for the Ethical Treatment of Animals but have since expanded on their activism to include several environmental and human rights issues as well. They've appeared on the *Today Show*, Oprah.com, The Kitchn, *BUST* magazine and numerous other media outlets, publications, and food festivals promoting compassionate living. Their first book *Betty Goes Vegan* won *VegNews* magazine's Cookbook of the Year award in 2013. These days Annie gets to focus full time on veganizing everything, writing, and fighting crime Angela Lansbury style. Dan is Senior Strategy Director at Purpose, where he helps non-profit organizations build more engaged communities of supporters. This solar system's yellow sun gives him a wide range of super powers. You can follow their adventures at MeetTheShannons.com.